COPING AND PULLING THROUGH

Coping and Pulling Through

Action Processes in Vulnerable Situations

Edited by

VIVIANNE CHÂTEL
University Paris V-La Sorbonne, France and
University of Fribourg, Switzerland

MARC-HENRY SOULET
University of Fribourg, Switzerland

Translation by Margaret Lainsbury
revised by John Richardson

Published with the help of DGXII (EU) and
Federal Office for Education and Science (CH)

Routledge
Taylor & Francis Group

LONDON AND NEW YORK

First published 2004 by Ashgate Publishing

Reissued 2019 by Routledge
2 Park Square, Milton Park, Abingdon, Oxon, OX14 4RN
52 Vanderbilt Avenue, New York, NY 10017

Routledge is an imprint of the Taylor & Francis Group, an informa business

Publisher's Note
The publisher has gone to great lengths to ensure the quality of this reprint but points out that some imperfections in the original copies may be apparent.

Disclaimer
The publisher has made every effort to trace copyright holders and welcomes correspondence from those they have been unable to contact.

A Library of Congress record exists under LC control number:

ISBN 13: 978-0-8153-8823-4 (hbk)
ISBN 13: 978-1-138-61917-3 (pbk)
ISBN 13: 978-1-351-16104-6 (ebk)

Contents

List of Tables

List of Contributors

Robert Castel, Professor of Sociology, École des hautes études en sciences sociales, Paris (France).

Vivianne Châtel, Senior Researcher in Sociology, University ParisV-La Sorbonne, (France) and University of Fribourg (Switzerland).

Jean-Marc Ferry, Professor of Philosophy, Free University, Brussels (Belgium).

Jacques Fierens, Professor of Law, Notre Dame de la Paix University, Namur (Belgium).

Danièle Laberge, Professor of Criminology, Université du Québec, Montreal (Canada).

Daniel Mercure, Professor of Sociology, Laval University, Quebec (Canada).

Serge Paugam, Senior Researcher in Sociology, French National Center for Scientific Research, Paris (France).

Giovanna Procacci, Senior Researcher in Sociology, University of Milan (Italy).

Shirley Roy, Professor of Sociology, Université du Québec, Montreal (Canada).

Franz Schultheis, Professor of Sociology, University of Geneva (Switzerland).

Marc-Henry Soulet, Professor of Sociology, University of Fribourg (Switzerland).

Introduction

Vivianne Châtel and Marc-Henry Soulet

The highlighting of the processes of exclusion and the great amount of attention that has been focused on this issue has, paradoxically, opened up the field of sociological analysis in two directions: the forms of survival in a situation of deprivation and the mechanisms of inclusion from a weakened position. Admittedly, earlier work has looked at the practices of the dominated, the pretence and the diversion of stigma, the logic of the collective mobilisation of the exploited, at the cultural frameworks of poverty. But the question what it is to act in a situation of vulnerability, and what forms this takes, have never been addressed directly.

During a recent international symposium, we sought to investigate the relations between acting and vulnerability. The attention was focused on how situations of insecurity and deprivation could be dealt with, with the aim of investigating, theoretically and empirically, the existence of specific forms of acting in a context of vulnerability. What resources can be mobilised and how, in a state of material and symbolic deprivation? What alliances can be formed and what supports can be found in a condition of structural inequality and in the absence of any possibility of reciprocity? How can the social experience be reconstructed once it has been undone? How can one take support from a spoiled identity and undertake a transformation of identity and of the situation? How, when enclosed in a situation of radical otherness, can one launch oneself into the issues of conventionality?[1]

A better understanding of the complexity of the issues raised by these questions requires understanding the situations of vulnerability themselves as well as the relations between vulnerability and action. Two lines of thought characterise this problematic: 1) In what ways does the issue of vulnerability express a key logic of present-day societies? What is the general trend in which it is rooted? What are its effects on the status of the individual in society? What are the likely impacts of this trend on the elements of contemporary social cohesion?; 2) How does a situation of vulnerability influence the nature of acting? What form does acting actually take when the conditions of an 'ordinary' form of acting are no longer present? In fact, what does acting entail in situations of great material and symbolic deprivation that make the very possibility of acting problematic?

The present work seeks to consider this and to sketch the outline of an understanding of action in a situation of vulnerability. Certain authors attempt to trace the frameworks of understanding situations of vulnerability and the implications for the status of the human being in society. Others try to identify forms of action in situations of vulnerability, particularly by the characterisation of these situations.

The introductory contribution of Vivianne Châtel links vulnerability to two areas: first, the situation where trust has been destroyed and where flexibility is increasingly demanded with regard both to living and working conditions; second, mode of acting which begins from the position of dignity and narrativity, prior to concentrating on the notion of vulnerability itself (moral vulnerability as utmost responsibility for Others and social vulnerability as weakening of the act of appearing to the world).

Daniel Mercure, solicited for a socio-economic overview of vulnerability, focuses his contribution on the analysis of phenomena of insecurity with regard to work and, particularly, the consequences that the various forms of flexibility have on the organisation of work. The resurgence of vulnerability in contemporary societies can only be understood through examination of the crumbling of labour relations and the splintering of the forms of employment. Both labour relations and employment were vital contributions to social cohesion, during the second half of the twentieth century. Flexible assignment is characteristic of the dynamic of the transformation of the organisation of work and of new forms of employment. As such it is of essential importance in framing the forms of acting in society, as it is conducive to a continual weakening of the individual.

Robert Castel continues this reflection by anchoring it in a socio-historical approach. He seeks to explain the foundations of the constitution of man, as an individual, in society in order to account for the reappearance at the forefront of the social scene of vulnerability. In modern society the individual has been able to constitute himself as such thanks to the existence of supports, firstly private property and then social property, which have served him as a basis. Today, the vulnerable individual is thrown back onto the status of a person made vulnerable by the crumbling of the mechanisms of social protection. Unequally supported individuals find that they are weakened and vulnerable as the supports that had been put into place to enable them to fulfil promises of autonomy are eroded. Deprived of these supports, they are doubly condemned, on the one hand, to act without attachments and stable supports, on the other, to have just themselves for reference and perspective. Mass vulnerability, created by a loss of belonging to collectives which gave them the right to certain claims and granted protection, results in over-exposure, making all form of action costly.

But these two approaches would not suffice to apprehend the complexity of the issues of vulnerability. Jacques Fierens, basing himself on a socio-juridical interpretation, seeks to put vulnerability back within the broader issue of Human Rights, and particularly within the assertion of equal dignity that they contain. This assertion proves to be the compensatory counterpart to the power of acting through which the human being in society defines himself. The fact that dignity is appealed to over and over again underlines the extent to which social situations and experiences of denial and vulnerability confront many members of society with the powerlessness to act, or at the very least with the difficulty of doing so. At the same time, it is hard to put dignity formally into law as it is so susceptible to interpretation. It constitutes, in fact, a reference basis, a matrix principle, which needs to be subject to, and included in, the public debate so that everyone can participate in defining the content. All the more so, because only the dignity of those who have a voice, preferably a public voice, is recognised.

Jean-Marc Ferry, favouring a socio-philosophical interpretation, seeks, within the framework of an opening up of the public argument to the vulnerability of human dignity, to define what could be the basis of political justice. He demonstrates the opportunity that exists to broaden the spectrum of political justice, through the use of reconstructive ethics based on the unique individuality of the social actors. Taking the expressive strength of narration and argumentation as support, this form of ethics participates in the structuring of a place that is receptive to the expression of social suffering, and which is essential for its political translation.

Thus the question of access to citizenship in a context of vulnerability arises. Giovanna Procacci, exploring the socio-political sphere, aims to clarify the relationship between these two concepts. Prior to being a system of rights, citizenship is a principle of recognition, particularly of the right of having access to these rights. In this sense, it is not just a political bond, although today it is often reduced to this. Citizenship is also the vehicle of a social bond that is challenged by exclusion. Intervention policies too often omit this element, thus concentrate on the individual, who is condemned to re-integrate himself at the same time as he is made vulnerable in his places of belonging. Paradoxically, such intervention policies contribute to the creation of a structural context which renders the people they target even more vulnerable, thus also limiting their capability to act. This situation analysed for various contexts by contributors of this volume: Serge Paugam (occupational precariousness), Danièle Laberge and Shirley Roy (survival and homelessness) and Franz Schultheis (specific state assistance programmes).

In the analysis made by Serge Paugam, occupational precariousness effectively weakens the feeling of belonging to the group and the very meaning of the action within (and for the) group, although it is necessary to distinguish between several types of insecurity. On the basis of a typology of incomplete forms of professional integration Serge Paugam looks at both the relationship to a job and to the conditions of employment. His analysis shows that the invalidating form of integration, marked by powerlessness and the lack of confidence, makes the greatest contribution to a distancing from political and collective action as well as action of solidarity.

Danièle Laberge and Shirley Roy explore the problem of the continuity of self in a context of survival. For itinerant or homeless people, who face situations of extreme vulnerability, one of the major problems in terms of action is to maintain their physical and psychological integrity. Holding on and coping with the situation, before even thinking about getting out of it, constitute costly operations that entail heavy consequences. The maintenance of a positive self-image in extreme conditions, the preservation of a congruence of identity in a world that seriously deconstructs, the neutralisation of negative and stigmatising representations, are so many operations that suppose resources and skills, strange as this may seem. Cognitive operations and symbolic work are combined with a composite use of the scarce and uncertain resources offered by the environment to be able to successfully carry out this work of continuity of identity.

Franz Schultheis reminds us that vulnerability is always set, to a greater or lesser extent, in a relationship of domination. He takes as his theme the forms of action developed by precarious populations, people seeking state assistance, within the framework of a special programme aimed at the combating of vulnerability. By analysing the material and symbolic exchanges within a structure which fundamentally assigns status unequally, the paradoxical result leads to a reinforcing of vulnerability of those with the least lack of cultural capital through the effect of stigmatisation, and to an established vulnerability for those who are the most lacking in resources through the effect of dependence. Only the intermediate categories in this programme, conceived as being destined for a homogenous population, fully benefit from the resources offered and construct alternatives to the offer imposed on them.

In conclusion, Marc-Henry Soulet seeks to outline a model of understanding what acting is when individuals are situated at the limits of the possibility to act, using an analysis framework based on situations of vulnerability understood as being an action context marked by a weakening of the ordinary and stable action structures.

Note

1   *Faire face et s'en sortir. Agir en situation de vulnérabilité.* Symposium of the International Association of Francophone Sociologists organised by the Chair of social work (Department of social work and social policies) of the university of Fribourg, 27-28 September 2001.

References

Châtel, V. and Soulet, M.H. (2002), *Faire face et s'en sortir.* Volume 1, *Négociation identitaire et capacité d'action.* Volume 2, *Développement des compétences et action collective,* Éditions Universitaires, Fribourg.

Chapter 1

Acting in a Situation of Social Vulnerability: Constructing the Problem

Vivianne Châtel

To situate this attempt at a problematisation, I would like to set it in the context of a story, a commonplace story like one of those stories that we all know, the only difference being, perhaps, that this one is not about people who are excluded – as per the usual categories – or people with a disability, or about (multiple) drug-addicts, in other words, it is not about any of the categories usually understood as being vulnerable. It concerns a highly-qualified female person, employed in a state-owned company. After years of official employment and services rendered, this person was not given a permanent appointment for purely extra-professional reasons. The reason being, a fact which was, moreover, common knowledge well before she took up her post, a long-term relationship with another member of the work group. What is it that makes this situation interesting, given that it is, after all, banal in the face of the recent and future redundancies made by large companies?

Simply because it is a fairly good presentation of the mechanisms of vulnerability and of the way that action mechanisms are weakened as a result, but also because it concerns social categories *a priori* considered as non-vulnerable and thus forgotten by the fields of analysis. Additionally this, especially, within the framework of our contemporary societies where work tends to retain a place of major importance, that it gives identity.

This story enables us to highlight several issues, notably that of trust, that of the contradiction internal to economic discourse and that of the capability of acting, issues which should allow us to outline the question of acting in a situation of vulnerability and especially to distinguish the prerequisites.

The first issue then is that of being placed in a situation of vulnerability by negation of the trust placed in the company. To understand this negation, it is important to return to the organisational principles of contemporary society. Many analyses have appeared over recent years concerning the place of work in the present-day world. They all agree on acknowledging the essential place that work occupies, an essential place that prompts us to wonder about the employee / place of work relationship (where the place of work refers to any place of work, be it in a public institution, a small, medium, large or very large company). The requirements of the world of the place of work aim to establish a relationship of trust. In this trust means that the person places his/her future in the hands of the company. Trust, also means the internalisation of the principles which guide the professional act in the current work context. This tends to accentuate the concern for an appropriateness between the values of the employee and that of the company, an appropriateness between official rules and unofficial rules from which no place of work can escape. Trust also, inasmuch that is guided by implicit knowledge and socialised into certain work codes, the person invests himself/herself in a relationship which is intrinsic to a history which gives him/her a meaning and an end (permanency in the job, mobility or something else). Finally, trust, when in the normative professional world, investment as loyalty are both recognised and approved criteria. In the example evoked, which will serve as our main thread, trust placed in the professional sphere turns out to be profoundly affected, even betrayed. The criteria that are generally effective are not functioning. For one face, one name, one history, investment and loyalty are not acknowledged.

Trust has only recently been studied by sociology, despite the fact that it is a key issue in social relations. It is essential insofar as it is independent of, or is a substitute for, contracts and other co-operation agreements which have a juridical basis. There is no need for a written or oral promise, or for a legal contract. Trusting Others, is as it were, thinking, though without being completely sure, that Others will keep their commitments, even, and especially, if these are implicit, which of course has consequences for the situation or the action context. In other words, if I trust Others, I act in reference to the fact that Others are supposed to keep their commitments, commitments which are not necessarily explicit promises, but which take into account the action context and the behaviour expectations. Here we encounter the acquisitions of Weberian sociology where social activity and typification (to use the terminology of Alfred Schütz) are inextricably linked. Thus trust is inherently a weakening, because it is partly based on official rules but also on implicit knowledge. Trust supposes not only an analysis of the interests of the various parties involved, but also an inevitable risk, that of betrayal. Hence, our idea of a weakening, insofar as it is difficult to count on the idea of a reputation to defend in a socio-cultural world where, finally, only individual performance is what matters. In the contemporary perspective of social relations which are guided by individual success and indifference to the future of Others, trust becomes dependence. Somewhat in the logic of the economic contract denounced by Émile Durkheim as incapable of creating social cohesion, simply because today's ally would be tomorrow's enemy. Trust and dependence are thus linked because everything hangs on protagonists who connect their actions to the degree of capability that they assign to their allies of keeping their unspoken commitments, of respecting a word that is also unspoken, but which is embedded in customs, or perhaps in interpretable official codes. Each action situation is a situation of interpretation, inherently dependant on the real-life world of the participants. The values and ways of being of some do not completely tally with the values and ways of being of others, and this is true even within a same social group. Unfortunate experiences during holidays shared with best friends are just one testimony to the distress caused by promises not being kept and trust being betrayed.

Therefore, besides the issue of knowing whether trust today still constitutes a transmitted and internalised value, or more exactly whether its near equivalent, respect of commitments and codes, is still a recognised and reasserted social practice, it is important to understand that dependence, which stems from trust, is not a reciprocal principle. In fact, the idea of trust conceals the idea of power and especially of *power over* (to take Paul Ricœur's phrase), knowing that:

> It is difficult to imagine situations of interaction in which one individual does not exert a power over another by the very fact of acting. (Ricœur, 1992, 220)

In other words, it conceals the idea that there is never an exact equivalence between the *power of* Others and the *power over* Others. Trust is abused when this fundamental Kantian distinction between a person as an end in himself/herself and a person as a means disappears, leaving the way free for *power over* to exert itself, without any possible reciprocity, even without risk. Basically, the idea of trust, especially in a world of the fundamental differentiation of social positions and thus in a world of social inequalities (whether visible or not), takes us back to the idea of social justice and even more so to the application of moral criteria. It is particularly based on the idea that *power over* will not be exerted in a way that breaches fundamental freedoms, or more exactly the social codes and practices that govern a given institution.

Now, in our example, *power over* is exerted in opposition to the established codes and practices. Trust being a category which drives social relations in their entirety, it is a particular motor of professional relations. In the world of work, which is subject to the imperatives of profitability and competitiveness, trust proves to be essentially dependent and subject to, the (non) application of moral imperatives, insofar as it cannot merely be reduced to the idea of the evaluation of risks. This reduction would then mean that the person who gives their trust has the power to not give it. But to what extent can *power over* be subsumed under ethico-juridical considerations, particularly in a world where the media of Power and Money dominate? To what extent, in such a world, is trust reduced to nothingness, which, moreover, seems to be the status accorded it by the juridical proceedings of our societies, in which the search for a perpetrator is ever more intensified. The consequence is the creation 'of a society of victims, everyone seeking to appear to be one so as to benefit from compensation' (Engel, 1995, 17).[1] Trust then is relative. In such a societal context, it is particularly subordinate to the capability of the participants to not be totally dominated by the possible gains resulting from a lawsuit should an injury be incurred, especially because the activity is freely agreed (in which each participant is aware of the risks that he/she is taking in the activity).

If, as a result, trust is approached as being a mainstay of social cohesion, it merits all our attention. In our story, the breaching of trust is a breach of the capability to act. Simply put, it weakens the *power to do* of the actor who, while being the author of his/her acts, no longer has control over the consequences. Anyone in a position of subordination, unless they have the capacity to harm, is weakened when the aims of the protagonists differ. In order to face this, self-esteem which Paul Ricœur likens to 'the dignity attached to the moral status of the human person' hardly counterbalances the logic of interest (Ricœur, 2000, 138). Indeed, this self-esteem is denied as a skill or as vehicle for the idea of the subject. Consequently, trust betrayed, leads to low self-esteem rather than to the acknowledgement of a Self-subject-capable of imputation.

The second issue actualised by our story concerns the contradictions inherent to the discourse of the economic world. In the past, it was obligatory:

> not only to work, but to work within the framework of traditional structures, accepting a wage which was also unalterably fixed; and not only idleness, begging and itinerancy were condemned, but also any attempts to negotiate the wage or to seek another job with better conditions. (Castel, 1989, 12-13)

Today, it is still obligatory to work, but more, especially, to be flexible. Idleness, begging and itinerancy are still condemned – some politicians do not hesitate to take anti-begging measures. But it is the ways in which job legislation is regularly undermined which particularly deserve our attention (e.g. the transfer of manufacturing to a developing country). In fact, over the last few years, identification, mobility and flexibility have become essential and dominating values. The economic world effectively has the habit of suggesting that a career is (or will be) divided between several posts – different jobs, different places, different social positions. This claim brings into play one of the elements of the economic and financial sphere, without concern for the people involved, even without concern for the world – to repeat the fears of the advocates of sustainable development. Flexibility, like work time, subject only to the requirements of the company and without any other criteria being taken into consideration, and mobility within the sphere of employment, are dominant values in the economic world. They form the point where the organisation of contemporary society pauses, as though the latter were completely conquered by, or had sworn allegiance to economic demands.

In a recent, rather polemic work, Pierre-André Taguieff wonders, not irrelevantly about *le bougisme* (unsettledness) or what he also calls *le mouvementisme* (shifting), as a mark of contemporary society (Taguieff, 2001). Within this perspective, the economic sphere calls for mobility, flexibility, constant adaptation, for a kind of constant movement, but also for permanent availability. Employees of all types must continually be the best, the most capable, the most competent, the most competitive, the most driven... In order to 'go with the flow', to take the terminology of advertising or the media, you have to move, have drive, go for it. But to go where? Living in the world certainly presupposes adapting oneself, but adapting oneself to what, in the end, and according to which norms?

We are seeing the appearance, alongside the gulf that is forming between rich countries and poor countries, alongside the environmental issues, a split at the very heart of the western world. This split between two worlds, vis-à-vis this new requirement for flexibility and mobility, is characterised by two aspects. On the one hand, there are those who surf this wave of mobility, so fervently demanded by the economic sphere. On the other, there are those who are uneasy, not with regard to investment in work, but with regard to permanent geographic mobility, or an imposed flexibility, who consequently become victims of this pliability of the frameworks, flexibility which becomes insecurity, which is undermining. Furthermore, this split rests on two other contradictions, one internal to the very discourse of large companies with this demand for total flexibility/mobility, and at the same time, the demand for the identification of the employee with the company. The other is internal to the political world which condemns the failure of parents to take responsibility for the education of their children and simultaneously, does not call into question this flexibility, which is translated into elastic working hours rarely compatible with parental responsibility. It does not ask any questions about the minimum social conditions necessary for the exercise of this parental responsibility.[2]

In other words, to return to the first contradiction, the economic sphere suggests, and demands, a near-total identification of the person with his/her place of work. However, it does not hesitate to call this investment and this identification into question and to deny it all relevance. This demand of the economic world for total flexibility/mobility seems to forget the social and normative background which guides and defines the work relationship of thousands of people, while several ways of imagining the work relationship are identifiable, such as the mobility model and the professional model (Francfort, Osty, Sainsaulieu and Uhalde, 1995).[3]

The first model reflects an over-determination of the personal trajectory in the implication of the individual in the place of work. It is not the values of the company that validate this implication, but primarily the idea of amassing experience, accumulating skills, gathering professional reflections and observations; it is, to use current terminology, improving one's 'employability' by a diversification of lived experiences. Mobility is, in this sense, an asset laid claim to and perfectly well-assumed. In other words, there are no qualms about the company. What guides the acts of the employees who fit this schema is only defined by the knowledge or the new skills that they can acquire, or by the positive experience for their own curriculum vitae, or an interest may be purely personal (financial, symbolic, cultural). No consideration is given to the fact that the employee is not attached to the company and can get a high price (when there is no economic crisis of course) for his/her skills, his/her experience, or his/her know-how. In this sense, the employee perfectly fits the 'unsettledness' era. Free of all attachments, free of all constraints. Free, or rather detached, in the sense of having no attachments, but also without real ties, apart from potential ones.

To return to the strategies of the actor, this perspective cannot be shared by everybody. In fact, a certain number of considerations – social, familial and cultural – must be taken into account to explain the strategies of the actors at this level. Thus, family obligations often put a stop to this demand for mobility, to this call for 'unsettledness', together with life histories, experience, illusions and disillusions, or commitments. This mobility strategy concerns *in fine* a very small part of the population which is easily identified.[4] Whether a person is young without attachments, married with child(ren) at school and has a spouse who works in a responsible job with a high level of social recognition, or unmarried but with a strong local family or social involvement, all affect the possibility of being mobile. The same considerations apply to flexibility: who *in fine* can allow themselves to accept open-ended working hours? The person who has no choice (because of the burden of family expenses), or the person who can capitalise on his/her experience. Though the reduction in working hours (to 35) in France has resulted in supplementary days of rest for some selected professional categories, for others (notably factory workers), it is just another way of making the worker more exploitable because he/she is subject to the demands of the factory. Flexibility, in this framework, simply becomes a disguised way of adapting working hours to the ups and downs of production. It is not a way of improving living conditions, of favouring family time – which is not time spent on household tasks. Also it does not encourage participation in social, cultural, civic activities, in other words participation in activities with high symbolic value – activities which are not remunerated, but which have great potential for integration.[5]

The other model of relationship to work that interests us here is the professional model, marked by the content of work and the way that the individuals see it. The concern for work well-done, for service rendered, skills developed, constitutes a mark of belonging, a certain socialisation in ways of being, of thinking and acting, which today perhaps are marginalised, but are still active. It is commitment, not necessarily to the company, but to the work, to its content or its symbolism, which is the determining factor.

Here we can recall *hussards* of the French Republic, those teachers strongly imbued with the republican ideal or again, in a completely different category, the *compagnons*, those aesthetes of wood and stone who have marked, and still mark, the great restorations of historic monuments, and who are indisputably the worthy representatives of *homo faber*, driven by the search for the durability of the object. But some people are subjected to this 'shifting' associated with a logic of the disposable, of consumption here and now, without any concern for durability. Does not the fact of always producing more in order to always consume more finally tend towards the absurd, transforming contemporary society into the disposable society?

But what of the other point of contradiction raised above: the demand for a common identity? Various seminars, company conferences or coaching and other study days all have the same single aim: to define a culture which is common to the members of a company, often, but not only, under the pretext of globalisation, of the grouping of companies, or just simply for reasons of efficiency, or for the image of the institution – as much places for the formatting, for the pinpointing of the potentialities and weaknesses of people, as places for the development of a common company culture. *In fine*, this is where the paradox lies: on the one hand, the demand of the professional world is for increased competitiveness, inordinate profitability and complete investment, total identification with the company. On the other hand, the person is finally a toy that one moves around, that one makes redundant, depending on how one feels, depending on stock-market profits (for large companies), or on displeasure, jealousies, resentment and, especially, depending on games of power or manipulation. It is futile to think that a same company culture can soften, or even wipe out, the effects of power and manipulation. On the contrary, the company culture is there to reinforce the feeling of belonging to the company, the need to invest in the company. In the context of production stakes, of profits for the shareholders, of results to be attained, it is characterised by a concomitant development of feelings of rivalry and of competition. This can not only be counter-productive, but can also contribute to a sense of ill-being and a vulnerability which are hardly recognised.

Here there is a clash of spheres of values. The values of implication, of service rendered, of identification, versus the values of flexibility or again, and more really, of the availability of self, or again versus the values of manipulation, of power which many actors do not have the required resources to deal with. This confrontation takes place to the detriment of other values, and by no means the least important ones, in particular, the responsibility of the employee vis-à-vis his or her family commitments.

Consequently, does this make it essential to understand the workings of reactions in situations of vulnerability, in a crisis of trust, in a confrontation of values? Apart from the question of the very possibility of acting, several reactions are likely in such a context, such as, among others, nonchalance, a re-definition of priorities, or the loss of self-confidence, in other words the developing of low self-esteem. Not only the capability of acting in a situation that calls into question the human being, but also the shaping of the action, will, to a great extent if not exclusively, depend on one's capital of social and cultural, psychological, not to say psychical resources. The possible responses suppose specific resources which directly inform the life course and the person's motivations for acting. In other words, not just anybody can be nonchalant about such things, certain skills are required to be able to take that attitude. Here, the mechanisms of vulnerability come into play, mechanisms which call on the social resources of the person concerned, on his social anchorages but also on the chain of experience which, in the end, constitutes his real-life world. Family socialisation, acquired values, the social trajectory, possible situations of betrayal which lead to a precarious identity, everything can finally converge towards a vulnerability which is not latent but real. Consequently, vulnerability is no longer restricted to the domain of the badly-integrated or excluded, it touches the whole of the social world.

In this context how do we face vulnerability and come through? This question certainly comes back to the issue of supports for the action. In order to act, does the person have the benefit of clear frameworks, of conditions which are guaranteed, i.e. which are predictable, whether these be structural resources, reticular resources or community resources (Castel and Haroche, 2001)? However it also returns, apart from these resources which are generally emphasised, to *the capability of putting one's vulnerability into words, which here constitutes our third issue*. To take an example which, admittedly, is extreme: what was experienced through the concentration camps has shown just how difficult it is to find the words to tell the incredible. It has shown the limits of speech and words themselves in the act of communication for the act of saying not to alleviate but merely to signify. How to say things without the putting into words becoming a support for justification?

> You can tell all about this experience... Even if you remain caught up in it, prolonging death, if necessary – reviving it endlessly in the nooks and crannies of the story. Even if you become no more than the language of this death, and live at its expense, fatally. But can people hear everything, imagine everything? Will they be able to understand? Will they have the necessary patience, passion, compassion, and fortitude? I begin to doubt it, in that first moment, that first meeting with men from *before*, from the *outside*, emissaries from life – when I see the stunned, almost hostile, and certainly suspicious look in the eyes of the three officers. (Semprun, 1997, 14)

Certainly everything can be said, but can everything be listened to and heard? How can we listen to the inconceivable? How can we accept the unacceptable? It is, as it were, the anguish of credibility.

In this same perspective, is the vulnerability lived in the company and/or in society quite simply capable of being put into words? Does the actor in this situation run the risk of being more greatly discredited at the very moment when all attention is turned towards the intensification of the Self, of competence, of strength, of professional success? Will the others have the necessary 'rigour' to hear, and thus to go beyond the prejudice of incompetence and to refuse just to pity? Is not someone who fails quite simply classified under the heading of incapable, incompetent? In the current logic of 'shifting' to go back to the expression of Pierre-André Taguieff, is not the fact of recounting one's vulnerability, running the risk of being considered, not only incompetent or weak, but also backward, lacking innovation, incredibly outmoded? Is it always easy and possible to say that you have been fired despite your investment and your dedication? Does not the actor, in this situation, run the risk of being disowned, disrespected insofar as the person who invests himself, who is dedicated and competent cannot possibly be fired, except in cases of great economic crises? It is simply not credible and it is the entire register of trust that collapses. In the end, on what does the credibility of the interlocutor hang?

Between fascination and despair, the excluded, the weak, the victims, suffer (...) the shame of their situation and of the logic that sweeps them along. Furthermore, the perversion of the code and the perversion of the prevailing discourse work to make them responsible to the point of feeling guilty. (Diet, 1994, 160)

Thinking themselves guilty of an uncommitted error which only serves to undermine their credibility. We are obliged, in order to understand acting in situations of vulnerability, to mobilise the chain of experience, the chain of illusions/disillusions which mark the trajectory of a person, enabling us not only to understand hi/her relationship to Others, his/her relationship to the company or to the institution, but also to his/her moral commitments. This is where the question of narration becomes relevant.

To understand the acts, and even more, to imagine them, we need to be able to have access to the history of a life, to these social and cultural experiences, to this capital which orients, defines and structures attitudes. Hence, the importance of narration at the basis of interaction, maybe even, of the possibility of social cohesion. But does not the possibility of narration itself depend on these experiences, this chain of illusions/disillusions? What finally guarantees access to narration, that is to say the putting into words of self? Does vulnerability not constitute an obstacle to this narration, to the very possibility of this narration, due to the degree to which the skills, the potentialities of the person are called into question by vulnerability. In another text we put forward what seemed to us to be one of the major obstacles to the exercising of the theory of communicational activity, namely being educated in discursive language, as all members of the society do not possess the same capability of putting things into words (Châtel, to be published). Which is what Paul Ricœur's analysis confirms with remarkable pertinence:

What is immediately obvious is this basic inequality of people as regards the mastering of speech, inequality which is much less determined by nature than by a perverse effect of culture, when the powerlessness to say things, results in effective exclusion outside of the sphere of language; in this respect one of the very first forms of equality of chances concerns equality on the level of being able to speak, of being able to say, to explain, to argue, to debate. (Ricœur, 2001, 90)

If speaking is to create a common world, then it is also necessary for exchange to be possible, and an exchange which is not organised into a hierarchy. But is the vulnerable person in the same place, on the same level as the non-vulnerable person? Even if he/she has the benefit of *being able to speak*, this does not mean that his/her words are going to be considered as being equally relevant or are going to be given the same attention. By being vulnerable, by considering himself/herself vulnerable, he/she loses the strength of saying, even though he/she has benefited from this strength at some moment in his/her life. We should recall, to show the strength of the link between vulnerability and (in-)capability of saying, Georg

Herbert Mead's belief that socialisation is constructed around interactions which are mediated by language (1934).

How, finally, can we enter into a *reconstructive dialectic* (Ferry, 1996), aiming to explain misunderstanding, aiming to explain differences of interpretation and aiming to resolve conflicts or incomprehension when people are denied as people? In vulnerability, everything hangs on trust and credibility, and thus recognition. If one of the fundamental limits of communicational activity resides precisely in the practical impossibility of the ideal situation for argumentation (both the lack of access of everybody to the place of discussion and the not taking into account of everybody in the same spirit of equality of speech), is this not precisely because, in the face of events, of experiences lived, recognition is not obligatorily acquired, too marked as it is by the register of what is just and what is unjust, of the credible and the incredible?

Narration/reconstruction as a possible way of overcoming misunderstandings, sufferings lived seems finally to deny, or seems to not take into account, the very logic which ends in the denial of some by others. If narration is a guarantee of sincerity, of soundness, even of truth, are one's conditions of possibility not however linked to one's self-esteem? In other words, if one considers himself/herself as worthless, useless and without qualities, can one still talk about himself/herself? In fact, denying the other skills, or simply setting him/her in the circle of the negation of self, is this not finally refusing Others their dimension of an acting and speaking subject? Is narration at all possible within the framework of a lack of self-esteem? Is it at all possible within the framework of vulnerability? Is vulnerability not then an obstacle to social participation, even to social life? In refusing Others their dimension of an acting and speaking subject, that is to say of a responsible subject, as a principle of belonging to the world, it is the very possibility of social cohesion which is called into question.

Is society at all ready to hear about these chains of misfortunes and suffering which are connected to these lives made vulnerable, lost, deprived, and is it ready to act? Is society at all ready to hear the inconceivable, or that which it defines as inconceivable, such as child workers, slavery, desocialisation or, as in our example, the refusal of a permanent post for extra-professional reasons?

These various issues (trust, flexibility and the possibility of narration which punctuate the possibility of acting) constitute the bases of my reflection. In other words, in a sociological context which is strongly marked by the affirmation of the subject – though perhaps it would be more fitting to speak rather of the individual – in an economic context strongly marked by the idea of profitability and competitiveness, even of self-development through and in the place of work, it seems relevant to ask ourselves questions about acting in a situation of vulnerability. It is reinforced because this vulnerability calls into question the very notion of subject, if by subject we of course understand this capability to act and to think in a responsible and autonomous manner, i.e. by oneself and with a critical mind, resumed by the Kantian maxims:

(1) To think for oneself; (2) to think from the standpoint of every one else; (3) always to think consistently. (Kant, 1973, 152)

The individual is *product* and *initiator*. The dimension of initiator being undeniably subordinated to the social history (which is an entanglement of histories) of the person, i.e. subordinated to these chains of frustrations, negations, and disillusions which, over time, make up the identity framework of the person. These drive the course of his life and which *in fine* inform his construction of identity, in other words, it is considerably subordinate to that which constitutes the individual as product.

Action, or mastery of situations, presents itself as a circular process in which the actor is at once both the *initiator* of his accountable actions and the *product* of the traditions in which he stands, of the solidary groups to which he belongs, of socialization and learning processes to which he is exposed. (Habermas, 1987, 135, authors's italics)

Understanding acting in a situation of vulnerability supposes then turning our attention to this socialisation process which has stamped, and continues to stamp, the life course of the actor, his actions as much as his decisions, his strength as much as his weakness. Also the vagaries and the delights of life do not stamp life histories in the same way. There is no point here in returning to the lessons of Pierre Bourdieu on capital and habitus. It is, however, worth recalling their importance in the current socio-economic context in which the individual is only defined by his professional position, and repeating their fecundity for the understanding of acting in a situation of vulnerability.

The *habitus*, a product of history, produces individual and collective practices – more history – in accordance with the schemes generated by history. It ensures the active presence of past experiences, which, deposited in each organism in the form of schemes of perception, thought and action, tend to guarantee the 'correctness' of practices and their constancy over time, more reliably than all formal rules and explicit norms (...) Because the *habitus* is an infinite capacity for generating products – thoughts, perceptions, expressions and actions – whose limits are set by the historically and socially situated conditions of its production, the conditioned and conditional freedom it provides is a remote from creation of unpredictable novelty as it is from simple mechanical reproduction of the original conditioning. (Bourdieu, 1990, 54-55)

Habitus is then, to take the established expression, a structuring structure of the social world, but also of the individual. In the form of internalised arrangements, it orients experiences, encounters, and is redefined, remodelled by these experiences, these encounters, these frustrations, illusions and disillusions. It initiates the capability of the individual to free himself from his past, whilst being profoundly marked by this past.

> Because he always depends on the other, the subject finds himself determined by a prehistory, a historical and cultural social context, discourses, values and norms which preside over his genesis. (Diet, 1994, 160).

But what happens when, finally, under the operative rule of efficiency and of profitability, these symbols, these reference points which enable the individual to form himself as subject, as a complete subject, i.e. autonomous and responsible are broken up.

> The production of appearance, voluntary falsification of information, appeals for 'realism', all manner of means are implemented to destroy the very possibilities of a making sense of, and of critically examining oneself and the other. Xenophobia, racism, contempt for the other, hatred of difference and of thought seep through social cohesion. Trivialised, from then on they rule communication, which is reduced to the transmission of efficient information whose only function is to seduce or to terrorise.(…) Efficiency and productivity, in a world of management, where the Stock Exchange, succeeding to the Throne and the Altar, is the only reference, reduce subjects to things, objects produced and manipulated whose right to existence depends on their economic and social utility. (Diet, 1994, 161)

So what then becomes of all those who are without acknowledged social and economic utility?

How to be a subject in a world that denies you your status of subject, capable of imputation, that is to say, in a world of vulnerability? How to be a person in a world of vulnerability? Though it is here a question of trust, of issues of conventionality, all social constructs that go well beyond internalisations, disillusions, sufferings and misfortunes, it is also a question of social recognition. It is also and especially a question of responsibility for Others, in the strongest sense of the term, i.e. of feeling oneself responsible for Others, whoever these Others may be, and of belonging to a common humanity, of belonging to the public place. Leaving aside the vulnerability which is intrinsically linked to the mortal status of the human being,[6] apprehension of this concept takes us back to two registers distinct in their conceptualisation but particularly fruitful in reaching this side of vulnerability, namely. Firstly, vulnerability as being specific to the responsible human being, a vulnerability of a moral nature, as it were, and secondly, vulnerability making it impossible for a person to appear to the world, in other words a vulnerability of a social nature.

First register then, vulnerability as consequence of an extreme responsibility. All of the problematics of sustainable development, echoed by the Rio Conference, and constantly repeated and evoked, testifies, on the environmental level, to the massive destruction of eco-systems, to the plundering of nature, sometimes through the intermediary of particular social groups (e.g. the plundering of the genetic patrimony of entire populations, such as that of the inhabitants of the Islands of Tonga or of Iceland), to the unlimited and irreversible force of technology and science. On the socio-economic level, to the globalisation of exchanges, to the poorest populations being exploited unscrupulously and in a way that is beyond the most elementary of human rights, to the loss of social reference points, to the constant search for pleasure, making the need for an examination of the question of responsibility an urgent one. This unlimited seeking of responsibility is often condemned as *in fine* counterproductive because it restricts to inaction. To be master of one's destiny supposes at the least being capable of determining the consequences of one's acts (whether this be at the level of scientific and technical discoveries, or at the level of our most everyday acts imbued with the relationship to the Other). Without this approach, the individual remains an individual and cannot accede to the status of subject because he quite simply remains under the yoke of masters and tutors, incapable of thinking for oneself; to take one on the Kantian maxims. Man, master of his destiny, or, on the contrary, being vulnerable because he is totally subjected to the imperatives of the all-powerful economic-financial force via the exploitation of man by man and via the massive destruction of the environment?

Without denying the relevance of the *responsibility principle* of Hans Jonas[7] (1984), here we shall refer to another concept, that of responsibility for Others, borrowed from Emmanuel Lévinas. This, notably, insofar as responsibility for Others is not via the awareness of the unlimited power of man over nature, an awareness which is most certainly pressing, but via the awareness of existence, in their social nakedness, of the Other person. The main intention in the work of Emmanuel Lévinas can be conveyed by the idea that concern for the Other is specific to humanity. It is the imperative of the face which solicits my responsibility for Others. And I cannot turn away from these sufferings, I cannot turn away from this summons. In this encounter with a face in its nakedness, the face makes an appeal to me and to nobody else. Others, enigmas, both similar and different, are lived as an assignation of responsibility.

In this perspective, where Others becomes an injunction for oneself, thus an ethical injunction before being a moral one, this responsibility for Others becomes a practical value even if the infinite of my responsibility (which supposes responsibility for Others) constitutes a challenge, even a practical impossibility. Consequently, this concept of responsibility for Others becomes particularly fruitful for our wish to understand acting in a situation of vulnerability. Agreeing to this influence of responsibility for Others, is to agree to be a hostage, Emmanuel Lévinas would say. Although this interpretation is profoundly singular because non-reciprocal, it supposes and questions the impossibility of taking refuge behind the fatalism of powerlessness that leads to inaction. To the 'each of us is guilty in everything before everyone, and I most of all' of one of the Karamazov brothers (Dostoïevski, 1992, 289), which continues the idea of responsibility for Others, many analysts reply with the impossibility of responsibility due to a limited action horizon.[8]   This only takes on meaning in the proximity which is immediately perceptible and spatially limited, simply because our measurable and personal actions in response to exploitation, to slavery, to genocide, to glaring inequalities, to non-recognition and to contempt for human beings who have become units of accountancy, is particularly insignificant. And yet! How can we accept to live alongside thousands of men, women and children who are excluded, useless to the world, enslaved or starving? How can we so easily turn away from these sufferings, from this glaring vulnerability? How can we accept to be borne along only by concern for oneself, the pursuit of self? How, finally, can we accept the indecency of this pursuit of self when it rubs shoulders with the most complete dehumanisation? Or again, why do we see the sense of all human action only in gain, easy money and power?

'It is in the interhuman perspective of *my* responsibility for the other, without concern for reciprocity, in my call for his or her disinterested help, in the asymmetry of the relation of *one* to the *other*' (Lévinas, 1998, 101, author's italics) that we see vulnerability. From this viewpoint, vulnerability asks the essential question, and admittedly this is unexpected because it is despite the processes of civilisation and the process of *Aufklärung*, of the relationship to Others, of the relation to Others.

> Nobody can remain in himself: the humanity of man, subjectivity, is a responsibility for others, an extreme vulnerability. (…) It is a question of the subjectivity of the subject – non-indifference to others in unlimited responsibility, – because it is not measured in terms by commitments. (Lévinas, 1996, 109)

It is then in and by the social relationship that man learns this responsibility for Others. To approach these Others, is to constantly call oneself into question. But does not man take refuge behind the mask of social success, of affirmation of self to stave off this appeal, to stave off this injunction? How can we content ourselves with a 'limited and egoist fate of him who is only for-himself, and washes his hands of the faults and misfortunes of others' (Lévinas, 1999, 116). Though the fact of fraternity precedes the liberty of the subject, responsibility for Others precedes social belonging. Thus it precedes typification. It precedes the expectation of behaviour. Responding to the potential (social) vulnerability of the Other person, is the vulnerability of he who responds and who not only 'always has one response more to give' (Lévinas, 1999, 134) but a responsibility which is inexhaustible. Vulnerability, because it is an injunction of responsibility that I cannot ignore.

> Here there is proximity and not tenth about proximity, not certainty about the presence of the other, but responsibility for him without deliberation, and without the compulsion of truths in which commitments arise, without certainty. This responsibility commits me, and does so before any truth and any certainty, making the question of trust and norms

an *idle* question, for in its uprightness a consciousness is not only naivety and opinion. (Lévinas, 1999, 120)

Through this responsibility for Others, Emmanuel Lévinas challenges all recourse to reason, to science, to knowledge. The responsibility that is assigned to me proceeds from the denuded man to whom I am a hostage. Responsibility for Others is situated then prior to social relations even if it remains consubstantial to the relationship to Others, but a relationship to Others which is de-socialised or more exactly pre-socialised. Concern for Others is indeed the sign of the human, but it is previous to the social knowledge of the Other, and, above all, it is previous to (and has priority over) concern for oneself. The definition of the ethical act lies, for Emmanuel Lévinas, in this acceptance or this acknowledgement of this priority of the Other over all other considerations. This responsibility for Others constitutes what is specifically human and which resides precisely in this openness to the Other. But in the act of negation of the Other, in the refusal to see him, not only does the Other find himself locked in a closed world, but the 'I' (which excludes) also finds itself locked in a closed world, in its world to which only those who are the same have access. In this confinement/blindness, I can no longer experience either plurality or singularity.

This responsibility for Others interpellates us on several levels: first of all it obliges a re-interpretation of the relationship to Others, a redefinition of Others other than through a relationship of utility, of equality, even of reciprocity because:

Other as another is not only an alter ego; he is what I am not and this not because of his character or because of his physiognomy, or because of his psychology, but because of his very otherness. (Lévinas, 1994, 75)

Consequently, responsibility for Others obliges us then to rethink the issue of social cohesion. In the shift of attention to Others, the subject becomes vulnerable. The subjectivity of the subject, writes Emmanuel Lévinas, is vulnerability, as exposure to the Other for whom I am responsible and for whom I am irreplaceable. To the concern for being oneself (borne by the concern for oneself, obsessed only by one's own image), to the purely egoistic logic of contemporary times, to the pursuit of self, responsibility for Others opposes the lack of concern for the Other and thus constitutes an extreme vulnerability (how to answer for Others?). Extreme vulnerability as this responsibility for Others assigns me the suffering of Others or responsibility for the acts of Others ('the uniqueness of the self is the very fact of bearing the fault of another' (Lévinas, 1999, 112)). Extreme vulnerability as this responsibility for Others condemns me, *a minima*, to the extent that the position of Emmanuel Lévinas is confined to the incommensurable and the impossible, to not be anaesthetised, to not suffer from amnesia, to not be blind. Therefore it also obliges us to interpellate ourselves on the conditions of belonging to a common humanity, such is the permanence of the misfortune, of the persecution and of the humiliations that perpetuates the tragedy of man.

The second register is therefore, vulnerability as the impossibility of acting. If we take the lessons of Hannah Arendt, the world can be interpreted as a plurality of perspectives, which corresponds to a plurality of human beings. It is 'the public space – which is constituted by acting together (...) the world-namely, the thing that arises between people and in which everything that individuals carry with them innately can become visible and audible' (Arendt, 1960, 9-10). Turning to Hannah Arendt after Emmanuel Lévinas may be surprising. However, it seems to us that responsibility for Others only takes on its entire force in a society where it is impossible to live alongside Others, without seeing them. For there to be responsibility for Others, there must be Others. The Face, even stripped of its socio-cultural attire, only exists if it appears. But in the current and incessant pursuit of Self, which generates total indifference to Others, Others simply do not exist – at least a certain number of Others. Hence, this detour via the notion of public place as a manifestation of the will to live together. The common world is defined as the place of appearance of beings who are both unique and similar. What makes the essence of the subject, is this belonging to a common world, is this possibility of appearing to the world, of being acknowledged in the world. To be excluded from it – that is to say to be excluded from an acknowledged place in a common world – is to be excluded from humanity. Hannah Arendt concludes her analysis of imperialism by these words, which are so terribly prophetic and pessimistic:

> The danger is that a global, universally interrelated civilization may produce barbarians from its own midst by forcing millions of people into conditions which, despite all appearances, are the conditions of savages. (Arendt, 1967a, 302)

So does vulnerability not do just this, destroy all possibility of public (and even private) production of self? Is vulnerability, not just precisely this, deprivation of an acknowledged place in the world? In the story of vulnerability evoked above and which serves as a common theme linking our analysis, it is in fact this deprivation which concerns us. Simply because the person concerned finds herself thrown back on just the private sphere, deprived of appearance in the world, deprived of participation in the world, deprived of recognition. She finds herself thrown back onto the status of a person who is not credible, a lack of credibility that is not related to falsification, but to a violent challenging of otherness, of her otherness. Setting someone apart and outside the world, putting them out of the game, is putting them outside of the rules of the world and notably outside of its rules of sociality. How then, when that is the case, can one still participate in its places of sociality, how can one still take an interest in the game of the world when one has been excluded?

Vulnerability, from this point of view, is basically experiencing something that is nonhuman, an experience that consists in being an object for other people.

Part of our existence lies in the feeling of those near to us. This is why the experience of someone who has lived for days during which man was merely a thing in the eyes of man is non-human. (Levi, 1995, 178)

Though Primo Levi is actually referring to the experience of the concentration camps, this interpretation, to his eyes, is no less true for other experiences where a person is first and foremost an object before being Another, where a person exists, firstly and uniquely, to the extent that he is useful,

in short, (for) all those cases where one spontaneously asks oneself whether humanity, in the personal sense of the word, has been kept or has been lost, whether one can recover it. (Levi, 1998, 139)

This negation of the Kantian imperative to never use Others as a means, thus as an object, did not stop at the gates of the concentration camps, whatever the ideology that supported them. Thousands of men, women and children today continue to be exploited, enslaved, placed in inhuman living conditions, in non-developed countries, but also in the so-called rich countries.[9] How can they hear the first article of the Universal Declaration of Human Rights which reads 'All human beings are born free and equal in dignity and rights. They are endowed with reason and conscience and should act towards one another in a spirit of brotherhood'? This is also true for all of those people who find themselves unacknowledged on the social stage, thrown back on just the private sphere, excluded from the register of the human being.

Vulnerability returns inevitably to the experience of not belonging to the world. 'To be superfluous means not to belong to the world at all' (Arendt, 1967b, 475). This means the experience of being nothing. But belonging to the common world, is also the place of trust, the trust of Others, the trust in Others, sharing and communication. Inaccessibility to this public place or common place commits a person to solitude, but a devastating solitude as it is without confrontation with the Other which is only a human principle. This solitude is forlornness, i.e. a relationship with oneself, deprived of contact with the common world, with Others, without reference to a common world, to Others. It is a closing in on oneself and only oneself, which is not dialogue with oneself as implied by the critical mind or the quality of the subject who acts, speaks and judges.[10] A closing in upon oneself which constitutes an incapacitating vulnerability because it is a support to a negation of the subject, that is to say to a negation of the subject as initiator, capable of imputation, capable of responsibility. A closing in upon oneself that is a losing of interest and a retreat from the world. The ultimate principles of the person are simply no longer acknowledged on the public stage.

This question of acting in a situation of vulnerability, apprehended through belonging to the world, inevitably leads to a re-examination of the issue of the conditions of access to the status of human being, but also to the review of the issue of social cohesion. Precisely because with the banality of indifference to Others, the banality with which contemporary society accepts contempt for Others, the banality of inhumanity, it is all the force of the will to live together that disappears and it is the expression of freedom itself that is parenthesised.

For the story of vulnerability evoked earlier, we have finally highlighted several directions for analysis. Firstly, it enables vulnerability not to be limited to clearly identified and specific categories, such as the homeless, people with a low employability rating, the poor, (multiple) drug-addicts. On the contrary, it opens up the field of investigation to social logics which are at work in society, social logics that are determined by the principles of a market society where everyone is seeking to maximise their advantages, and this without concern for the Other. The idea then is to understand the mechanisms of making people vulnerable and especially to come to understand the mechanisms of socialisation that facilitate vulnerability, and all this independently of the social places. Next, it encourages reflection on the very definition of trust, trust in oneself, trust in Others, trust in institutions, and questions the very source of the action. What is acting in a climate of suspicion, even of betrayal, of an implicit promise not kept, etc.? It also obliges us to reflect on the nature of the action. Though all action is production of self, it is fundamentally interaction. We see aid associations springing up here and there, aid to self-development, assistance in the development of skills, associations which may or may not be based on the idea of social networks, but whose near-immutable principle is the re-mobilisation of people in a situation of vulnerability. *In fine* woe betide anyone who does not participate, he is immediately stigmatised as being beyond redemption, as being a-social. But is this idea of the re-mobilisation of unavowed resources (potential skills), based on the taking into account of the person, as an acting and speaking subject, i.e. on an acknowledgement of the person as a responsible subject. Or is it rather based on an attribution of skills linked to pre-defined socio-cultural schemas, Others only being acknowledged insofar as they incarnate a (social) place and a place which fits precise social codes?

To try to grasp the issues of acting in a situation of vulnerability by identifying the resources to be mobilised and the means to mobilise them, or by relating it to the issues of the contemporary world, such as the question of the relationship to work or to trust in social relations has a certain and essential interest. But is this not to forget the very basis of vulnerability, namely contempt and indifference for Others and their negation, the sending of them outside of society, thereby implying a fundamental calling into question of the will to live together? Is it not to forget that a vulnerability exists which is this side of social vulnerability, i.e. a vulnerability of an ontological nature, preceding the very understanding of both the issues and the complexity of social vulnerability?

Notes

1   Note the example of two mountaineers, the leader falls causing his fellow climber to fall with him. In a lawsuit brought by the second protagonist, the first was held responsible even though he had committed no offence, 'though no error had been committed, but

simply because the action undertaken inherently comprised the possibility of this injury' (Engel, 1995, 17).

2   Numerous accounts in the Employment features of daily newspapers touch on this impossibility of assuming one's parental role insofar as working hours are often incompatible with a regular presence at home. Cf. for example, sales or cleaning occupations. Cf. the reports on Employment of the daily newspaper *Libération*. Along the same lines, the important opposition of employees to the process of the 35-hour week in France is often vindicated by flexible working hours, often imposed in return for the obtaining of the 35-hour week; flexibility which translates into the reality of making it impossible to manage one's time and into increased availability that only benefits the company.

3   The authors have thus identified four other ways of imagining the relationship to work: the regulation model, the community model, the public service model, the entrepreneurial model.

4   We only have to take *Actors and systems* by Michel Crozier and Erhard Friedberg (1980) to be reminded of the diverse strategies of the actors. 'Taking the respective resources of the actors in a power relationship into account thus complicates the initial design considerably. It becomes clear that, faced with the same power relationship, different actors do not share similar alternatives or temporal horizons. In short, their capacity to *proportion their commitment* or adjust their investment, thereby limiting the risks to themselves which inevitably accompany relations of power, is not the same. By dint of their social situation, actors have different "strategic capacities"' (Crozier and Friedberg, 1980, 36).

5   We could also see in this the possibility of developing the quaternary sector, the counterpart of universal allocation that Jean-Marc Ferry defines 'first and foremost as that of *personal activities*' (Ferry, 1995, 111).

6   We do not include this form of vulnerability here as it is linked to the condition of being alive, to the finiteness of a being which makes any life vulnerable, by definition, whatever the social conditions of existence.

7   Karl Otto Apel already stated this in an essay on ethics written in 1967. 'For the first time in the history of the human species, men are confronted in practice with the task of assuming, on a planetary level, collective responsibility for the consequences of their activities' (Apel, 1987, 46).

8   Jean-Luc Marion (1991, 129-130) refutes this idea of responsibility in these terms: 'It is not me as an individual who is responsible for malnutrition, for drought, for unequal exchange, for so-called freedom wars, for terrorism and totalitarianism, etc. This responsibility is not directly mine and for a very simple reason: my concrete, effective measurable decisions, in short, that which depends on my free will, which remains the only thing that can give us just reason to respect ourselves, have no influence whatsoever, at least not directly, on these permanent and structural ills. And if I am responsible, it is first and foremost for my neighbour: a task which sufficiently exhausts my spontaneous altruism.' For Paul Ricœur (2000, 33), 'an unlimited responsibility would make action impossible'.

9   The Committee Against Modern Slavery fights against modern forms of slavery in the western countries.

10 For the distinction between solitude and forlornness, the reader should refer to the analysis of Hannah Arendt (1978).

References

Appel, K.O. (1987), *L'Éthique à l'âge de la science. L'a priori de la communauté communicationnelle et les fondements de l'éthique*, Presses universitaires de Lille, Lille.

Arendt, H. (1960), *Men in Dark Times*, R. Piper, Munich.

Arendt, H. (1967a), *The Origins of Totalitarianism*, part 2, *Imperialism*, The World Publishing Company, Eleventh Printing, Cleveland and New York.

Arendt, H. (1967b), *The Origins of Totalitarianism*, part 3, *Totalitarianism*, The World Publishing Company, Eleventh Printing, Cleveland and New York.

Arendt, H. (1978), *The Life of the Mind*, volume 1, *Thinking*, Harcourt Brace Jovanovich, New York and London.

Bourdieu, P. (1990), *The Logic of Practice*, translated by Richard Nice, Stanford University Press, Stanford.

Castel, R. (1989), 'La question sociale commence en 1349', *Vie sociale and Les cahiers de la recherche sur le travail social*, 'Le Social aux prises avec l'histoire', 1.

Castel, R. and Haroche, Cl. (2001), *Propriété privée, propriété sociale, propriété de soi. Entretiens sur la construction de l'individu moderne*, Éditions Fayard, Paris.

Châtel, V. (to be published), *Analyse des théories du lien social. De la conscience collective à l'activité communicationnelle*, Éditions universitaires, Fribourg.

Crozier, M. and Friedberg, E. (1980), *Actors and Systems: The Politics of Collective Action*, translated by Arthur Goldhammer, University of Chicago Press, Chicago.

Diet, E. (1994), 'De culpabilité en responsabilité', *Autrement*, 'La Responsabilité', 14.

Dostoïevski, F. (1992), *The Brothers Karamazov*, translated by Richard Pevear and Larissa Volokhonsky, Vintage Classics, London.

Engel, L. (1995), *La Responsabilité en crise*, Éditions Hachette, Paris.

Ferry, J.M. (1995), *L'Allocation universelle. Pour un revenu de citoyenneté*, Éditions du Cerf, Paris.

Ferry, J.M. (1996), *L'Éthique reconstructive*, Éditions du Cerf, Paris.

Francfort, I., Osty, F., Sainsaulieu, R. and Uhalde, M. (1995), *Les Mondes sociaux de l'entreprise*, Éditions Desclée de Brouwer, Paris.

Habermas, J. (1987), *The Theory of Communicative Action*, Vol. 2, *Lifeworld and System: A Critique of Functionalist Reason*, translated by Thomas McCarthy, Polity Press, Cambridge.

Jonas, H. (1984), *The Imperative of Responsibility: In Search of an Ethics for the Technological Age*, translated by Hans Jonas, with the collaboration of David Herr, University of Chicago Press, Chicago.

Kant, E. (1973), *The Critique of Judgement*, translated by James C. Meredith, Oxford University Press, Oxford.

Levi, P. (1995), *If it is a Man*, translated by Stuart Woolf, Abacus, London.

Levi, P. (1998), *Conversations et entretiens*, Paris, Éditions Robert Laffont.

Lévinas, E. (1994), *Le Temps et l'autre*, Presses universitaires de France, Paris, 5ème édition.

Lévinas, E. (1996), *Humanisme de l'autre homme*, Le livre de poche, Paris.

Lévinas, E. (1998), *Entre nous: On thinking-of-the-other*, translated by Michael B. Smith and Barbara Harshav, Columbia University Press, New York.

Lévinas, E. (1999), *Otherwise than Being: Or, Beyond Essence*, translated by Alphonso Lingis, Duquesne University Press, Pittsburg.

Marion, J.L. (1991), *Prolégomènes à la charité*, Éditions La Différence, Paris.

Mead, G. H. (1934), *Mind, Self and Society from the Standpoint of a Social Behaviorist*, University of Chicago Press, Chicago.

Ricœur, P. (1992), *Oneself as Another*, translated by Kathleen Blamey, University of Chicago Press, Chicago.

Ricœur, P. (2000), *The Just*, translated by David Pellauer, University of Chicago Press, Chicago.

Ricœur, P. (2001), *Le Juste 2*, Éditions Esprit, Paris.

Semprun, J. (1997), *Literature or Life*, translated by Linda Coverdale, Viking, New York.

Taguieff, P.A. (2001), *Résister au bougisme. Démocratie forte contre mondialisation techno-marchande*, Éditions mille et une nuits, Paris.

Chapter 2

Capital Thinking and Social Vulnerability: The Effects of Flexible Assignation

Daniel Mercure

One of the main contributions of post-war social and cultural anthropology is to have shown that no society is safe from history, power struggles, conflicts and numerous forms of inequality, in short, to have highlighted one of the great myths of historical societies. In fact, every society turns out to be more or less fragile and, therefore, to include areas of vulnerability, sometimes ecological, sometimes social, often to include both. Our societies are no exception, indeed, far from it. However, while contemporary forms of social vulnerability are singular, so are the ways taken by different social groups to overcome such situations. The form of social vulnerability which will be the object of this article concerns the relationship to work, particularly job security, which can run the whole scale from chronic unemployment to a stable job, that is to say, can range from disaffiliation to complete and stable social integration.

In fact, over the last twenty-five years our societies have been marked by the return of old forms of social vulnerability, particularly as far as employment is concerned (Mercure, 1996; Mercure and Dubé, 1998; Mercure and Dubé, 1999).[1] During this period the post-war employment norm of permanent regular employment, has been eroded and replaced by various other forms of employment in which there is something of the employee relations of the beginning of the last century. The rapid development of part-time, temporary or even fee-based work, together with the greater use of subcontractors have resulted in a big increase in atypical employment as well as a sharp rise in the number of self-employed workers, the unemployed and those receiving social security benefits. With regard to the contemporary practice of direct or indirect subcontracting, this has now become so important, and takes so many different guises, that we may well be led to ask ourselves whether companies should still be considered as employers in the traditional sense of the term, or rather mainly be defined as givers of orders? Such changes in the forms of employment are of great importance, if only because work ties, and more particularly the form that these ties take in our societies, constitute one of the key elements of social cohesion, which is still, to a great extent, founded on employment and the regulation of employment. Examination of this issue means asking ourselves questions about the changes taking place in our societies, and even about the future of our societies.

The objective of the present article is to suggest some markers which may be able to help us to understand the contemporary changes taking place in the forms of employment, changes which are at the source of a great many of the new forms of social vulnerability. In order to define a crucial aspect of the social context of these changes in employment, we shall present a few historical reference points regarding the current changes in the relations between company dynamics, the organisation of work and the forms of employment. To do this, we shall first clarify what exactly is now being challenged, namely the Fordist mode of regulation, as elaborated in the mid 1930s, and especially in the form that dominated our societies during the course of the thirty-year boom period after World War II, up until the first oil crisis of 1973-1974. We shall then take a more detailed look at recent changes in western economies, with a view to understanding current company dynamics and, as a result, the return in a new guise of certain forms of social vulnerability which are characteristic of our societies. The dynamics in question seem to take a particular form for which we shall use the term flexible assignation. We shall return to this point later on.

Work and Employment in a Fordist Type of Society

Modern employment history is closely linked to the three main phases of the industrial revolution. Beginning in the middle of the eighteenth century in England, the first phase was marked by the rise of capitalism and the emergence of the proletariat. Based on the textile, coal and steam industries, this first phase was followed, at the end of the nineteenth century, by a second phase characterised, among other things, by the discovery of oil and electricity, the massive use of steel and the expansion of big companies. The third phase of the industrial revolution, which began in the middle of the previous century, represents a crucial period during which the nature of work and the forms of employment underwent great changes in western societies. From the middle of the twentieth century, this industrial transformation has had a completely new scientific and technical character, as testified by the use of innovatory sources of energy, such as nuclear energy, the development of automation – due, in particular, to rapid developments in cybernetics and electronics – the spectacular advances made by the chemical industry enabling the manufacture of many synthetic products, the progress made in the field of data processing, as well as the unprecedented growth of the service sector.

Moreover, the period of strong economic growth which began after World War II, the so-called 'Trentes Glorieuses' (the thirty-year post-war boom period), was marked out by an innovatory mode of economic development and regulation of our societies, the Fordist mode of regulation, which denotes three realities with which we are familiar. Firstly, mass consumption, i.e. a manufacturing system characterised by the mass production of standardised goods, using long assembly lines and low-skilled workers. Secondly, an increase in the number of wage earners and in the global level of unionisation, that is, wage-labour relations based on a long-term employment contract, the existence of job security and salary increases in line with productivity gains. Finally, the increase in the standard of living of the population and the rapid development of the welfare state, in other words a system of accumulation of wealth characterised by the increased purchasing power of wage earners and the setting up of state mechanisms for the distribution of wealth, particularly through various social security and income support measures. A similar type of system for the regulation of society accompanied the economic growth of the industrialised countries from the post-war period up until the first oil crisis of 1973-1974.

Based on scientific discoveries, technical developments, strong state regulation, a high level of unionisation and an employment norm characterised by the strong presence of regular and permanent jobs, this period of our history profoundly changed the way organisations operated and, consequently, our ways of working. On the one hand, the public and private service sector experienced phenomenal growth, to the point of becoming the main source of employment in our societies. On the other hand, the composition of the active workforce changed, as testified by the spectacular rise in the number of women and university graduates on the labour market. Companies also innovated production methods in several ways and continually increased their level of productivity in a context of a big growth in demand and in employment. Big companies also developed various logistic support services for production, placing ever increasing importance on their management practices, and recruiting ever greater numbers of technicians and managers. Furthermore, the qualification profile of the latter was substantially modified, to the point that the notion of skill gradually became associated with that of specialisation, that is to say with the acquisition of detailed knowledge limited to a particular field, enabling the solving of concrete problems and the carrying out of clearly defined tasks. The result, of course, was a high degree of compartmentalisation of theoretical knowledge and practical skills. In short, the ideal managerial qualification model was that of the specialist. Their place of work was, more often than not, a company dedicated to the production of standardised goods and services, having market-based divisions, organised into a strict hierarchy and subject to the integrated planning of its activities and careful control of its performances.

Together with mass production, the Fordist mode of regulation also demanded a body of practical knowledge, characterised by technical rationalisation and the standardisation of tasks. Specialised training and the separation of conception and execution was the principal credo of this period. A good example of this phenomenon is the case of production employees, who were governed by skill principles characteristic of the scientific organisation of work. It is a fact that Taylorism tended to increase the efficiency of work by separating the tasks of conception and execution and, above all, by breaking down work activities into basic and repetitive tasks. Experience, practical knowledge of the work environment, manual or mental dexterity, a fast work pace and the obeying of instructions were synonymous with performance. The difference between the training profile of the subordinate employees and that of the managers was striking, except for two points: the specialisation and the compartmentalisation of both their technical and practical knowledge. The work model that we have just described was essentially based on the mass consumption of standardised goods in an expanding market. Though this model of society was founded on the collective accumulation of wealth, paid employment, steady, permanent jobs, the rapid growth of the middle classes and the presence of extensive social protection, it nevertheless turned out to be marked by forms of work which were alienating, particularly because of the degree to which the division of labour governed daily production activities.

A Changing Economy

It was in the mid 1970s that this work model was seriously challenged. At this time, the main industrialised countries had to overcome new economic pressures, initially related to the oil crises of 1973-1974 and 1979-1980, then to increased competition from Asian countries. Diversification of demand, increased quality requirements, the rapid growth of new information and communication technologies, as well as the increasing globalisation of markets further added to an economic process which had already been marked by several turbulent periods. It was the end of the post-war boom years.

For big companies, this situation generated uncertainties and, in many cases, was even the cause of a serious competitiveness crisis. Consequently, organisations were forced to question the validity of their growth and capital investment strategies, as well as their management policies for production, employment and work relations. Very quickly, most of the difficulties encountered by companies were attributed to their lack of flexibility. For example, many managers highlighted the inadequacy of the rigidity built into their means of production, as compared to a market characterised by frequent fluctuations; they also condemned the high number of government regulations, as well as the lack of flexibility of the collective agreements which governed a part of their activities. In many companies, bold work rationalisation policies were drawn up and implemented.

Thus, the pursuit of flexibility soon came to be seen as the best way to increase competitiveness and profitability, becoming a question of increasing the ability of companies to adapt to variations in demand and to market fluctuations. Various measures were taken with a view to attaining this objective, such as the introduction of flexible production methods so as to be able to produce a greater variety of products or to be able to modify assembly lines quickly. Organisations also drew up management policies favouring greater versatility in work activities, greater flexibility in the modification of the forms of employment, of the size of the workforce and of work regulations, ranging from methods of payment more and more closely linked to company productivity gains to the renegotiation of collective agreements judged to be too rigid. Thus, these changes challenged most of the foundations of the Fordist mode of regulation, not only as far as the organisation of production and the management of work were concerned, but also as regards the forms taken by employment.

Moreover, these changes were accompanied by a structural transformation of the economy of our societies, and particularly by the emergence of what Nuala Beck calls the 'New Economy' (Beck, 1992), which is essentially based on four strategic areas of growth. These areas are effectively the new driving forces of North American economic development, namely the computer, semiconductor and software sector, the health and pharmaceutical product sector, the communications and telecommunications sector and finally, the vast sector of instrumentation and optics.

In fact, the new economy appears today to be at the centre of a redefinition of the nature of work and of the forms of employment. For example, there is no doubt that the role of intellectual work in the economic performance of our countries has increased, all of the sectors considered to be the driving forces of the new economy are distinguished by the fact that they are knowledge-based, as testified by the popular and very appropriate term of knowledge economy (Landry, 1997; Winslow and Bramer, 1994). However, this undeniable fact is part of an economic and social process of greater magnitude, marked by a huge swing in the direction of the pursuit of flexibility on the part of large organisations and states. This phenomenon is seen, not only in the growth of ultra-free market ideology and the practices that accompany it – particularly the globalisation of markets and the redefinition of the role of the state – but also in the important changes in company development strategies. So, it is by a detailed examination of these new flexibility issues that we shall try to understand the current dynamics of companies and, consequently, present-day changes in work and the forms of employment.

Ultra-Free Market Ideology and Flexibility

However, before going further, it is necessary to emphasise the fact that such economic changes are part of a wider debate marked by the return of free-market, or even ultra-free market, ideology. In fact, the flexibility debate is not a new one. The very notion of flexibility has always been one of the key words of free enterprise. From this perspective, flexibility goes beyond the framework of the organisation of work and raises the question of the global conception of society. Already for Adam Smith, this notion carried a heavy ideological load, associated as it is with the free movement of goods and capital, with the non-interventionism of the state, in short with the benefits of market regulation guided by 'the invisible hand' of individual interests (Smith, 1950). Also, from the 1930s, the supporters of classic liberalism criticised the *New Deal*, implemented in the United Stated by Roosevelt to check the crisis, for conveying an idea of society which was too rigid.

In the 1970s, it was the turn of the ultra-free marketeers to appropriate the idea of flexibility, brought out by the forceful essays of Murray Rothbard (1982) and David Friedman (1973). These writers concern themselves with proving the social validity of an ideology founded on a return to complete laissez-faire by making flexibility and 'market freedom' the salient points of their analyses. The ultra-free sense of the term flexibility means shielding society from politics. This discourse has its origins within the Austrian school of economic thought, in particular with Ludwig von Mises (1949) and Friedrich von Hayek (1973). After having inspired the economic policies of Great Britain (Thatcherism) and the United States (Reaganism) during the 1970s and 1980s, this same discourse was at the heart of the far-reaching negotiation of new free-trade agreements between several countries, agreements which form the spearhead of the current globalisation of markets. In addition, this vision of the world governs the elaboration of a series of management policies implemented by larger companies. A cursory listing of the various forms of flexibility introduced by the latter in the industrialised countries is itself a reminder of recent employment history; and this history has led to a serious challenging of the forms of employment which characterised the post-war period. Let us now give a broad outline.

Companies Seeking Flexibility

The first wave of change destined to increase flexibility in companies began in the mid 1970s and mainly concerned technical and functional flexibility.

Technical flexibility rests on a series of innovations in the work environment based on computing, such as the introduction of digitally operated machines, of computer terminals for various jobs, or of computerised production control systems. For the most part, technical flexibility is thus closely linked to advances in office automation and robotics. It is distinguished by the introduction of easily adaptable production techniques, with the idea of being able to quickly modify the production line and of being able to manufacture a greater variety of products, especially in the sectors which are closely linked to mass consumption. The pursuit of this objective generates innovative production methods, aiming to overcome the limits of rigid production lines by the installation of multi-purpose, automated equipment allowing the production of small runs and the adaptation of products to variations in demand. The case of the car industry, particularly the Japanese just-in-time method of production, is an excellent illustration of this form of flexibility (Coriat, 1990). The adoption of flexible technologies ensures the integration of various production elements, the manufacture of better quality products and the optimal management of stocks.

However, flexible technologies require workers to have broader skills and make greater demands of their knowledge and expertise. Also, the pursuit of technical flexibility was rapidly associated with another form of flexibility, namely functional flexibility. This is the product of management policies which bring about increased versatility in work activity. This type of flexibility requires workers to have a series of skills in order to be able to master the different aspects of the production line. The organisation of work also appears to be founded more on responsible autonomy and employee initiative, according to methods which, on the one hand, have the effect of breaking down the barriers between jobs, and on the other hand, between the work itself and its related tasks – for example machine maintenance. This method of organising work tends to lead to an increase in the versatility of the workforce, in internal mobility, as well as in the co-operation between jobs. All things considered, technical flexibility contributes to broadening job content and leads to many changes in how work is organised, such as the development of work in autonomous and multi-skilled teams.

Of course, the changes that we have just described aroused anxiety, firstly because they required considerable modification of jobs, then because they were likely to involve a great number of redundancies. Nevertheless, they also kindled great enthusiasm in many observers of the employment scene. In fact, several of them saw in these changes the dawn of a new age, characterised by the reprofessionalisation of work. Were we not witnessing the realisation of a great hope, namely that of the return of the primacy of man over the tool and, more globally, the primacy of man over work? For example, the German sociologists Horst Kern and Michael Schumann (1984) defended the thesis of the end of the division of labour. Their study, which analyses the forms taken by the rationalisation of work in various sectors of German industry at the beginning of the 1980s, led them to conclude that, for the main part of industrial production, the organisation of work was increasingly dependent on a lessening degree of task division, on a modification of the role of the worker in the production process, on a greater and more independent employee capacity for intervention, as well as on increased skills. For many researchers, a new era was taking shape: that of the end of the division of labour.

However, the important economic recession of the beginning of the 1980s tempered this enthusiasm. In fact, this particular recession was marked, among other things, by a big increase in the interest rate. This phenomenon prompted companies to develop greater financial flexibility. Financial flexibility denotes a series of practices which aim to adjust investment costs to market fluctuations. To do this, organisations try to limit their investment costs, not only by the establishment of new methods of stock control and by a better spreading of their supplies, but also by the increased rationalisation of work and, above all, by a modification of the forms of employment, notably by the implementation of subcontracting.

It was in the mid 1980s, then even more so at the beginning of the prolonged recession of the 1990s, that the worst fears of the main trade union groups were confirmed. During this period, companies attempted to increase their competitiveness by determinedly embarking upon a particular form of financial flexibility, namely flexible wage systems. The basic principle of this type of flexibility is to ensure that wages are much more sensitive to both the intensity of the production activity and the supply and demand situation of the labour market. With a view to attaining this aim, employers tend to ease the legal measures concerning the minimum wage, challenge the principles of equal pay and of wage indexing, and apply themselves to reducing non-wage costs. In the same context, they favour the continuous review of wages and especially the adjustment of wages to company performance, i.e. to real productivity gains rather than to anticipated gains; this practice amounts to calling into question one of the essential principles of our collective system of bargaining and social control, namely wage rises negotiated over a fixed period. The effect of these practices was to undermine the old Fordist way of regulating work.

As was only to be expected, wage flexibility was immediately teamed with numerical flexibility, the final stage of this far-reaching evolution towards the pursuit of flexibility on the part of employers. Numerical flexibility is characterised by adjusting the size of the workforce in accordance with market fluctuations. To do this, employers often renegotiate employment contracts, including job security, and resort more and more to part-time, temporary or fee-based work, and increasingly have recourse to a series of subcontracting practices, all of which has echoes of certain company employment policies of the beginning of the last century. The result is a dramatic increase in the number of insecure jobs which are at the source of new forms of social vulnerability.

Obviously, the practices which ensue from numerical flexibility policies have accentuated the decline of Fordist employee relations and caused the polarisation of the forms of employment, which is beneficial to companies. On the one hand, traditional employment is now the reserve of certain fractions of the workforce who constitute a primary core of wage earners. On the other hand, the spread of atypical forms of work on a so-called secondary market assure large companies the flexible regulation of a part of their workers. This results in a dual labour market based on a two-tier employment system, causing new social inequalities (Osterman, 1984). As a result, it is the entire system of social regulation, slowly built up since the Second World War, which is being called into question. This renting of the social fabric makes new employment forms a vital contemporary issue, together with, of course, the issue of social solidarity; it also inevitably raises fundamental questions about new forms of social vulnerability, and particularly about the ability of our societies to halt this destruction of the social fabric.

As for the employees of large companies who still hold a regular job, it is by greater functional flexibility that they contribute to the attainment of the organisational objectives of total flexibility. In fact, the requirements for versatility are ever greater, while the intensity of work goes on increasing. Furthermore, the pursuit of functional flexibility is changing the traditional forms of negotiation between management and labour, though the principle of a basic collective agreement has not been completely rejected. In general, the new social compromise is still based on a long-term employment contract in accordance with Fordist practice, but the scope of this solution often seems to be limited by a greater individualisation of work relations, in particular by the introduction of new forms of employee flexibility. Obviously, the result of the implacable process that we have just outlined is to put trade unions in a defensive position. Faced with an agonising choice they have really only one option: the negotiation of functional flexibility rather than enduring the anguish of numerical flexibility.

All of these changes, which have taken place over a period of almost twenty-five years, have had the effect, on the one hand, of completely transforming the general dynamics of companies, and on the other hand, of modifying the nature of work and the forms of employment. Let us first look at the new configuration of companies, in other words, the organisational bases of their innovative development strategy, which attempts to reconcile, in a coherent way, all of the forms of flexibility which we have just described.

Flexible Assignation: the Strategic Foundations of a New Company Dynamic, the Source of a Radical Modification of Work and of the Forms of Employment

We suggest the use of the term flexible assignation to indicate the concurrent presence of all of these forms of flexibility in companies (Mercure, 1996). At the heart of the process there is, on the one hand, the rapid development in the practices of the outsourcing of work, or assignation, and especially in those practices which are connected with the new direct and indirect forms of subcontracting and, on the other hand, the pursuit of wholesale flexibility, particularly in the matters of financial, technical, functional and numerical flexibility.

Obviously, this type of synthesis remains very general, given that flexibility practices inevitably vary depending on the company, the sector and the country. For example, certain organisations depend more on one or the other of these various forms of flexibility. Incidentally, it is possible for certain types of flexibility to contradict other forms of flexibility. To illustrate this point let us take numerical flexibility, this may lead to too high a turnover rate of the workforce, thus reducing worker support of the company objectives, which can very well be an obstacle to functional flexibility. Nevertheless, most researchers acknowledge both the importance of practices of this type and the fact that they are significantly changing the face of work in our societies (Badham and Mathews, 1989; Mercure, 1997).

Regarding the new company development model based on a process of flexible assignation and its effects on the forms of employment, three features seem to us to be fundamental, as much because of their intrinsic importance, as because of the degree to which they are generalised in several sectors of our economy (Mercure, 1996). The features in question are to do with the way that production, work and work relations are managed. The first feature is at the heart of the new methods of combining direct and indirect subcontracting practices; the second, at the core of increased demands for versatility; the third, the spearhead of the current restructuring of work relations and the forms of employment. Let us briefly summarise them.

Regarding the way that production is managed, the changes observed lie in the shifting of strategies with a view to securing a return on capital, thus focusing more on the global dynamics of the organisation. In fact, in large companies, we have noticed that a return to profitability is more and more associated with the installation of new forms of equipment and the co-ordination of production, supply and distribution activities. In other words, production policy is no longer the way favoured for capital productivity; the direction being taken is now rather that of a flexible equilibrium between what companies do themselves and what is done outside of the company. The management model under consideration is based on a wide-ranging strategy of assignation, drawn up in accordance with new methods: the outsourcing of production is no longer based, as it was in the past, on the classic choice between *make or buy*, depending only on the logic of market price. In fact, the new methods of co-ordinating supply, production and distribution activities integrate four principle types of inter-company relations, these being: vertical integration of a part of the production operations; the quasi-integration of legally independent subcontractors; co-operation in the form of economic partnership with subcontractors; the purchase of components from and the sale of products to several different distributors and suppliers on the market, under differing contractual terms. These various types of inter-company relations are always set up in such a way so as to conform to a logic based on flexibility, cost, the assurance of supplies and market security. The global logic is flexible and competitive, and each solution is itself endowed with great adaptability: flexibility within flexibility. This new way of achieving growth is thus based on an approach which favours big savings on investment; it is also supported by new policies of the regulation of stock and supply. The nerve centre of the company is shifted, in the sense that production operations are subordinated to a logic of competitiveness, which is itself subject to the policies of flexibility, productivity and security.

As far as the organisation of work is concerned, the company model under consideration is part of a process consisting not only of technical and functional flexibility, but also of high work productivity. In fact, the organisation of work is orientated towards the optimisation of work activities within an organisational framework which is based on concern for both increasing the flexibility of the production apparatus and limiting the stoppages endured by the company, as a part of the fixed costs are now the responsibility of the subcontractors. The organisation of work is based more and more on methods which allow for a greater versatility in the tasks undertaken, the increase of internal mobility, the development of teamwork and co-operation between jobs, as well as an increase in the number of related tasks. This reorganisation of work is often accompanied by measures seeking to increase the intensity of work.

As for work relations, they are the subject of important changes. Work relations are based on both collective agreements and on the increased individualisation of the ties between the employer and the employees. Admittedly, the principle of the collective employment contract remains in force. However, employee management policies are more and more personalised and the new agreements which are negotiated tend to ease employment rules and to initiate a payment structure based more on a particular type of wage flexibility, namely that of relating pay to the performance of the company, according to various forms of employee participation in the company's economic results. In reality, the model desired by managers is that of payment directly related to the intensity of the production activity, that is to say, to the production capacity used. The global rate of payment also appears to be more and more susceptible to the cost price of potential subcontractors. Furthermore, employment policy is characterised by, among other things, the rapid expansion of subcontracting, reductions in the size of the workforce and the modification of the employment rules and regulations of a large proportion of wage earners. Also, the efficiency link between payment directly related to the intensity of the production activity and the forms of employment is conveyed by the rapid increase in the many forms of fixed-term employment and by the growing use of part-time and independent workers.

In short, flexible assignation is characterised by a series of qualitative changes which aim to reconcile three objectives, these being the assurance of supplies and market security, the flexibility of the production apparatus, including the workforce, and high work productivity. This management model is based on a new organisational trajectory, the principle reference points of which are as follows: firstly, the emergence of performance strategies tied to the global dynamics of the company; the presence of forms of co-ordination and integration of productive activities based on a logic of flexibility and assignation having recourse to various forms of subcontracting; finally, the setting up of systems for managing work and work relations that are not only adaptable, but also versatile and competitive. These are what we feel to be the principle distinguishing features of this new company dynamic.

The Effects of Flexible Assignation on the Forms of Employment

Let us now try to better define the effect of this company development model on the evolution of work and especially on the new forms of social vulnerability resulting from company employment policies. We have indicated several aspects throughout our discussion. So we shall limit our observations to a few main points.

First of all, it appears that technical and functional flexibility tend to lead to an increase in skills for several categories of workers, at the same time as contributing to increasing the versatility of tasks and the intensity of work. In fact, this pursuit of flexibility has significantly modified jobs and human resource management strategies, notably as regards the skill profile required of managerial staff and of employees for the fulfilment of their tasks (Mercure and Dubé, 1998; Mercure and Dubé, 1999). In the main, we can observe that the work specialisation model, favoured by employers during the post-World War II boom period, though still of great interest, is now teamed with, and generally subordinated to, the versatility model, entailing a whole range of abilities which enable complex processes to be mastered and varied tasks to be carried out. In other words, these new qualification models do not completely eliminate specialisation; rather they tend to reconcile this aspect with flexibility and versatility, in accordance with a process that aims to attain several objectives, i.e. the consolidation of analytical abilities, the avoidance of compartmentalisation between different professional practices and greater ability to adapt to rapid and numerous changes. In short, within the framework of our skills studies we have observed that a general skill model, combining flexibility and specialisation, is often to be found at the heart of the various sub-models of skill favoured by employers, observations which are in keeping with one of the key aspects of the dynamics of flexible assignation presented above. Let us add that, for companies, the pursuit of flexibility is not only a question of multi-purpose training having a field of specialisation matching the job to be filled, but is also a series of professional, social and personal aptitudes. With a view to attaining good economic performance, organisations now depend more on flexibility and life skills, rather than just on knowledge and expertise. In fact, for a part of their workforce, they are less and less concerned with buying labour power, and more and more concerned with associating themselves with and mobilising the totality of the worker's human potential to their own ends. However, it must be remembered that for another part of labour power used directly or indirectly, organisations have increasing recourse to a series of practices related to numerical flexibility.

Next, and most particularly, assignation practices and numerical and employee flexibility policies contribute to the deterioration of the employment conditions of a large proportion of the workforce, and thus to the modification of the post-war employment norm. Also, assignation practices, and the practices associated with the pursuit of wage and numerical flexibility, raise what we might well call a serious problem for society.

On this issue, the fact that forces itself most clearly on the observer is undoubtedly the decline of the work and pay conditions of a large proportion of the workforce. As we have already stated, employers try to adjust the size of the wage bill to company performance, which sometimes results in the lowering of wages and welfare benefits, and often in the implementation of a remuneration system with different levels of payment for the same type of work. This latter practice creates strong wage polarisation between the various categories of workers, for example, between independent workers, whose numbers are growing because of the boom in subcontracting policies, and the employees of big companies.

The growing importance of assignation practices and numerical flexibility also encourages organisations to have more and more recourse to part-time, temporary or fee-based work, and to make greater use of a series of subcontractors. As we have already indicated, the result is an increase in the number of atypical jobs. For many workers, this situation means that they can no longer count on spending their entire career within the same company, as was often the case for the post-war generations. In many cases, the policies of flexible assignation also result in a big reduction in the number of employees, achieved sometimes through early retirement for a part of the employees, sometimes through massive collective redundancies. Some workers who have been made redundant manage to find a lesser-paid and insecure job with one of the subcontracting firms. Others become 'regular' employees of a fast-expanding type of business, namely the agencies specialising in temporary employment. Still others, in competition with young unemployed qualified people, try to set up their own micro-businesses and embark upon the chasing of contracts, most often micro-contracts.

More and more taxed by corporatism, trade unions barely have a choice: they do their best to protect jobs, often at the price of big concessions on wages and the organisation of work. It is obvious that, nowadays, unions no longer try to fight against the fact of work being 'en miettes' (in crumbs, or in pieces), according to the formula proposed by Georges Friedmann in the 1950s, but against having only 'les miettes' of work. This trade unionism crisis is accentuated by the fact that the changes taking place often provide companies with the opportunity to limit the role of the unions and even to abandon them.

Of course, one of the most visible effects of flexible assignation is to uproot work, that is to say to radically modify the nature of social cohesion between workers and companies. In fact, the new policies of numerical flexibility raise the thorny question of the future of the wage-earning class as the modern form of social integration and individual identity. Reacting to this deterioration of employment conditions, some people herald the emergence of a civilisation marked by the end of work; others condemn the economic horror bequeathed to the younger generations of workers (Méda, 1995; Rifkin, 1995; Forester, 1999). As for the supporters of the ultra-free market, they set us an enormous challenge: to count on the fact that the victims of flexible assignation will be the standard bearers of a new form of enterprise, which will be the source of renewed economic growth, founded on their dynamism. In this scenario, it is to be noted that this talk is less and less of the great avant-garde of the captains of industry, i.e. the avant-garde which, often after having been backed by the state, initiated flexible assignation and is still managing it today. The avant-garde on which our hopes rest is, in fact, a sort of 'micro-avant-garde'...

So, in order to confront the new market conditions, companies have chosen to adopt assignation and flexibility. Organisations have also radically modified work in accordance with a complex process, the main guidelines of which are, on the one hand, an increase in subcontracting and the multiplication of atypical forms of work and, on the other, a substantial transformation of our ways of working, Moreover, the demands of versatility are ever higher, at the same time as the intensity of work is increasing, expressed by an increase in skills as well as by an increase in the number of cases of professional exhaustion, all in an employment context which is marked by insecurity.

However, as we have already indicated, flexible assignation does not merely have the effect of modifying work content or challenging social cohesion within the company. This practice, because it radically changes the conditions of employment in our societies, has the more dramatic effects of not only making a large part of the population vulnerable, but also of undermining all of the old forms of social solidarity. In fact, there are now entire sections of the workforce who find themselves unemployed, or who are obliged to take early retirement, to accept insecure jobs, or who are employed in workplaces do not fully implement current employment laws, who are swelling the ranks of the unemployed and the impoverished. Thus, work and the wage-earning class are becoming less and less representative of the main ways in which our societies ensure social integration, and this raises many questions. To illustrate the point, we shall mention just three. Firstly, is this just a transitory period, or on the contrary, are we experiencing a real transformation of society? In other words, over the next few years, will work and the wage-earning class once more become the main areas of social integration as they were in the past, and particularly since the Second World War? Secondly, if this is not the case, does this mean that in the coming years we will witness such a great transformation of society that it will challenge the construction of social identity through work, as well as all of the advantages associated with the wage earner's position, such as the systems of social protection, the ways in which status is attributed and the forms of income distribution? Thirdly, if such a scenario should come to pass, what would be the foundations of the new regulation of society?

Is it possible to curb such a phenomenon or, at least to signpost the prejudicial effects for the workforce, of the new dynamics of flexible assignation, particularly in the matter of employment? Several ways are open to us, among which, somewhat timorously, is that of a re-examination of our employment laws, of our social policies and, above all, of the way we choose to co-ordinate the latter with the features that characterise our way of producing wealth. However, the analysis of a phenomenon of such magnitude, and of its numerous effects on the new forms of social vulnerability, must be accompanied by a thorough consideration of the future of work and of the wage-earning class as a basis of social cohesion and, even more fundamentally, by a public debate about social justice in societies characterised by affluence.

Note

1   This chapter reprints, with the permission of the editor, large extracts from an article entitled 'Les mutations contemporaines du travail' published in a special edition of *Laval théologique et philosophique*, the title of which is *Mutations culturelles et transcendance* (special issue, first quarter 2000).

References

Badham, R. and Mathews, J. (1989), 'The New Production Systems Debate', *Labour and Industry*, 2.

Beck, N. (1992), *Shifting Gears: Thriving in the New Economy*, Harper-Collins Publishers, Toronto.

Coriat, B. (1990), *L'Atelier et le robot*, Éditions Christian Bourgois, Paris.

Forester, V. (1999), *The Economic Horror*, Polity Press, Cambridge.

Friedman, D. (1973), *The Machinery of Freedom. Guide to a Radical Capitalism*, Harper and Row, New York.

Hayek, F. von (1973), *Law, Legislation and Liberty*, Routledge and Kegan, London.

Kern, H. and Schumann, M. (1984), *The End of Division of Labour*, Beck, Munich.

Landry, F. (1997), *La Révolution du savoir dans l'entreprise*, Éditions Transcontinental, Montréal.

Méda, D. (1995), *Le Travail, une valeur en voie de disparition*, Éditions Aubier, Paris.

Mercure, D. (1996), *Le Travail déraciné. L'impartition flexible dans la dynamique sociale des entreprises forestières au Québec*, Boréal, Montréal.

Mercure, D. (1997), 'Les formes de la flexibilité', *Sciences Humaines*, 78.

Mercure, D. and Dubé, A. (1998), *Les Entreprises et l'emploi. Les nouvelles formes de qualification du travail*, Publications du Québec, Québec.

Mercure, D. and Dubé, A. (1999), 'Les nouveaux modèles de qualification fondés sur la flexibilité: entre la professionnalisation et la taylorisation du travail', *Relations industrielles*, Vol. 54(1).

Mises, L. von (1949), *Human Action*, Yale University Press, New Haven.

Osterman, P. (1984), *Internal Labor Market*, MIT Press, Cambridge.

Rifkin, J. (1995), *The End of Work*, Putnam's Sons, New York.

Rothbard, M. (1982), *The Ethics of Liberty*, Humanities Press, Atlantic Highlands.

Smith, A. (1950), *An Inquiry into the Nature and Causes of the Wealth of Nations*, Methuen, London.

Winslow, C. and Bramer, W. (1994), *Future Work: Putting Knowledge to Work in Knowledge Economy*, Free Press, New York.

Chapter 3

Individuals without Supports

Robert Castel

It is important to accept that the notion of vulnerability is central to understanding the significance of the changes taking place in the social sector and to try to give it a precise meaning. The problems that this sector faces today can, to a great extent, be expressed by the hypothesis of the *resurgence of vulnerability*. Vulnerability, uncertainty of the future, being obliged to live from 'hand-to-mouth' as it used to be called, was once a fact of life for the working classes. However, the situation was stabilised by the strengthening of the wage earner's position, the development of employment law and social protection. Since the mid-seventies, some of the rights acquired by the workforce have been questioned and it could be argued that the expression 'resurgence of vulnerability' well encapsulates the effects: the weakening of social positions, the uncertain nature of professional careers, the lack of resources to confront the future, now all pose problems which are not a repetition of the vulnerability of the past. These problems are new ones because individuals, who do not belong to the classic category of 'clients' in social work, are now seeking help. Indeed this led people to the debate about the 'new poor' in the eighties. The term is debatable, but it expresses the acknowledgement that new categories of the population have begun to pose problems. These now include people who were integrated in the world of work and have lost their status, or others, particularly young people, seeking employment and who are not able to find a stable place in society.

This means that 'acting in a situation of vulnerability' poses some particularly difficult problems because we do not have established techniques to deal with these situations. New professions are being sought, and it is from the field that the practical responses will come, wherever possible. Thus, we must first listen to those who are trying to take up these challenges through their practical experience. Secondly, a contribution to the consideration of vulnerability can be made by trying to characterise *the status of the vulnerable individual*. We must try to give a precise meaning to the term 'vulnerable individual' to avoid confusion with other categories. He, or she, is not only a poor person, lacking economic resources, or someone who is 'excluded' and rejected by society, but very often someone who has been *made vulnerable*, weakened, swept along by a process of loss of belonging and of resources. This is why it is a question of a precise and new type of modern individual. It could be argued that the resurgence of social vulnerability, which is the consequence of changes to the structure of paid employment, has given rise to this new profile of a contemporary individual, whose supports have been eroded, undermined by recent social changes.

In order to validate this hypothesis it is essential to try and reposition this vulnerable individual on the trajectory of the historical development of the individual. Thus, the vulnerable individual could be understood to be the result of a process of the promotion of the individual, now in crisis because this individual lacks the supports necessary to guarantee his or her solidity. It is, therefore, important to explain how support is to be understood here.

The core of this hypothesis is that *individuals are unequally supported to be individuals*. In other words, there are individuals and individuals, and the prevailing idea of the individual in our culture, the reference value, does not exclude other representations of the individual. Of course, the individual is generally valued and since the Declaration of the Rights of Man and the Citizen, probably the central value of democratic societies, the citizen at the political and moral levels, the subject responsible for his or her acts and autonomous. This is confirmed *a contrario* by the model of totalitarianism: totalitarianism appears to us to be absolutely wrong because the individual is denied all value and is turned into an automaton.

Obviously, it is not disputed that the individual is an eminent value, but there are different ways of being an individual. Take the example of the vagabond. In pre-industrial societies the vagabond represented practically the only possible profile of an individual. Because in a society of orders, estates and statutes, where everyone was assigned a fixed place in traditional networks of dependence and inter-dependence, the vagabond was the only one to exist on his own, removed from family, territorial and hierarchical ties. But to be an individual in such a way is something dreadful. Vagabonds were pitilessly hounded, locked up, branded, sent to the galleys and many were even executed. A truly negative example then, of being an individual, merely an individual, and nothing else with no supports at all.

The objection could be raised that the vagabond is an old historical figure and has all but disappeared today. However, if we consider the case of a truly contemporary individual, an unemployed person who was once well-integrated, who seemed protected, and in possession of the resources necessary to living his or her own life in an independent way. But now this person has been forced out of this configuration because, for example, the company has decided to invest somewhere else, where labour costs are lower. At the same time, this person loses the ability to control the future. He or she is most definitely still an individual and, as long as resignation does not set in, is even exhorted to act like an individual: make telephone calls, write CVs, make appointments, attend job interviews, etc. But it is an uncomfortable and low-status – vulnerable – way of being an individual, without reliable signposts, living with the threat of an uncertain future.

This reintroduces the idea of *supports*. It is not enough to declare the merits and the eminent value of the individual. It is also important to consider the conditions necessary to being an individual, in the full sense of the term, endowed with a minimum of independence. Because it is also possible to be an individual lacking supports, an individual by default, and ultimately to be, like the vagabond, an individual in a negative way, completely alone and completely naked.

This idea can be developed further and the question asked, what is the nature of these supports which the individual needs to have at his or her disposal in order to be able to exist in a positive way? A response may be that these supports can take several forms and that they have varied throughout history. Social history shows that there is a construction of the modern individual having used different supports as the basis for independence. It is possible to establish the history or genealogy of this construction of the individual, which would involve following the changes to these supports. This could start from the moment when the modern conception of the individual began to assert itself in Western Europe – around the 17th-18th century – up until its present-day form or forms.

Of course, I do not intend to set out this history here, which I have already outlined elsewhere (Castel, 2001). But it is important, however, to briefly indicate the importance of the two main supports which have successively given strength to the modern individual. The first is private property and, secondly, what could be called social property, that is to say a combination of resources, rights and protections incorporated into the conditions of the working people. The point being not history for history's sake, but to try to understand modern vulnerability, and the contemporary status of the vulnerable individual, as a form of disconnection with respect to the supports of social property.

To take the first point, very briefly: even if it may seem shocking, the first support necessary to enable the modern individual to assert him or herself with a minimum of independence was private property. What was it that stabilised the vagabond mentioned earlier, drifting between the cracks in a society of orders and statutes? It was the ability to gain a hold on property – otherwise, he would have continued his wanderings, making him an individual without substance. John Locke, who at the end of the 17th century was a perceptive witness of this moment of departure from the holistic society, said 'man is master of himself, and proprietor of his own person, and the actions or labour of it'. On the basis of this property, a product of his work, he not only gained material independence, but also social independence. He ceased to be someone else's 'man' as it was called in ancient feudal law, that is to say, kept in the hierarchical relationships of dependence and interdependence of traditional societies. He could thus exist for himself, take possession of his own being on the basis of private property.

There is no other way of understanding why property is ranked as an inalienable right in the Declaration of the Rights of Man and the Citizen, nor why, for example, a mind as revolutionary as Saint-Just dreamt of a Republic of free and independent smallholders. It is less a question of class attachment to 'bourgeois' property, than the realisation that property is the necessary condition for the independence of the citizen. It is the heart of what Crawford B. Macpherson called 'possessive individualism' and is at the core of the modern, and primarily liberal, concept of the individual: the individual needs property to exist positively because property makes it possible to exist by and for oneself, to escape dependence. But there is a major implication in this independence of the individual being based on property: what status can the individual without property have? It is essentially the question of the status of the worker, the employee. Employees in their roles as workers participate in the activity of appropriation. However, an employee does not appropriate for him or herself but for others, for the employer. It is the question of the separation of work and property that is at the heart of the modern social question. As regards the individual, it can be interpreted thus: 'Is the worker, the employee, an individual in a positive way?'

The answer is no. A person living or surviving by work alone cannot be an individual in his or her own right. The separation of property and work splits up into two conflicting ways of being an individual: individuals endowed with the ability to be independent, and those who remain in a position of subordination, and also of poverty and the indignity of social nonentities.

This is not an ideological or political interpretation, but rather a quasi-sociological statement of the workers' condition, how they are obliged to live and how they are treated. To take one account among others, already quoted above, but which is particularly significant. It is from l'abbé Sieyès, known to have been the great inspirer of the Declaration of the Rights of Man and the Citizen, which we may accept as the great manifesto of the affirmation of the modern individual, of his dignity and of his rights. However, in a note written a few years before 1789, l'abbé Sieyès describes the workers of the day thus:

> These poor wretches destined to hard labour, producers of he enjoyment of others, barely having enough to sustain their suffering and needy bodies (...) lacking freedom, lacking morality, this immense mass of biped instruments possessing only their miserably paid hands and an absorbed soul. (Sieyès, 1985, 81)

L'abbé Sieyès's account is lucid enough. These individuals 'possessing only their miserably paid hands' are the manual workers of the end of the 18th century. 'Producers of the enjoyment of others', they are not producing things for themselves. They are the small wage earners of the time, living a miserably hand-to-mouth existence, unskilled workers, day labourers, drudges. They are obviously wretched, but they are particularly despised because they represent social nonentity *par excellence*.

So this 'non-property owing class' as they begin to be called from the 18th century is made up of individuals lacking any of the positive qualities ascribed to individuals at the time and displayed in the Declaration of the Rights of Man and the Citizen. But this issue, which doubtlessly shows the fundamental contradiction of liberal thought, and which Sieyès expresses in its rawest form, is pursued further during the 19th century. For these 'instruments bipèdes' are in fact, the nucleus of modern wage earners which will be developed through urbanisation and industrialisation. They will engender the proletariat of Marx with 'nothing to lose but their chains', and who the descriptions of pauperism represent as a mass of 'new barbarians', immoral and dangerous. The social question they pose is political because they risk destroying the bases of the social order by revolutionary subversion. But it is also anthropological: is modern society condemned to allow the proliferation at its heart of masses of so-called 'instruments bipèdes' in a state of permanent instability, threatened with ruin because they lack the minimum of resources for the attainment of independence?

How did we extricate ourselves from this intolerable situation? *By adding protection and rights to work.* The worker can thus build up his own security from his work, giving him something equivalent to private property.

Take pensions, for example. Before pensions the situation of the old worker who, no longer being able to work, offered a particularly dramatic illustration of the miseries of the people. If he was lucky enough to have children, they could perhaps just about look after him, but he would often be left to languish before dying in the poorhouse, which meant utter degradation. A pension does not grant a life of luxury, but at least it gives a minimum of security, enabling a person to exist independently and to meet his or her needs. And this security is a right acquired through work: the old worker has 'entitlements', he has a right to the security set down by law and guaranteed by the state. This right to security frees him from dependence on charity or any kind of elective assistance. Thus a pension is *homologous to* private property for non-property owning individuals, it gives them a support on which to base their independence.

A pension is just one example of this new type of resource guaranteed by the state and which could be called social property, different from private property, but assuring property for security. It would be an onerous task to set out its ramifications, particularly during the period following the Second World War, peaking in Western Europe in the seventies and providing what can be called *social reintegration of non-property owners*. But to take just one example illustrates the fact that this development of social property enabled the generalisation or, more preferably, the democratisation of a positive status of the individual in the wage-earning society.

The example is a technician, or the manager of a company in the sixties. He does not necessarily own anything, except perhaps his car, his stereo and a few other personal goods. But he earns a reasonable salary and, most importantly, he is insured against the main social risks and his future seems to be guaranteed, on the basis of the stability of his professional career and the rights and protections he is accumulating, including for when he stops work (his retirement). In terms of security and independence, he compares favourably with the person of independent means, nervously defending his patrimony. Thus we have *a model of a positive individual constructed from protected wage earners*. He is probably even the model of the modern individual *par excellence*: dynamic, enterprising, interested in culture and travelling, concerned with his professional advancement and his social image, he will send his children to university, etc. Is he not the paradigm of the positive individual of modern mythology?

But this individual is the way he is because *he has stable supports at his disposal*. His freedom and his independence rest on the basis of social rights and protections. It is also a way of saying that the old vulnerability of the people has been vanquished, together with the poverty of the workers. In the wage-earning society of the 1960s to 1970s the vast majority of workers had attained stability. These protected employees were able to feel themselves to be relatively invulnerable, at least as long as these systems of rights and protections of social property remained strong.

But that is the point, they did not remain strong. Although often described incorrectly, 'the crisis' of the seventies saw, not the total disappearance, but the crumbling of these supports linked to paid employment. Through mass unemployment and the undermining of work relations, gaps appeared in social property and the main effect of this 'great change', to echo Karl Polanyi, was undoubtedly, as stated above, *the resurgence of vulnerability*. The uncertainty of the future, being forced once again to live a hand-to-mouth existence, the instability of professional positions and social insecurity have again become common situations. Thus, mass vulnerability, which had apparently been eradicated, seems to be resurfacing and individuals who were previously stabilised are once again placed in a situation of vulnerability.

How exactly does this resurgence of vulnerability affect the status of the individual? To understand this, it is important to reflect on a paradox.

For a majority of workers the possibility of attaining positive individuality was achieved *because of their inclusion in collectives*: worker collectives and union collectives, collective agreements, collective regulation of employment law and social protection. It is the collective status of employee which 'devulnerabilised', if this is an appropriate term, the individual worker, gave him or her strength and stability.

But what is occurring today is a decollectivisation, or a re-individualisation, firstly of work relations, but also of the various elements of the position of the wage earner. Which is why this is a paradox in the effects of the processes of individualisation, or decollectivisation, which are today traversing the organisation of work, and beyond that, large sectors of the social experience. People are required to act as individuals more often than when they were part of the large collective mechanisms. But this generalised individualisation is problematic because many individuals lack the resources necessary to play these new roles and, on the contrary, lose their supports, which are undermined by this process. So they risk finding themselves 'individuals by default'.

Hence, a split in the constitution of the very status of the modern individual and this can give rise to two contrasting profiles. Many people can indeed turn this new situation to their advantage, maximise their chances by freeing themselves from collective constraints, which can, in fact, be very burdensome (see Taylorism and the division of labour). Moreover, this is made much fuss of by business management, and more generally in the neo-liberal attitude: do something, make an effort, take initiatives and risks by freeing yourselves from collective, bureaucratic and state constraints. And some people really do come out of it well, they are the winners of the current *aggiornamento* of capitalism. But it is because they have the supports to play this game or, as Pierre Bourdieu would say, the capital, not only the financial capital, but also the social, relational and cultural capital, to which the social rights and social property could be added.

But for those who do not have these resources at their disposal, the demands of individualisation result in a loss of status, a return to vulnerability, and even a total disconnection with respect to collective belonging, which I have called disaffiliation. They undoubtedly remain individuals, but they become overexposed individuals, and are no longer protected. They are on the front line, backs against the wall and without reserves, and they are obliged, as people say, to 'make a real effort'.

This is a general outline that appears to synthesise the main and, as stated above, ambiguous effects of the individualisation processes currently at work in our society. But a more specific analysis is necessary, particularly of the characteristics of these individuals in need of supports. At the outset the long-term unemployed were considered. It is also possible to consider the young person in search of a first job, who wanders from training scheme to training scheme and from one casual job to another, sometimes living a fairly makeshift existence. 'Having a tough time of it', as people say, is an excellent example of contemporary vulnerability. The beneficiary of income support is another example of a particularly vulnerable individual. He or she generally does not have a job and often experiences integration difficulties with the people around him or her and his or her family. But this person is also told: 'make an effort', 'do something', 'make plans', 'sign a contract' – things which individuals following a better signposted path are not asked to do on a daily basis. Thus, there are some individuals who seem almost condemned to be individuals. They are individuals in a very problematic way because they do not have any reserves at their disposal and are particularly vulnerable to the risks of life.

This chapter has simply outlined the problem by sketching the link that can exist between social situations of vulnerability and the status of the vulnerable individual. Obviously, further examination of how to 'get out of' these situations is necessary. If it is true that the fragility of these individuals stems from a disconnection with respect to protective supports, or the impossibility of connecting up again, then it is possible to construct the hypothesis that it is a question of *re-*

affiliating these individuals by getting them supports. These may be classic supports of social property, or supports that have yet to be created. However, this proposal remains very general and abstract and it is doubtful whether it can be made much more precise from the reflexive level on which the above is placed. As stated at the outset, these new circumstances present us with new situations and we do not have the formulas *a priori* to deal with them. It is thus most probably by following and analysing the practical ways of trying to meet these challenges in the field that we shall be able to increase our theoretical knowledge of the questions raised by the resurgence of vulnerability.

References

Castel, R. and Haroche, Cl. (2001), *Propriété privée, propriété sociale, propriété de soi. Entretiens sur la construction de l'individu moderne*, Éditions Fayard, Paris.
Sieyès, E.J. (1985), *Écrits politiques*, Éditions des archives contemporaines, Paris.

Chapter 4

Is the Juridical Establishment of the Principle of the Respect of Human Dignity Effective?

Jacques Fierens

À quoi servent mes poèmes
Si mon père ne sait me lire?
Mon père a cent ans
Il n'a pas vu la mer
Ce soir il viendra
Épeler mes lettres
Et demain il saura
Lire
Dignité

Rachid Boudjedra,
Pour ne plus rêver, Alger, Sned, 1965.

People in sometimes extreme situations of vulnerability, have always struggled and striven to change their living conditions and especially their relationship to others. When social structures did not seem very open to change (from Greek and Roman Antiquity up until the end of the Ancien Regime), their efforts were often perceived as being aimed at improving their material situation, later (especially since the Socialist and Marxist movements), as the staking of a claim to a place in political and economic life, coming to be seen more recently (since the Second World War), as clearly having a legal perspective. In fact, beyond approaching poverty in terms of material hardship, after the concept, developed in the 1960s of the idea of a lack of security being a form of 'social exclusion', present-day analysis often favours the theme of rights and, of course, primarily that of so-called fundamental rights, human rights.[1] The possibility of acquiring material goods, a decent income, participation in government, the possibility of living as a family, access to knowledge and culture are all essentially based on legal relationships.

Behind the assertion of rights, one often finds more and more, both in the claims of those grieved and at the heart of legal discourse itself, the assertion of the *dignity* of every human being. Contrary to what one might think, this insistence is relatively recent.

This is probably what led the organisers of this meeting to set down, among the main lines of thought, the study of 'the concern for being treated with respect and dignity'. It is to this that we propose to make a contribution from a particular perspective: let us start from the hypothesis that this concern is real and with the observation that the notion of human dignity has permeated law. What is the origin of this reference? Does it have a content? Should its vagueness be combatted? Should its assertion be encouraged? In short, is the legal assertion of human dignity effective or is it more a kind of incantation? Are there conditions attached to its effectiveness?

The Appearance of the Notion of Human Dignity in Philosophy

Dignity

The word 'dignité', in French, is attested around 1155 (Rey, 1992, 604). It is derived from the Latin *dignitas*, itself a translation from the Greek *axia*, which is usually translated by worth, or *axiôma*, used by Aristotle for 'axiom', 'first principle of reason', 'that which is accepted upon being stated'.[2] From the same root *axios*, which can be translated as 'worthy', means still more fundamentally 'that which carries weight in itself', 'that which influences by its own weight', or 'that which has worth in itself'.[3]

Greek and Latin also had a meaning that we still find today: dignity is also a responsibility, a function, a distinguished title or even an attitude stamped with nobility and solemnity.[4] Thus we can differentiate between 'a' dignity and 'the' dignity. In the first sense, the idea is characterised by the fact that it marks a difference between people, but once this becomes 'human dignity', it is, on the contrary, used to describe an essential sameness.

Human Dignity

When dignity is the dignity of every person, a new concept appears which takes us back to that which is supposed in every general representation of the human condition, to an attribute of the human race, of which the origin was first thought of as being divine, then as 'natural'. This expression of a fundamental human attribute in terms of dignity finds its source in Renaissance thought. The Middle Age had the tendency to emphasise a pessimistic conception of the nature of man, insisting on his sinfulness and his decay. However, from the thirteenth century, Lotario de Conti, who was to become Pope Innocent III, after having written a tract on human wretchedness in 1195 (*De miseriae humanae conditionis*), resolved to write another on the dignity of man, without, however, actually having been able to do so. The subject was taken up again two hundred years later, in 1447, by Bartolomeo Fazio (*De excellentia et praestantia hominis*), and in 1452 by Giannozzo Manetti (*De dignitate et excellentia hominis*). In 1486 and 1487, at the age of 24, Jean Pic de la Mirandole wrote his *Discours sur la dignité de l'homme*,[5] which is probably the first great assertion of human dignity. The *Discours* took a new, radically optimistic, direction, intending to exalt the greatness of man.[6]

In the seventeenth century, Pascal, who was also seeking the greatness of man through his own wretchedness, asserted a universal principle in the sense that it is valid for all men, and a particular principle in the sense that it differentiates man from all other creatures:

> Man is obviously made to think. It is his whole dignity and his whole merit. (1940, 45)[7]
> All the dignity of man consists in thought (...). But what is this thought? How foolish it is. (1940, 100) It is not from space that I must seek my dignity, but from the government of my thought. (1940, 97)

Thus Pascal took up the old Greek theme of rationality and self-consciousness as a specific difference between man and other creatures – *anthrôpos zôon logon échon* – but expressing it this time through the notion of dignity.

A century later, it was Immanuel Kant who best prepared the way for the legal notion (was he not, according to Jean Lacroix (1969, 66), 'the man of the Law'?). At the same time as he mobilised the concept to establish the primacy of morality, he also returned to the most original meaning, the Greek sense of 'worth in itself', having no equivalent.

> In the kingdom of ends everything has either a price or a dignity. Whatever has a price can be replaced by something else as its equivalent; on the other hand, whatever is above all price, and therefore admits of no equivalent, has a dignity (...) but that which constitutes the condition under which alone something can be an end in itself has not merely a relative worth, i.e., a price, but has an intrinsic worth, i.e., dignity. (Kant, 1983a, 40)

Dignity belongs to humanity alone because only humanity is capable of morality, that is to say, of acting through pure duty. Morality is a law and that is why Immanuel Kant's thinking is of a legal type. The capability of being a moral being and of acknowledging others as being capable of morality is the ultimate foundation of human dignity:

> Now morality is the condition under which alone a rational being can be an end in himself, for only thereby can he be a legislating member in the kingdom of ends. Hence morality and humanity, insofar as it is capable of morality, alone has dignity (Kant, 1983a, 40-41). Humanity itself is a dignity; for a man cannot be used merely as a means by any man (either by others or even by himself) but must always be used at the same time as an end. It is just in this that his dignity (personality) consists, by which he raises himself above all other beings in the world that are not men and yet can be used, and so over all *things*. (Kant, 1983b, 255)

Thus, the assertion of human dignity enabled, as we have seen, the reaffirmation of 'humanity' as a whole, which had already been an insistence of the stoics.[8] In time, that is to say from the status of the Nuremberg Tribunal in 1945, 'humanity' also became a legal notion, enigmatic subject of a collective right, as seen in the reinforcement of notions such as that of 'crimes against humanity' (Fierens, 2000).

Respect

Besides the connection with humanity, the emergence of the concept of the dignity of man is inseparable from that of respect (Audard, 1993). Dignity commands respect and the latter is the measure of an equality between men. Immanuel Kant again:

> In the system of nature, man (*homo phaenomenon, animal rationale*) is a being of slight importance and shares with the rest of the animals, as offspring of the earth, an ordinary value (*pretium vulgare*)... But man regarded as a person, that is, as the subject of morally practical reason, is exalted above any price; for as a person (*homo noumenon*) he is not be valued merely as a means to the ends of others or even to his own ends, but as an end in himself, that is, he possesses a *dignity* (an absolute inner worth) by which he *exacts* respect for himself from all other rational beings in the world. He can measure himself with every other being of this kind and value himself on a footing of equality with them. (Kant, 1983b, 230)

Respect is the relationship of esteem to dignity, it is the relation of one reasonable subject to another. It is by nature fundamentally lawful, legal, even if, as we know, for Immanuel Kant law is moral before being political:[9]

> For nothing can have any worth other than what the law determines. But the legislation itself which determines all worth must for that very reason have dignity, i.e., unconditional and incomparable worth; and the word 'respect' alone provides a suitable expression for the esteem which a rational being must have for it. (Kant, 1983a, 41)

Human Dignity in Law

Appearance in Texts

The first allusion to human dignity in a normative text seems to be that of Article 151 of the German constitution, known as the 'Weimar' constitution, adopted on 11 August 1919, which mentions 'life in dignity'.[10] The context here is that of the constitutional emergence of economic, social and cultural rights which this text is also one of the first to sanction.[11] We shall see that the invocation of dignity in order to obtain debtors' rights is criticised, but it is however in this context that the notion is asserted for the first time in law. It is also perhaps not purely by chance that this assertion was made after one of the humanitarian cataclysms of the twentieth century, the First World War.

'Human dignity' then appears in international public law in the Preamble to the United Nations Charter of 26 June 1945,[12] before being mentioned twice in that of the Universal Declaration of Human Rights of 10 December 1948, as well as in Articles 1, 22 and 23, § 3.[13] On the subject of the first Article, we know that René Cassin, who wrote the first draft, was inspired by the French Declaration of 1789. The latter declared: 'All human beings are born free and equal and rights.' René Cassin wrote: 'All human beings are born free and equal *in dignity* and rights' (Verdoodt, 1964, 59-60).[14]

Since 1945, the notion of dignity has run the entire gamut of the hierarchy of the normative texts of many countries. It has been included in treaties,[15] constitutions,[16] laws[17] and regulations, and it is becoming very difficult to note all of the occurrences.

In Jurisprudence

Today, the courts, for their part, often turn more and more to human dignity to justify their decisions.[18] The fact that it is no longer always a question of interpreting a legal text mentioning it is noteworthy. The idea is often used in the absence of any legal reference, or rather *because* no adequate legal reference exists, to justify the solution (Martens, 2000). Human dignity is thus raised to the rank of a general principle of law, of a 'matrix principle' (Mathieu, 1995, 211), even of a 'suprapositive' rule.

In chronological order, we can first quote the European Court of Human Rights, which evokes the safeguarding of dignity as one of the main aims of Article 3 of the Convention, together with the protection of physical integrity.[19]

On 9 July 1990, in the case of *John Moore*, a patient from whom doctors had taken tissues without his consent, the Californian Supreme Court mentions dignity.[20]

In the context of electricity being cut off because of a failure to pay bills, the Appeal Court in Brussels found that 'every person must be protected if his right to lead a life worthy of human dignity is compromised'.[21] In the same context, The President of the County Court of Charleroi was to find that the use of the plea of non-fulfilment 'contradicted the notion of human dignity' when it resulted in making 'a person with two children live without gas and electricity, in the middle of winter'.[22] So, we see again that reference to human dignity is also used to guarantee a debtor's right, here that of being supplied with electricity.

The French Constitutional Council decided in 1994 that 'the protection of human dignity against all forms of oppression and degradation' is a 'principle of constitutional value'.[23] The same Council then declared that the principle of the protection of human rights is an 'objective of constitutional value'.[24]

In the same sense, on 16 October 1997, the Constitutional Court of Rumania, asserted that human dignity is a supreme value of the Rumanian constitutional state.[25]

The French Council of State, in the famous 'tossing the dwarf' case, said that respect for human dignity is one of the constituents of public order.[26] One of the interests of the case, which received extensive commentary from a variety of angles, was to show to what extent the notion of human dignity could be solicited to conflicting ends. The person being thrown, and thus directly concerned by the case, asserted, in the name of his own dignity, that the show which was being criticised had enabled him, for the first time, to earn a reasonable living and to become a star. The banning of the show would result in his 'exclusion'. The Doctrine, therefore, wondered whether an offence against human dignity must be assessed on the 'subjective' level of the person who is subjected to the treatment, or on the 'objective' level of the facts considered for themselves. This is largely an incorrect question. As always in law, it is a question of the relationship between human beings, and not the situation of a single individual, to the extent moreover, that such an approach is possible. Law is not only concerned with relations. The spectators, or even just the people acquainted with the organisation of the game, in their relationship to the participants, and to the dwarf himself, are also subject to a treatment. It is this reciprocal relationship that has to be assessed. The fact remains that the violation of the principle of human dignity in the case in point did not obviously appear to all of the commentators and, in this respect, the ruling was globally disapproved of by doctrine. On the theoretical level, the decision of the French Council of State shows the link that can be established with another idea of variable content, but which is less criticised, that of public order.[27]

With its decision of 28 May 1996, the Court of Appeal of Paris, ruled that a Benetton advertisement evoking the HIV virus used 'a degrading stigmatising of the dignity of people implacably suffering in their bodies and in their being, thus abusing the freedom of expression'.[28] The plaintiffs encountered a special difficulty because they were obviously not personally targeted by the contested advertisement and could cite neither a direct personal wrong, nor a breach of an individual right. 'Classic' human rights were of no use here. As an annotator of the ruling pointed out, human dignity was, in a way, taking over from human rights (Edelman, 1989).

Criticism of the Notion of Human Dignity

Human dignity has thus permeated law and jurisprudence. It is on the way to becoming considered as an anterior principle, superior even to human rights which illustrate the various aspects of it. Its establishment is not, however, above criticism from philosophers or jurists, indeed, far from it.

The Criticism of Hannah Arendt

Hannah Arendt's criticism of reference to human dignity seems particularly forceful, notably because it is based on experience of the Holocaust. In short, she says that the invoking of dignity risks being tragically useless if certain conditions are not fulfilled. A man cannot have rights, and cannot therefore see his dignity respected, unless he is part of a political and legal community (Arendt, 1967).

Thus, human rights were not able to prevent the horror of the Nazi extermination camps because the human beings who perished there no longer had any legal status. Moreover, Hannah Arendt maintains that the victims themselves never invoked their fundamental rights. Human rights and dignity cannot content themselves with concerning an 'abstract' man (here we have an echo of Karl Marx[29]), who does not exist anywhere, but must necessarily refer to the man included in a political community, to man as citizen. Deprived of citizenship, man can only assert his dignity. At the same time, Hannah Arendt reminds us of the lesson of Aristotle, for whom man is fundamentally both he who has speech (*zôon logon échon*) and he who is a citizen (*zôon politikon*), both things being intimately related.[30] Without the power of speech and without citizenship, the establishment of the respect of human dignity is in vain. Immanuel Kant also established the link between citizenship and dignity, going so far as to reconcile, up to a certain point, 'a' dignity and 'the' dignity, by asserting:

> Certainly no man in a state can be without any dignity, since he at least has the dignity of a citizen. The exception is someone who has lost it by his own *crime* because of which, though he is kept alive, he is made mere tool of another's choice (either of the state or of another citizen)... (Kant, 1991, 139)

But, Hannah Arendt observes that a person can be deprived of citizenship because of what that person *is*, and not because of what that person has *done* as Immanuel Kant suggests:

> Before this, what we must call a 'human right' today would have been thought of as a general characteristic of the human condition which no tyrant could take away. Its loss entails the loss of relevance of speech (and man, since Aristotle, has been defined as a being commanding the power of speech and thought), and the loss of all human relationship (and man, again since Aristotle, has been thought of as the 'political animal', that is one who by definition lives in a community), the loss, in other words, of some of the most essential characteristics of human life. (...) Man, it turns out, can lose all so-called Rights of Man without losing his essential quality as man, his human dignity. Only the loss of a polity itself expels him from humanity. (Arendt, 1967, 297)

The genocide committed by the Nazis, just like the Rwandan genocide or other crimes against humanity, are the tragic reductio ad absurdum of the pertinence of Hannah Arendt's reflection. The Third Reich, or the government that was in power in Rwanda until 1994, each within its own cultural sphere, progressively denied Jews or *Tutsis* respectively, the quality of 'subjects of dignity', systematically preventing them from speaking out, and leading to the possibility of the ultimate negation of this dignity.[31] The scandalous poverty of millions of human beings, unprotected by human dignity, is a result of the same absence of conditions necessary to the respect of it: rather than being able to be explained by economic mechanisms, it is due to the absence of citizenship and the lack of a voice for the people who suffer from it. The same can be said of the fate reserved for people seeking refugee status in many countries: their legal status, or rather the lack of acknowledgement of their fundamental rights, whether in theory or in practice, is the cause of their terrible vulnerability. The assertion of dignity is not enough. Citizenship, national or international, and access to the language that is listened to are indispensable.

The Criticism of the Jurists

Few commentators who are jurists do not criticise the notion of human dignity. The reproaches are many: the notion is 'vague' (Saint-James, 1997, 67), it is 'by definition a-legal' (Théron, 1998, 296),[32] capable of being manipulated to the extreme. The courts, and especially constitutional judges, find in it the basis of a power and of responsibilities abandoned by constituents (Martens, 2000) and reference to dignity is a threat to freedoms. It allows the imposition of subjective moral ideas.[33] The attempt to assert a 'matrix principle' of human rights introduces confusion in terms of their value. More particularly, on the subject of the ruling of the French Council of State relative to the tossing of the dwarf, dignity is 'an alibi for the extension of the components of public order' (Saint-James, 1997, 67). The hidden concept of human dignity is that of public morality 'flying the flag of convenience'.[34]

However, none of these objections seems diriment.

For the Notion of Human Dignity

An Aspiration of the Holders of Rights

The notion of human dignity must be maintained and strengthened in law. The first reason for this is that it expresses much better than others the aspirations of those whose fundamental rights are the most obviously flouted. A Frenchman who had been kept prisoner for nearly twenty years in the Gulag was interviewed on a French television channel by Jean-Marie Cavada who asked him what had caused him the most suffering during his imprisonment. Without mentioning the hunger, the cold, the brutality, the prisoners who died in front of his eyes, he replied, 'the humiliation'. The testimony of Nazi camp survivors is in a similar vein (Levi, 1995; Antelme, 1957). The same type of assertion is also found when speaking to people living in great poverty, whether they live in the south or the north of the world: 'The hardest thing to bear is the shame'. Pride and dignity are the first things that people aspire to, before, or beyond, all material claims. This constant in the words of those whose most basic rights are compromised must be taken very seriously by law.

The Indispensable Role of Law

To the criticism according to which there is cause for resisting a more general phenomenon of 'juridicalisation at all costs' (Théron, 1998, 303-304) having the erroneous premise 'the nature of law is only to protect individual prerogatives', the response could be given that, in fact, law does not have the monopoly of this protection, but that within its sphere of competence, only it can establish citizenship and speech, that is to say the democratic debate which is the result, and only it is able to mobilise civil authorities and the constraint over which it has the monopoly, to guarantee the conditions of dignity and to prevent its violation. Many other ways, as well as law, need to be explored in order to allow or to protect dignity (education, access to the arts, to spirituality), but they always *also* have legal implications (the examples taken obviously correspond to 'classic' fundamental rights, such as the right to education, to freedom of expression, freedom of thought and religion). It would be better to say that, in order to guarantee dignity, law is indispensable, but insufficient.

Law, Ethics and Morality

Criticism of the moralisation of the notion has the shortcoming of lacking depth. Of course human dignity is firstly a moral assertion. How can we not admit this when we see that the most obvious origin of its introduction into modern law is the insistence of Immanuel Kant, for whom the requirement for morality constitutes the real human condition? Without going as far as he does (the weakness of Immanuel Kant lies precisely in the fact that he could not imagine a morality which would transcend law and rights to become a real ethics of freedom), it should be remembered that the discussion is as old as law thought: is law separable from ethics? It was already the question Socrates and Plato asked of the sophists. The split between justice and power, initiated by Machiavelli, the positivist illusion which still so well feeds our attitudes and our universities, the splitting of law and ethics all proved to be not only impossible, but also dangerous. Besides the responsibility of a Kelsen in the tolerance of odious legal orders, did we not see, under the occupation, the most renowned French jurists discussing the (real) problems posed by 'the Jewish label', without the ethical question being asked? (Lochak, 1989, 252) Law as an organiser of human actions, ethics as a way of reflecting on the meaning of those actions, and morality as a rule of behaviour not sanctioned by any authority outside of our innermost selves, are all inevitably and eternally closely linked, especially when the most fundamental rights are at stake. Their influence is reciprocal and circular.

It is not a question of knowing whether law concerns morality or ethics – it is obvious that the answer is yes – but of knowing which instance is the origin of the legal norm and according to which procedure it will exercise its authority. What counts today in our secularised democracies, is the preponderance of civil authority over moral or religious authority in the elaboration of the norm and of judgements. This does neither mean that law has nothing to do with morality, nor that a moral notion does not have its place in law.

Notions of Variable Content

The notion of human dignity is admittedly unspecified. It leaves the way open to differing interpretations and excesses which have, in fact, occurred in jurisprudence. The Belgian Council of State succeeded in qualifying it as a 'principe limitatif' (restrictive principle) regarding the organic law of 8 July 1976 for public welfare centres, which declares welfare as being commensurate with what is necessary to the respect of human dignity.[35] The notion, according to the high administrative court, refers to a sort of maximum rather than to a minimum of legal guarantees, which is absurd. As Paul Martens humorously remarked, the invoking of dignity can serve the cause of all tendencies: 'lymphatic positivists, lively positivists, beatific jus naturalists, shifty jus naturalists, touchy materialists, edifying constructivists or Foucaldian moaners...' (Martens, 2000, 574-575). But in this respect, jurisprudence can also play the unifying and regulating role which is classically expected of it, by progressively and flexibly identifying 'in the light of present-day conditions' as the European Court of Human Rights would put it, the legal content of dignity. The utility of the notion lies precisely in the fact of its not having any exact content. In law, human dignity is a functional, evolutional, operating principle. It is far from being the only one (Perelman and Vander Elst, 1984), but nevertheless, today, it could be said that it is focused upon by critics who could well target other notions. The foundations of law can only be expressed through these notions of variable content, such as 'public order', 'democratic society', 'accepted standards of good behaviour', 'offence', 'inhuman treatment', and so many others, up to and including the fundamental concept of 'reasonable'. These notions are the means available to the judge to achieve a balance of interests, rather than applying a supposed judicial syllogism which would, in fact, imply a prior and precise content. Human dignity indicates a sense and a measure to the legislator and to the judge, and that is enough for the drawing up of laws and the passing of judgements. Maybe it is its relative newness, or the fact that is ever more frequently used, that makes human dignity the object of more criticism.

The Example of the Right to Social Security in Belgium

In Belgium, when the right to social security was established as being that which enables someone to live in a way that is 'worthy of human dignity', the legislation department of the Council of State gave its opinion that this single reference could not establish a subjective right, moreover, as it happens, a debtor's right. However, the legislator deliberately refused to be more specific about the notion that would be specified by the courts and that would evolve with time.[36] We have seen that excesses have occurred, such as that of the administration department of the Belgian Council of State, which asserted the existence of a restrictive principle. But the risk could be taken. In spite of some slips, after a quarter of a century of the implementation of the law on social security and thousands of administrative and legal decisions, no-one defends the idea anymore that the notion of dignity is inopportune, illegitimate or ineffective, and social security performs its function very concretely to the benefit of thousands of people, whose situation would be different if the law establishing human dignity did not exist.

The Need for a Democratic Debate

Should we complain about the power thus given to judges by the legislator, explicitly if a text mentions human dignity or implicitly if the principle is a matrix notion, a general principle of law, an unwritten constitutional principle? Admittedly, the power of the judge is considerable, but the court is one of the places par excellence for the exercise of citizenship and speech. The invoking of dignity is legitimate if it is the result of a debate: an informal and prior debate in the relationship between the holders of rights, a formalised debate in the elaboration of democratic law, a debate which is regulated in form and in content before democratic courts.

> This then is how the procedural function of law is carried out: it no longer imposes, it proposes, it no longer excludes, it integrates, it does not close the discussion, it opens it. We do not really know anymore where to place human dignity, or how to foresee what it has in store for us since it has become juridical. But we have at our disposal all of the elements necessary for participation in the debate and henceforth the solution cannot be imposed upon us by those who are supposed to know. (Martens, 2000, 576)

Speech and Equality

But let us go further and conclude: it is not enough for the debate to exist, it is also necessary that everyone participates, especially including those whose dignity is the most compromised: the humiliated, the tortured, the poor, foreigners, those who are socially excluded for whatever reason. Dignity only protects those who are able to speak out, which also means to speak out publicly. In order to be able to participate in the debate, it is necessary to be a citizen, in the sense explained to us by Hannah Arendt, otherwise, effectively, the establishment of the respect of human dignity, as a principle of law is useless. The gaining of access to the language does not just mean having learned to speak, but also the means of having the possibility of being listened to. Aristotle already understood this twenty-four centuries ago, when he linked citizenship and *logos*, though he did not then think that this language should be that of all human beings, fully equal by right, that citizenship should be that of everybody. This principle – this *axia*, this 'axiom', this dignity through the right to equality – was only established on the theoretical level in a much more recent age, with the Enlightenment for philosophy[37] and with the American and French Revolutions for law.[38] This acquisition is certainly not a definitive one. Nazism needed only a decade to take a hold in a Europe which had had two centuries of egalitarian tradition behind it. It also remains for us to make the legal principle of the respect of human dignity effective.

Such is, when all is said and done, the condition of the legitimacy and the effectiveness of the notion of human dignity in law: may everyone be able to contribute as equals in the public debate to define its content.

Notes

1   We are familiar with the definition of the French Economic and Social Council, proposed by the ATD Fourth World Movement and now current within the instances of the UN: 'The lack of basic security connotes the absence of one or more factors enabling individuals and families to assume basic responsibilities and to enjoy fundamental rights. The situations may become widespread and result in more serious and permanent consequences. The lack of basic security leads to chronic poverty when it simultaneously affects several aspects of people's lives, when it is prolonged and when it severely compromises people's chances of regaining their rights and of reassuming their responsibilities in the near future' (*Journal Officiel*, 1987). This definition must be qualified. The lack of security targeted, the accumulation of which may lead to chronic poverty, no longer always has the consequence of depriving people and families of the *enjoyment* of fundamental rights, but of exercising them. Today the range of rights destined to protect people from poverty, from a lack of security, from exclusion, is, in fact, very complete. The problem is to create the conditions necessary for them to be effective.
2   Aristote, *Métaphysique*, B, 2, 997a and ff; *Arist. lat.*, XXV/2, 45, 21 s., IV, c 3, 1005a20 and b33 (64, 26s); c. 3, 1090 a36 (265, 5) – Boetius, *De hebdom.* PL 64, 1311B; *De differentiis topicis* I, PL 64, 1176 – D. Albertus Magnus, *Metaph.*, I tr. 1 c.8, Cologne 16/1, 12, 43s.; III tr.2 c.2, 114, 29s; IV tr.2 c.1, 173, 9s – Thomas Aquinus, *Post. anal.*, I lect. 18, § 3; lect. 43, § 13. 'A demonstration principle is an immediate proposition. A proposition is immediate to which no other is anterior' (*Analytiques seconds*, I, 2, 72a, 7). A first principle immediately recognised is an *axiôma* which should not be confused with a thesis which is just as indemonstrable. The thesis, 'though not being susceptible to demonstration, is not indispensable to anyone wishing to learn something' (*Analytiques seconds*, 72a, 15). On the contrary, if 'its possession is indispensable to anyone who wishes to learn anything, it is an axiom. There are effectively some truths of this type'.
3   Cf. the quotations collected by Bailly, A. (1950), *Dictionnaire grec-français*, Éditions Hachette, Paris, 195.
4   Thus, for example, Jean Chrysostome refers to the *dignitas* of the priest (*Du sacerdoce*, III, 4). Pascal, quoted further on, evokes the 'royal dignity' (fr. 1132). The French Declaration of the Rights of Man and the Citizen of 17 August 1789 again evokes the eligibility of citizens 'to all dignities and to all public positions and occupations' (Art. VI). Immanuel Kant, who is also discussed further on, evokes 'political dignities' (Kant, 1983b, e.g. II, 1st section, § 47; II, 1st section, note D).
5   At this time, Jean Pic de la Mirandole was battling with the Roman censors. The text is an element in his defence. In short, for him, the dignity of man stems from his freedom. There is not first a human nature, but a movement, a sort of native power, through which man decides and realises his essence. That is to say that man is not born a man but becomes one, as if he were his own creator: hence he resembles God.

6   See also Erasmus (1466-1536) and his *Praise of Folly,* Thomas More (1478-1535) and his
    Utopia.
7   See also the critique of Zivia Klein (1968) and Thomas De Koninck (1995).
8   Simone Goyard-Fabre (1996, 87 and 171) indicates the probable influence of the Swiss
    Isaac Iselin (1784) on Immanuel Kant's reflection on humanity.
9   Law is only a place of practical reason. It is not the same as morality. Respect of the law is
    compliance with one's duty under the threat of constraint. Morality is duty because it is
    one's duty.
10 'The economy has to be organised on the principles of justice, with the goal of achieving
    life in dignity for everyone. Within these limits the economic liberty of the individual is to
    be secured.'
11 Economic, social and cultural rights appear in the French Constitutions of 1791 and of
    1793 and are then forgotten for more than a century.
12 'We, the Peoples of the United Nations Determined (...) to reaffirm faith in fundamental
    human rights, in the dignity and worth of the human person...'
13 Preamble: 'Whereas recognition of the inherent dignity and of the equal and inalienable
    rights of all members of the human family is the foundation of freedom, justice and peace
    in the world. (...) Whereas the peoples of the United Nations have in the Charter
    reaffirmed their faith in fundamental human rights, in the dignity and the worth of the
    human person and in the equal rights of men and women and have determined to promote
    social progress and better standards of life in larger freedom.' Art. 1: 'All human beings are
    born free and equal in dignity and rights. They are endowed with reason and conscience
    and should act towards one another in a spirit of brotherhood.' Art. 22: 'Everyone, as a
    member of society, has the right to social security and is entitled to realisation, through
    national effort and international co-operation and in accordance with the organization and
    resources of each State, of the economic, social and cultural rights indispensable for his
    dignity and the free development of his personality.' Art. 23, § 3: 'Everyone who works has
    the right to just and favourable remuneration ensuring for himself and his family an
    existence worthy of human dignity, and supplemented, if necessary, by other means of
    social protection.'
14 The preparatory works do not say anything about the insertion and the intention of the
    word. The author of the present paper has had access to the initial manuscript of René
    Cassin, a sheet of paper on which the very first draft of the Declaration was written. This
    object was given by Madame Cassin to Father Joseph Wrésinski, founder of the
    international movement A.T.D. Fourth World. The page contains many deletions, but the
    sentence mentioned was written uninterruptedly, without any alterations.
15 Cf. among others, the International Pact on Civil and Political Rights of 16 December
    1966, Preamble 1st and 2nd, and Art. 10, § 1 – International Pact of Economic, Social and
    Cultural Rights of 16 December 1966, Preamble 1st and 2nd, and Art. 13, § 1 – American
    Convention on Human Rights of 22 November 1969, Art. 5, § 2, Art. 6, § 2, Art. 11, § 1 –
    African Charter on Human and Peoples' Rights, Preamble 2nd, and Art. 5 – Arusha
    Agreement, Protocole relatif à l'État de droit, Art. 1 – New York Convention of 1 March
    1980, concerning the dignity of woman – New York Convention of 26 January 1990,
    concerning dignity of the child. The recent Charter of Fundamental Rights of the European
    Union of 7 December 2000 states in Article 1: 'Human dignity is inviolable. It must be
    respected and protected.' The title given to the whole of Chapter 1 is 'Dignity'. Cf. also the
    Convention for the Protection of Human Rights and Dignity of the Human Being with
    regard to the Application of Biology and Medicine of 4 April 1994 (Council of Europe).
16 Basic Law of the German Constitution 23 May 1949: '*Die Würde des Menschen ist
    unantastbar*' ('The dignity of man shall be inviolable'). The last revision of the Belgian
    Constitution introduced the word in Article 23, § 1: 'Everyone has the right to lead a life in
    conformity with human dignity.' – Rwandan Constitution of 30 May 1991, Preamble; Cf.

also Art. 12: 'The human being shall be sacred' and the title of this article, 'Human Dignity' – Federal Constitution of the Swiss Confederation of 18 April 1999, Article 7: 'Human dignity shall be respected and protected.' – Constitution of Cambodia of 21 September 1993, Art. 38, § 2: 'The law shall protect the life, honour and dignity of the citizens' and Art. 46, § 1: 'The commerce of human beings, exploitation by prostitution and obscenity which affect the reputation of women shall be prohibited.'

17 Cf. among others the Belgian organic law of 8 July 1976 on public welfare centres, Art. 1 – Belgian Judicial Code, Art. 1675/3, last paragraph, regarding the collective settling of debts; decree of 4 March 1991 relative to the assistance of young people, Art. 3 – New French Penal Code, Art. 225-14, 227-24, 433-5 and 434-24 – Cf. the very Kantian Art. 1 of the Act n°98-657 of 29 July 1998. Concerning the Campaign Against Exclusion: 'The struggle against exclusion is a national requirement based on the respect of equal dignity of all human beings and a priority of the whole public policies of the nation' – Art. L651-10 of the French 'code de la construction et de l'habitation' – for other references to French legislation, see Saint-James (1997, 62).

18 To date, the Belgian juridical data bank JUDIT has compiled a register of 231 decisions containing the word 'dignity' and 105 containing the words 'human dignity'. In Canadian law, see Huppe (1988, 724).

19 *Tyrer* ruling of 25 April 1978, series A, n°26. In the corroborating opinion that he adds to the *Tomasi* ruling of 27 August 1992, Judge De Meyer explicitly links Article 3 of the Convention, which forbids torture and inhumane or degrading treatment, to human dignity: 'With regard to a person deprived of his liberty, all use of physical force which is not made necessary by his own behaviour is a breach of human dignity and must, consequently, be considered as a violation of the right guaranteed by Article 3 of the Convention.'

20 'The ramifications of recognizing and enforcing a property interest in body tissues are not know, but greatly feared – the effect of human dignity of a marketplace in human body parts, the impact on research and development of competitive bidding for such materials, and the exposure of researchers to potentially limitless and uncharted tort liability.' To recap, Mr John Moore was hospitalised in 1976 in the Medical Centre of the University of California for the treatment of his leukaemia. Doctors discovered that his blood contained unique substances enabling the treatment of certain diseases. Over a period of seven years and without the patient's consent they took skin, sperm and blood cells from his body. In 1984, a stem cell line was patented by the pharmaceutical company Sandoz who went on to make three billion dollars from it. Cf. also Court of Appeal of California: Moore v. The Regents of the University of California, 249 Cal. Reptr. 494 (Cal. App.2 Dist. 1988) (249 Cal. Rptr. 503). See also Hermitte (1988, 20-21) and Edelman (1989, 225-230).

21 Brussels, 24 December 1992, Iuvis, January 1994, 203, note P. Bouwens.

22 Civ. Charleroi (réf.), 19 January 2000, *Journal des juges de paix et de police*, 590 and note Fierens, J., 'La dignité humaine, limite à l'application de l'exception d'une exécution'.

23 Constitutional Council, n°94-343-344 DC, 27 July 1994, *JCP*, 1994, III, n°66974bis – *D., Jur.*, 1996, 237 and Mathieu (1995).

24 Decision n°94-359 of 19 January 1995. It should be pointed out that this time it was a question of the right to decent housing, which again indicates that the principle can function to set limits to the autonomy of wills as well as by way of debts of the person with regard to authority. Cf. however the reservations expressed by certain writers, which we do not share, as regards the joining of 'social' rights to the principle of human dignity: Jorion, B., *A.J.D.A.*, 1995, 457 and Saint-James (1997, 62-63).

25 *Bull. jur. Const.*, 1997, 3, 108. This concerned the examination of a press law which did not make any provision for the taking of legal action against abuse or libel in the press.

26 C.E. fr., ass., 27 October 1995, *RFD admin.*, 1995, 1204, concl. Frydman; *D.*, 1996, *Jur.*, 177 and note G. Lebreton – *JCP*, 1996, II, n°22630 and note Hamon, 657 – R.T.D.H.,

1996 and obs. N. Deffains, 'Les autorités locales responsables du respect de la dignité humaine. Sur une jurisprudence contestable du Conseil d'État'. Imported from Australia and North America 'tossing the dwarf' consisted of throwing a human being, a dwarf, the highest or the furthest possible. The person thrown was adequately protected and landed on an inflated mattress.

27 See note Hamon.
28 Paris, 28 May 1996, *D.*, 1996, *Jur.*, 617 and Edelman (1989).
29 Cf. also the conclusions of the study by Klein (1968).
30 Aristotle, *Politics*, Book I, II, 9, 10.
31 Cf. note Fierens, J., 'La non-définition du crime contre l'humanité' – Fierens, J, 'La qualification de génocide devant le Tribunal pénal international pour le Rwanda et devant les juridictions rwandaises', to be published in *Revue de droit pénal et de criminologie*.
32 The author also criticises the relating of public morality and dignity. See also page 302: 'The dignity can't be, as such, a juridical norm.' Along the same lines, Le Pourhiet (1991, 213).
33 In particular this is an insistence of French doctrine following the 'tossing the dwarf' ruling, as this jurisprudence breaks with a definition of public order by Maurice Hauriou (1927) which has become a classic, summarising it as a material and external order.
34 G. Lebreton note under C.E. fr., ass., 27 October 1995, *D.*, 1996, *Jur*, 179.
35 C.E., 21 May 1981, n°21.190, Rec., 731. Article 1, § 1 of the Belgian Law of 8 July 1976, previously mentioned, reads: 'Each person has the right to welfare. This one has the aim to allow everybody to live in accordance with human dignity.'
36 Parl. doc., Ch., session, 1975-1976, Report n°923, 8.
37 Immanuel Kant linked dignity and equality. See above.
38 See also Janos Kis (1989, 123), where the writer insists on 'equal dignity' as an ethical concept which 'attributes human rights to each individual' and places the founding instance of rights in a 'consensual debate' inspired by John Rawls (1972).

References

Antelme, R. (1957), *L'Espèce humaine*, Éditions Gallimard, Paris.

Arendt, H. (1967), *The Origins of Totalitarianism*, part 2, *Imperialism*, The world publishing company, Eleventh Printing, Cleveland and New York.

Audard, C. (éd.) (1993), *Le Respect. De l'estime à la déférence: une question de limite*, Éditions Autrement, Paris.

Edelman, B. (1989), 'L'homme aux cellules d'or', *D.*, *chr*.

Fierens, J. (2000), 'La non-définition des crimes contre l'humanité', *La revue nouvelle*, 3.

Goyard-Fabre, S. (1996), *La Philosophie du droit de Kant*, Librairie philosophique J. Vrin, Paris.

Hauriou, M. (1927), *Précis de droit administratif*, Éditions Sirey, Paris.

Hermitte, M.A. (1988), 'L'affaire Moore ou la diabolique notion de propriété', *Le Monde diplomatique*, December, 20-21.

Huppe, L. (1988), 'La dignité humaine comme fondement des droits et libertés garantis par la Charte', 48 *R. du B.*

Iselin, I. (1784), *Über die Geschichte der Menschheit*, C.G. Schmieder, Karlsrule, 1st edition 1764.

Journal Officiel de la République française. Avis et rapports du Comité économique et social (1987), *Grande pauvreté et précarité économique et sociale*, 28 February.

Kant, I. (1983a), *Ethical Philosophy*, Book 1, *Grounding for the Metaphysics of Morals*, translation by James W. Ellington, Hackett Publishing Company, Indianapolis.

Kant, I. (1983b), *Ethical Philosophy*, Book 2, *The Metaphysical Principles of Virtue*, translation by James W. Ellington, Hackett Publishing Company, Indianapolis.

Kant, I. (1991), *The Metaphysics of Morals*, Introduction, translation, and notes Mary Gregor, Cambridge University Press, Cambridge.

Kis, J. (1989), *L'Égale dignité. Essai sur les fondements des droits de l'homme*, Éditions du Seuil, Paris.

Klein, Z. (1968), *La Notion de dignité humaine dans la pensée de Kant et de Pascal*, Librairie philosophique J. Vrin, Paris.

Koninck, Th. de (1995), *De la dignité humaine*, Presses universitaires de France, Paris.

Lacroix, J. (1969), *Kant et le kantisme*, Presses universitaires de France, Paris.

Le Pourhiet, A.M. (1991), 'Le Conseil constitutionnel et l'éthique bio-médicale', in *Humanité et droit international. Mélanges René-Jean Dupuy*, Éditions Pédone, Paris.

Levi, P. (1995), *If it is a Man*, translated by Stuart Woolf, Abacus, London.

Lochak, D. (1989), 'La doctrine sous Vichy ou les mésaventures du positivisme' in *Les Usages sociaux du droit*, CURAPP, Paris.

Martens, P. (2000), 'Encore la dignité humaine: réflexions d'un juge sur la promotion par les juges d'une norme suspecte', in *Les Droits de l'homme au seuil du troisième millénaire. Mélanges en hommage à Pierre Lambert*, Éditions Bruylant, Brussels.

Mathieu, B. (1995), 'Pour une reconnaissance de 'principes matriciels' en matière de protection constitutionnelle des droits de l'homme', *D., chr.*

Pascal, B. (1940), *Thoughts*, Dent and sons Ltd, London.

Perelman, Ch. and Vander Elst, R. (eds.) (1984), *Les Notions à contenu variable en droit*, Éditions Bruylant, Brussels.

Rawls, J. (1972), *A Theory of Justice*, Clarendon Press, Oxford.

Rey, A. (éd.) (1992), *Dictionnaire historique de la langue française*, Éditions Le Robert, Paris.

Saint-James, V. (1997), 'Réflexions sur la dignité de l'être humain en tant que concept juridique du droit français', *D., chr.*

Théron, J.P. (1998), 'Dignité et liberté. Propos sur une jurisprudence contestable', in *Pouvoir et liberté. Études offertes à Jacques Mourgeon*, Éditions Bruylant, Brussels.

Verdoodt, A. (1964), *Naissance et signification de la Déclaration universelle des droits de l'homme*, Éditions Nauwelaerts, Louvain-Paris.

Chapter 5

Reconstructive Ethics, Political Justice and Social Vulnerability

Jean-Marc Ferry

Concerning ourselves with questions of focussing political interest on social distress no doubt involves reflecting on the ethical workings of *political justice*. While wishing to avoid considerations that may be of a sentimental nature, it is important to defend the thesis that 'public reason', which is supposed to support the consent of society members to the principles of political justice, would gain by being broadened and made more flexible and open to real-life experience, in the sense of *reconstructive ethics*. The unavoidably expressive registers of such testimonies do not spontaneously accord with the idea that is generally made of reason and of that which is rational. The opening up of public argument to the *vulnerability of human dignity* does not undermine, in fact does the reverse, the need for a social and political critique firmly bound by strict consideration of what is 'reasonable'.

The theme of political justice emerged about thirty years ago in, especially liberal, political philosophy, accompanying or incidentally generating some divisive reviews of the intellectual world. This theme then served as a basis for a series of discussions which, among other things, resulted in the American polarisation: liberals *versus* communitarians, and spread in the form of oppositions; between, for example, liberalism and republicanism, or procedural democracy and substantial democracy, and, soon, on the European question, the 'battle of sovereignism' and the review of the cosmopolitical idea.

However, the issue of political justice is, in general, that of the *normative foundation of a just society*. Obviously, this concerns its fundamental constitution, its 'basic structure'. From this perspective, political justice is not just a matter of social justice, but includes it. Its references are particularly those of public law and so it does not merely concern internal organisation (with reference to *ius civitatis*). It also applies to international order and to relations between the people of the world (with reference to the Law of Peoples or *ius gentium*), up to the supreme level. Here, in the face of sovereign states, it is concerned with the law of the citizens of the world (or *ius cosmopoliticum*). At the tension-free interface of human rights and the rights of the citizen, political justice opens up the important perspective of a cosmopolitical justice.

With regard to content, political justice is readily set out in the form of principles; for example, the principle of personal freedom, together with the principle of collective solidarity between society members. Thus opening up the debate on substantial aspects of political justice.

With regard to status, it could be argued that, for example, political justice is the system that realises the pure concept of public law, or also, the intention of practical reason. It could also be presented as the application of a cardinal rule of method of equity, referring to a system of coherence or general compossibility of freedoms, of responsibilities, of solidarities. This opens up the formal (intentional or operational) aspect of political justice.

With regard to the conditions of acceptability, it could be argued that, for example, political justice is embodied in the society whose normative order unreservedly agrees with the public reason upheld by the unity – distributive or collective – of all those concerned, even though this agreement is reached by setting aside the specific tendencies of the society members: thus we can speak, according to John Rawls, of an 'overlapping consensus', which achieves a distributive unity of agreement; i.e. that agreement is reached by the confrontation of positions in the process of public argument: it is possible to speak of 'consensus through confrontation', which achieves a collective unity of agreement. Therefore, whether the perspective is that of *overlapping consensus* or that of *consensus through confrontation*, in both cases we are dealing with the procedural aspect of political justice.

Over the last few years, interest in political justice has largely been directed towards the procedural aspect, whilst unavoidably arousing 'substantialist' reactions. But the procedural aspect deserves to be distinguished from the formal aspect, as it affects the conditions of acceptation. In fact, this concern corresponds to the very ancient intellection, according to which, in order to be valid, it is not enough for a proposition to be true: it must also be true 'with reason'. In terms of contemporary philosophy, this corresponds to the preoccupation of *establishing a claim to normative validity*. It is true that, in the context of an applied proceduralist theory, the philosophic interest for this establishment seems to be giving way to the positive interest of delimiting, as finely as possible, the empirical development of the formation processes of the public norms. This is done by making the normative perspective of the theoretician 'immanent' to the point where the decision processes seem to merge with the justification and legitimisation processes. It is *one* way of reconnecting the assessment of public normativity with the consideration of evolutionary situations of interest.

How do the real processes work to bring about the definitions of situations, confrontations of interests and points of view, assessments of normative claims, arbitrations and decisions concerning the regulation of the social world? Also, how can the resulting public norms be considered valid from the various standpoints?

In its 'proceduralist' version, the issue of political justice undoubtedly summons different, even divergent responses, the confrontation of which may prove instructive.

But this interest does not dispense with substantial considerations. The procedural approach of political justice in no way means that it is imperative to have to keep to a proceduralist conception. No doubt it does mean looking at the theoretical and practical ways by which public norms can be accepted as norms which are just. But it does *not* mean that the normative contents can admit substantial justifications, or that philosophers and other citizens take up discussions based on spontaneous moral intuitions.

People ask, for example, which system of solidarity is just; or how can international relations be organised justly? The substantial developments of political justice go hand in glove with new rights, which enrich the concept of citizenship from the bottom up and the top down. Thus, it could be argued, there is an unconditional right of society members to a basic income which can be subject to very different doctrinal justifications: liberal or libertarian, republican or democratic, socialist or anarchist, while at the same time being obliged to take the contexts of application into account. Also, the right to interfere in the internal affairs of a state, which raises huge questions in terms of political justice, against the problem of a legitimate restriction of national sovereignties, even of a legitimate use of violence, exerted in the name of a cosmopolitical justice.

But how is it possible to go beyond the tension between *Welfare State* and *Workfare State* or, at another level, between the fundamental rights of the individual and the sovereignty of states? It is in these questions too that the substantial problematics of political justice, viewed from the perspective of social law on the one hand, and international law on the other, are formed.

This is where real discussions are possible which, once again, are substantially formed by our moral intuitions in the broad sense, relative to what seems to us to be just, good, desirable, recommendable, suitable, appropriate, generally valid, from a deontic point of view. Here we can put forward all sorts of empirical considerations, simply taken from our everyday experience. As long as this everyday experience is not lived as closed to the world, but on the contrary, is largely well-informed by what is happening in the near and far world, for which we have to take the mass media as an essential source of information, however great their faults may be. At this point, political justice has something to say. In fact, freedom of communication, understood in a positive and objective sense, going far beyond the individualistic concept of freedom of expression, includes the right to information and to the participation of citizens in the definition of public agendas, which furthermore would suggest a civic right to some form of training. Freedom of communication is thus an important element for democratic autonomy and therefore for political justice. This element was neglected by the political liberalism of John Rawls.

If it is necessary that reflections on political justice are in tune with the concerns of the many, i.e. beyond small intellectual spheres, it would no doubt be well advised to shuffle the *contents*, that is to say not to scorn the *substantial* aspects of political justice. The quarrel that pits 'substantialists' against 'proceduralists' is, in fact, a false one. False because there is no substantial justice that is going to oppose procedural justice. In practice this makes virtually no sense. In fact, *real* political justice (which is also political injustice, in this case), is better understood from a theoretical point of view, from the different aspects of: content or 'substance', intention or 'form', method or 'procedure'; and, depending on the approach favoured for the theoretical discussion, we can speak more precisely of a substantial, formal or procedural *aspect* of political justice.

A man in the street exclaims: 'It's unjust!' 'And why is that?' he is asked.

- 'Because I wasn't consulted'; and, he adds, 'It isn't *legitimate!*'

- 'Indeed' agrees the philosopher, because 'The only norms of action that can pretend to validity are those ones that are liable to be agreed to by all of the interested persons as participants in rational discourse'.[1]

This is a procedural aspect of political justice.

- 'Moreover', the man adds, thus encouraged, 'there was discrimination. Others having no more claims to consultation than me were taken into account by the authorities, and have obtained advantages which are of no benefit to me, on the contrary. It's not *fair!*'.

- 'Indeed', replies the philosopher, because 'Each person has an equal right to a fully adequate scheme of equal basic liberties which is compatible with a similar scheme of liberties for all'.[2]

This is the formal aspect of political justice.

- 'And anyway', the man concludes (further incited to take his stand as a citizen), 'I consider my right to participate to have been breached, and at the very least my right to express an opinion and to let it be publicly known. It's just not *constitutional!*'

- 'Indeed', confirms the philosopher again, because '*The right to communication is the most fundamental of all, and no breach of this right can be justified.*'

This is a substantial aspect of political justice.

So if we claim to set these three aspects of justice up against one another, we are, in fact, wrestling with theoretical angles of attack, conceptual strategies, rather than conceptions of justice. Moreover, the logics thus opposed are not, in this *opposition*, those of political justice, but those of the philosophical conceptions relative to this justice; and if we hypostatise these approaches as if they were types of justice, then substantial justice, to paraphrase Immanuel Kant's famous image, would be 'blind', and procedural justice would be 'empty'.

The aspect which we could call formal is also interesting: for example, when it is directed towards the problematics of judgement, particularly, judgement of application, while we endeavour to follow the logic of the mental or intellectual operations in detail; or when the analysis is directed towards the objective system of norms and values instituted from the point of view of internal global rationality, characterising the basic structure of a society that we would like to be well-ordered. But as this matter is not purely technical; on account of the fact that it is not a matter of pure cybernetic considerations, interest in the rationality of the basic normative structure or in the system of a just society ('well-ordered' in the sense given by John Rawls) is obviously inseparable from an examination of what I would call the 'semantic arrangements' of this structure. Thus, beyond a functionalist rationality aiming for the general compatibility of these liberties, solidarities and responsibilities, with regard to their *practice* in a societal framework, such a normative system itself relies on axiological definitions, thus, in practice, on supposed stabilised meanings, in an (at least potential) public reason. This goes together with a reference to a common sense, to a 'general experience of life', as Wilhem Dilthey said, which itself has its own background; and this background can in turn be regarded as a 'text' woven by virtual propositions, or again, a matter of 'thoughts' in the sense of Gottlob Frege, sorts of phrases which tell us, for example, what freedom, or what solidarity or responsibility is for us. But this semantic arrangement has not always been what it is, at least, in historical societies. As through the akashic annals of the Tibetans, the hermeneutics of the real-life world can also diachronically explore the history of these meanings or of their formation. The deeper Constitutions of our societies do not come from nowhere. We knew that they are not heaven-sent, but that they originate in a reasonable will of men. We also now know that this reason and this will do not definitively obey eternal and unchanging laws; that the nature of reason is not fixed and that it is more a question of an indeterminate process of formation, involving successive discoveries, disillusions, frustrations, 'disenchantment'; that furthermore, this process is fragile, exposed to catastrophes, regressions, destruction, even to annihilation, the risk of which we must not lose sight. We understand ourselves through others and, in these others, we include what we have been. Hence, the hermeneutic idea of a reconstruction, interested in the deep, historical constitution of general experience through which the elements of modern or contemporary sense have been able to be embedded, and the semantic arrangements to stabilise, and which the public reason practised reviews each time it examines sections of political justice from the aspect, for example, of freedom (types of freedom), or of responsibility (orders of responsibilities), or of solidarity (systems of solidarity). Our contemporary identity becomes inseparable from a recognition of self in the other, which also supposes a reflexive appropriation of the elements of shared values and meanings, constituting what we can also regard as an ethical community.

Reconstructive ethics has its theoretical sources in the idea that: 1) our understanding of the world in general, and our conceptions of justice in particular, are structurally dependent on a historical selection of inherited representations and beliefs made reflexive through processes of training and apprenticeship; that 2) this 'historical world' formed by representations, beliefs, mentalities, values and norms, institutions – in short, everything that makes up the study material of social sciences – has a symbolic objectivity which outlives the expressions of the actors, endowing social meanings with a relatively autonomous existence; and that 3) the social actors are individuals in the strongest sense in that they identify themselves in the attitude of an I which relates to a You in communication, so that they understand one another both as a *person in general*, capable of speaking, of acting, of knowing, and as a *particular individual*, who is irreplaceable because of their unique biography.

This third point, in particular, is full of consequence as regards the ethical dimension. 'Individuality' (Georg W.F. Hegel) is the characteristic which distinguishes man from animals; and awareness of such a characteristic can only be gained in and through the community, understood as being the group where the system of recognition relations is reciprocal between its members. The community is intrinsic to individuality, just as intersubjectivity is at the core of subjectivity, insofar as people construct their identity in the communicational attitude of an address to a someone, mediatised by reference to something.

At the same time, the second point, relating to the symbolic structure of the social world taken as the 'historical world' (Wilhem Dilthey), suggests to us that reproduction of cultural forms of life presupposes the establishment of a dialectic of dead and living communication: meanings which are currently in use socially, so that, for example, we take certain representations of what is just or unjust to be self-evident, though they are not heaven-sent; their apparent objectivity of 'prejudices' (Hans G. Gadamer) structuring a common sense is revealed rather as a sedimented result of earlier communications, serving as a support for later communications. It follows that these 'obvious', socially current meanings, can also be regarded as symbols which have formed compromises at the price of a certain repression of universalisable interests. Thus, it is possible to examine them from the standpoint of a possibly failed recognition between the partners of past interactions.

Which is why also the first point, concerning the structural dependence of our present conceptions with regard to past traditions, now suggests that these traditions are not 'innocent'; that their contents are not to be so obviously trusted; that the historical selection procedure, which has occurred in a near natural way, does not exclude a critical reappropriation, even a self-criticism of the meanings we have inherited.

This leads us, not merely to assume a new relationship to our own history and culture, but to expand the practical exercise of political and social criticism, by looking at complaints from the perspective of an argumentation which is not confined to a strategic mobilisation of commonplaces. This does not mean that public reason, where, in principle, demands for justice are set out, should be rendered erudite and sophisticated. But that when these demands are for more than simple quantitative improvements, such as, for example, those that concern living standards, buying power, weekly working hours, or the age of retirement, and which are thus within the conventional scope of trade-unions; when instead the demands aim to question prejudices or, at the very least, habits which are so firmly anchored at the heart of shared evidences that their questioning would seem to be incongruous. For example, the idea that one has to be employed to have an income, so that the demand for a dignified life, for the population, gets confused with the demand for full employment. It then becomes important to be able to question received ideas regarding social justice, and also, and perhaps most importantly, regarding the way in which definitions of social usefulness implicitly assert themselves. But this also presupposes that the actors are themselves in a position to destabilise the obvious facts, the normative 'spontaneous' meanings, naively taken as being self-evident. For example, in seeking to change the supposition that the part of income necessary to the practising of one's responsibilities as a citizen, or to feeling a sense of belonging to a social community in general, is conditional, that is to say, conditioned by access to the work-employment system, what matters is the fact of not purely and simply trusting in the obvious facts, spontaneously shared by this same community. What matters is being able to shake the sedimented prejudices and the institutionalised certainties that form the conventional background of our real-life world and forge the symbolic framework of our most routine social perceptions. Again, this does not suppose that social victims should be enjoined to argue at the lofty heights of doctrines, past and present, which have not been sensitive to the most fundamental conditions of a 'well-ordered society'. Rather, it supposes that they do not let themselves be overawed by the discourses presenting the existing order as a pure expression of the constraints of reality; that furthermore, they are capable of showing that the greatest injustice is not only that the distribution of wealth is unequal, but that certain individuals are excluded from all possibility of access to property in the broad sense of the term which includes security, freedom, possession; that it is unacceptable that the right to substantial autonomy and the material and spiritual dignity of individuals should depend on an uncertain distribution of the opportunities of access to primary social property. But so that these intellections, which are just in themselves, become socially sensitive, the most convincing 'argument' surely does not lie in an academic deconstruction of imperfect theories. Nor is it likely to arise from the rhetorical redundancies of political or trade-union cant. The really convincing argument on the subject, can only reside in the expressive strength of an authentic real-life account of social distress, on condition that this expression is also able to make everyone share in and experience the depth of the sense of injustice. In fact, the strength of political argument does not consist of a simple appeal to the emotions or to humanitarian feelings, but in the understanding and appropriate expression of ethical concepts and moral principles. However, moral argument only has practical strength if it is, so to speak, backed up by accounts of real-life experience appropriate to the sense of injustice.

In the moral world, there are zones which seem excluded from the rationalisation of systematic arguments. How, for example, can it be demonstrated that the death penalty is morally unacceptable, 'unjust', unless we turn to the –

weak – argument that we cannot exclude judicial error? This is a weak argument because it is not the core of the problem, which is rather: even supposing that the condemned person is guilty of the crime he or she is accused of, the death penalty remains unacceptable. How can that be argued with theoretical discourse? How can these means be used to destabilise deeply rooted prejudices which speak of justice, like a tariff, as matching the punishment to the offence committed? How can it be asserted that justice is not necessarily a question of an eye for an eye? It is the same for the spheres of questioning which touch the depths of our still badly thematised moral intuitions; and this is also valid for matters relating to social or political justice. Only the expressive strength of recounted real-life experience can, perhaps, shake the toughness of convictions anchored in prejudices that have themselves been reinforced over the course of successive generations. This expressive strength supposes a form of unity of *narration* and of *argumentation;* and such a unity is precisely that of *reconstruction.* Also, public reason, to be understood as the reason which, ideally, expresses itself in open and free social and political communication, the reason we would like to see at work in our public spaces, must broaden its *concept* in the direction of registers which are more 'sensitive' than those to which democratic culture, impregnated as it is with the spirit of law and juridical argument in its 'classico-modern' version, has accustomed us.

It could be asked: what is the connection between, on the one hand, this relaxing of public reason which we require to be more open to 'arguments', for the most part private, of real-life experience in the form of intimate convictions and, on the other hand, the sources that reconstructive ethics supposedly takes in the intellections, for the most part philosophic, of the historicity of the human mind, of the symbolic structuring of the historical world, and of the individuality of the social actors? It could be answered: in the reasons given by these relatively recent intellections, to take seriously moral intuitions which have not yet attained the objectivity of socially recognised obvious facts. Their consideration in a sphere sufficiently receptive to social distress, allowing the still private suffering that this causes to be expressed publicly, and therefore receive a political translation, does not only mean opening up the ethics of the responsibility of the economic and political leaders to the considerations of the ethics of solicitude towards social victims. It also enables the destabilising of the system of prejudices which, among all society members, limit normative expectations, particularly as regards definitions of the socially useful, anticipation of the politically feasible, as well as conceivable advances in global solidarity measures.

Europe today is not safe from a social, economic and political catastrophe. The insidious passage from *Welfare State* to *Workfare State*, in other words to the supposed 'active social state' implementing, in the name of individual responsibility, a general conditionality of social security, risks not only increasing the masses of those excluded, but of legitimising this exclusion, in an indirect way, by inscription of the false values of 'adaptation' and 'flexibility'. Serious political consideration of social suffering within, and even beyond, Europe supposes that the western states be capable of self-criticism as regards the guiding principles of their world policy and the dependence of this policy with regard to economic and financial powers. It also supposes that states become more clearly aware of the risk of disconnection from the governmental system, which has largely become supranational, with respect to national public opinion. This is particularly true for the European Union: on the one hand, the government system cannot be removed with impunity from broad democratic participation; on the other hand, this political participation, indispensable to the stabilisation of the European system, is itself impossible in the absence of a universal and unconditional base of material autonomy, guaranteed for all of the citizens of the Union. This could thus, in the eyes of the world, represent more than a functional accompaniment to market imperatives: a real political response which could also become a symbolic point of reference in a world disorientated by globalisation.

Notes

1 Definition of the *discourse principle* or 'D principle', Jürgen Habermas.
2 Definition of the principle of equal liberty or 'first principle' of political justice, according to John Rawls.

Chapter 6

Exclusion and Assertion of Citizenship

Giovanna Procacci

In considering the area of thought set for this symposium, the linking of the analysis of poverty to that of citizenship means examining the poor's need of recognition from a specific point of view. This has two aspects, namely recognition of them as subjects and recognition of their poverty – of their basic needs. This amounts to making the hypothesis that this recognition is a condition of their capability to act or react in a situation of vulnerability. Or at the very least, that it influences this capability, citizenship, before being a system of rights, being first and foremost a principle of recognition. More importantly, recognition of the titularity of these rights and of the interest that society as a whole attaches to this titularity.

This also raises some important conceptual problems: everything effectively depends on the definitions of poverty and citizenship that we use – all the more so because these concepts are far from being univocal in the current social sciences debate and have a normative character, determining such things as the measurement of poverty, identification of poor populations, and even the choice between expansive or restrictive policies of citizenship.

The idea that the need for recognition is a condition for action in a situation of vulnerability, thus involving the issue of citizenship, refers to a definition of poverty in terms of 'capability and functioning' which we owe to Amartya Sen. If measurement of well-being is not established simply by the indicators of income and consumption, but is given by the ability to participate in the life of the community (Sen and Nussbaum, 1993), non-participation in social life and its institutions is not the consequence of a poverty which marginalises, but one of the conditions to be considered in the capability of people to use their resources, including their income (Sen, 1992). Thus citizenship, insofar as it governs the criteria for access to rights and services, has a role to play in the reduction (or not) of poverty. This means it makes sense to look at the social policies addressing poverty with regard to their ability to further, or not, this need for recognition, this assertion of citizenship.

At the instigation of the European Community, there is a current prevalence for defining poverty as social exclusion; consequently, political action committed to dealing with poverty is thought of in terms of 'fighting exclusion'. And citizenship, under the yoke of a neo-liberal economic climate, tends to be interpreted as a political bond based on civil law and on a contractual model – both in its nationalist and its 'multicultural' version – while its social dimension, which we nevertheless consider to be an integral part of our present experience as citizens, is regarded as a relic of largely outmoded social policies.

It is important to raise a few questions about these policies against social exclusion, evaluating them from the point of view of citizenship, and point out the trends which seem to me to be both implicit in such logic, and to be the bearers of new dangers, notably the danger of subsequently intensifying the political exclusion of the poor – their 'decitizenship' (Rébérioux, 1994). I have suggested elsewhere (Procacci, 2000) that the concept of social exclusion should be treated less as an analyser than as the symptom of a more general process of the desocialisation of poverty, which tends to reduce it to the personal life courses leading to marginalisation, against which anti-exclusion policies set equally personal integration courses. Here, I would like to focus on these integration measures, which are the main feature of the policies against social exclusion promoted by the Community amongst the member countries, by: 1) first looking at their coherence with the so-called 'European Social Model' (ESM), 2) then looking at how they operate, 3) and finally examining the elements which, in the integration measures of the ESM, arouse fears of a regressive transformation of citizenship systems.

The 'European Social Model'

The European Union is the driving force behind the spread of these anti-exclusion policies. In fact, since the adoption of the fight against social exclusion as one of the research priorities of the European Community in 1989, and the creation of the 'EU Observatory on National Policies to Combat Social Exclusion' in 1990, anti-exclusion policies have been at the centre of a 'convergence strategy' amongst the member countries, who are supposed to harmonise their policies, reinforcing what the Community literature calls the 'European Social Model'.

This system combines the characteristics common to the member countries of the European Union: regulated market economies, broad systems of social protection and the concerted solution of conflicts, as opposed to the *deregulation* of the United States or South East Asia. Community policy would like to further develop these common features, highlighting a second aspect of the ESM: it not only expresses that which is common to national forms of capitalism, but also has a transnational significance, which means that it entails a tendency to converge towards a common model. It must organise and direct national policies, rather than being derived from them; it becomes the tangible proof that 'social policy in a single country' is no longer viable, as Fritz Scharpf (2000) has observed.

The general characteristic of this model is shown by the idea that 'economic and social progress go hand in hand and are mutually reinforcing factors; which is why our economies regard social protection as a productive factor'. It thus becomes crucial to analyse the changes made in the social protection system; from this angle, the policies against social exclusion promoted by the Commission of the European

Communities (1999, 347) become a vital key to understanding the very nature of the ESM.

The Recommendation of the Council of 1992 already clearly placed the policy of combating poverty in the broader context of the strengthening of social protection systems, which is an essential part of the aforementioned ESM. But the key text for social protection issues is the revision of the Amsterdam Treaty (1997-99). Article 136 confirms the need to base social policy on 'Fundamental Social Rights'; Article 137 extends this base to the combating of social exclusion, explicitly appealing for co-operation between member countries for better understanding and the development of innovation as regards fighting exclusion. Also, the Social Charter of the Council of Europe, revised in 1996, established in Article 30 that, in order to ensure the right to protection against social exclusion, measures against poverty must promote the effective access of everyone to fundamental social rights (employment, housing, training, education, culture, social and medical assistance).

However, in both texts it is interesting to note that these fundamental social rights are reduced to the 'fundamental right of the individual to sufficient resources' (Commission of the European Communities, 1998, 774), and therefore to the respect of the fundamental dignity of the person – though effective access to this right is subject to active participation in the labour market. Social law is therefore considered more as a *fundamental right of the person*, setting the basis for the current restructuration of social protection systems.

The second demand made of this restructuring results from criticism made of the central role played by wages in the construction of our social protection systems – which are supposed to have both increased labour costs and intensified the disparities between the labour market and unemployment. In order to correct such flaws, today's social policies are obliged to *separate the costs of social protection from wages*.

It is to be expected that these requirements are also valid for anti-exclusion policies. In the strategy of the European Union, the fight against social exclusion demands measures which fall within the remit of social law, but 1) they interpret this on the basis of the fundamental right of the individual to the resources necessary to his or her survival, and 2) they are thus closely related to employment strategy. So, on the one hand, these measures individualise a relationship, essentially based on assistance, to a person deprived of resources; on the other hand, they confirm that exclusion is first and foremost to be understood as the result of a lack of work, and they even become more and more '*employment friendly*'. The two objectives are combined in the incorporated integration strategies which aim to change passive measures of income support into active measures in the labour market – all kinds of training activities for unemployed people (Commission of the European Communities, 1999), accompanied by tax exemption measures for employers to encourage them to create jobs. I will come back to this 'activation' and its objective of integration later on.

But at least two important consequences can be noted from a conceptual point of view. Interpreting social exclusion as exclusion from the labour market implies a first consequence, namely concealment of the fact that today, in our advanced societies, it is not just the lack of work, but the work itself, and more importantly job insecurity, which produces poverty. However, the quantitative data shows that also in our countries, the number of *working poor* is rising considerably – it is even the category of poor people which is increasing the most in relation to other categories. Experts (EAPN, 1999) signal a downward spiral where unemployment, combined with many other factors including insecure and underpaid employment, plays a part in the production of poverty. The real problem, as Fritz Scharpf (2000, 219) notes, in situations such as that of liberal countries like Britain today, is that as inequality increases, so does the poverty of insecure and underpaid workers. Though the rate of poverty persistence is increasing significantly, notably in a country like Britain (where it is calculated that between 1990 and 1995 31 per cent of the population experienced poverty, against 18 per cent in Germany), and poverty severity is also increasing (Commission of the European Communities, 2000, 82), Eurostat data indicate that of the 65 million poor people in the European Union today (18 per cent), 53 per cent live in families where someone is employed, 28 per cent are employed, 24 per cent retired. This is enough to establish the need to reflect on the links between poverty and employment, instead of limiting ourselves to talking about unemployment!

The second consequence is that epitomising poverty as exclusion from the labour market amounts to denying the complexity of its causes, which are not only economic or income related, but depend also on unequal access to rights, insufficient social protection, age, sex, isolation, etc. (Sen, 1992) In a situation characterised by an increase in inequality, which threatens social cohesion, and therefore the very process of the construction of Europe, anti-exclusion policies give the impression that a new equilibrium between the labour market and social protection will ensue merely by adapting social protection to changes in the labour market, by persuading the most disadvantaged to accept underpaid jobs (Pioch, 1996), despite that fact that such employment will never lead them out of poverty.

Though it is acknowledged that social exclusion is the effect of structural barriers (Commission of the European Communities, 2000b, 79), though it is claimed that social protection has a central role in the ESM, social exclusion policies seem first to seek to rectify a state of extreme deprivation, but appear incapable of affecting, in a structural and preventative way, the factors which drive the processes of pauperisation.

Integration Measures

There are not only consequences of a conceptual nature, there are also political ones. The key to the anti-exclusion policies is in the *integration* measures, which are everywhere present, from local micro politics (of the type 'town policies') to the policies claiming to be 'macro', of the income support type. In turn, as we have seen, the process of integration is effected via policies of activation to employment, that is to say, it is considered as professional integration.

Integration thus conveys an economist image of poverty, identified with exclusion from the labour market – the archetype of exclusion – the solution to which would be successful re-entry into this market. Consequently, inclusion is also viewed in economic terms, rather than 'participation in the life of the community', as Amartya Sen suggests. In concrete terms, it consists of all kinds of training courses, for the most part sponsored by the state and entrusted to an individual contract, which is considered to be the means of activation *par excellence* – this contract concerns a course of training directed at the labour market. Hence, integration measures find themselves caught up in the contradiction that is exposed between the inconditionality of social law and the requirement to compensate the obtaining of social security benefit. So, there is an attempt to reformulate reciprocity between right and duty, unlike social law, which tried to combine the two. It is true that this form of reciprocity does not have the strict character of *workfare*, but the texts remain ambiguous and leave civil servants a fair amount of discretionary power – which explains, for example, the stopping of benefit because of a refusal to undergo treatment for drug addiction.

But what particularly invalidates such reciprocity is the fact that neither the labour market is easy to reach, nor is professional integration simple to achieve. The training activities do not, in fact, create many new jobs, except, of course, for instructors. Therefore, the contract becomes a paradigm for public action, not particularly because it actually manages to restore reciprocity, but because it aims to actively give the poor person a sense of responsibility for his or her integration.

Let it be said that the beneficiaries of these social policies are readily described as excluded in order to justify the financing of the policies by taxation, whereas they are, in fact, workers. Though these anti-exclusion policies respond to the paradigm of new social policies, in that they shift their labour costs onto public funds, they contribute to the consolidation of intermediate work situations, characterised by being atypical state-sponsored jobs, underpaid, under-productive, generally underrated as regards their social utility – in short, *substandard employment*. Rather than professional integration, they result in the creation of a new area based on *exceptions to the normal conditions of work*. To see this, we just have to look more closely at the integration measures implemented; the new law against severe poverty of 1998 in France is in fact a series of atypical work formulas, and of course of remuneration, which are thus legalised, under cover of combating exclusion, and exempt from labour laws (Assemblée nationale, 1998).

It is true that the difficulty of achieving professional integration has led to the concept of integration being broadened to now also cover social integration. While professional integration consists of all sorts of these training practices, the effects of which we have seen, social integration is conceived in terms of action on the individual and his or her environment, in order to make the poor person responsible for his or her own reintegration. These are the local actions of *active involvement* (town policies) which target excluded people in their immediate surroundings, and in fact revive a form of supervision well-known to philanthropic practices. Local, active involvement is a misplaced response to a demand for participation in social life and entails a loss of social appreciation of the sufferings related to poverty. A breakdown of solidarity attributable to a society's collective operational mechanisms is transformed into an intervention on the individual and his environment; the risk of poverty, considered by social law as a risk for the whole of society, thus becomes a personal life course. Basically, it is perfectly possible that Étienne Balibar (1992) was right, when he suggested that the aim of these policies is not so much to combat exclusion, but rather to avoid including the excluded.

Reintegration is only meaningful as a provisional objective; yet, it becomes permanent, it represents the 'long-term provisional', as the *Commission nationale d'évaluation du Revenu minimum d'insertion* (National Commission for the Evaluation of Income Support) in France (Roche, 2000, 88) already acknowledged in 1992. Integration measures, midway between integration and marginality, culminate in the establishment of a new status, that of someone (the poor person) who is constantly being integrated, continually being pushed to attempt integration – a status which is, in fact, coincides with the sphere of assisted employment.

By What Right?

Consideration of the statutory effects of these changes inevitably involves the question of the juridical foundations of rights. The revival of logic of assistance (with all the stigmatisation, means testing, reduction of services, etc. that it entails) is, in fact, taking us further away from a social services system based on social law, which was once the mainstay of the institutions of social citizenship. Citizenship was not just a principle of access to services or a principle for the financing of them; it also provided the framework for admission to social rights, independently of the market value of the subject, and thus to the policies of redistribution.

The redistribution objective led to the construction of a complex system of social protection, where the distribution of social services, essentially insurance based, was only the most dominant form, alongside which and in spite of everything, assistance continued to be just as important. The evolution of assistance away from its private forms happened under the influence of the state, because of the risk of socialised poverty. Social protection systems thus represented a sort of equilibrium between the dominant measures of social insurance concerning wage-earners, and complementary assistance measures, both being based on a logic of social rights involving citizenship, not means testing.

From the mid-seventies and during the whole of the eighties, we witnessed the questioning of this equilibrium and the resurgence of assistance – particularly of private and religious assistance. This shift not only included a change in the form of financing, moving further and further away from distribution towards financing by taxation, but also the questioning of the juridical fundaments of social rights. The individualised nature of the anti-exclusion policies characteristic of both the social integration measures and the life course of the poor person undergoing reintegration, also actually drives a process of the destabilisation of rights, of social law, in the direction of *human rights.*

In fact, the new anti-exclusion policies coherently model social law on the fundamental rights of a person to the minimum means of subsistence, as we have seen in the 'European Social Model' promoted by the European Union. But if human dignity is the focus of human rights, it must be admitted that survival is not life. We are seeing the reopening of the contradiction between the natural man of human rights and the real man, living in a given society, for which social rights had tried to provide a political solution. Hence, we return to a juridical concept of the person, transcending any precise social context. Poverty is therefore no longer seen as a shared social risk, to be taken care of collectively, but as an individual right to avoid famine.

Social rights had a specific statutory standing, which harmonised both the advantage of the individual and his or her inclusion in society (Borgetto and Lafore, 2000, 291). When human rights become the reference principle of social policies, they run a great risk of guaranteeing no more than a precarious status. Their sole aim would seem to be that of maintaining a minimum of social cohesion by organising a programme of assistance for the most destitute, the limits of which could drop even further.

Yet, the rhetoric of rights is omnipresent in the contemporary political debate, which seems, moreover, never to have gone beyond the dichotomy between legal rights and moral rights, despite the altogether central role that the latter have had in the construction of the social services (Sen, 1996). Social rights in particular have often been accused by jurists of having a fundamental juridical weakness, even of not being real rights, in the name of the force of constitutional law. Today, human rights seem to be in a position to subsequently encourage such criticism, particularly in relation to the subject of citizenship.

In fact, they accompany the analysis of so-called *post-national* citizenship, according to which citizenship only represents a series of rights, from which non-citizens remain excluded. Which is why Luigi Ferrajoli (1994) comes to denounce citizenship as the 'last privilege'; and he expresses the desire for all social rights to be re-transcribed in terms of fundamental rights of the person, which, in his opinion, would be the only way to reinforce them constitutionally and shield them from political arbitrariness. For immigration experts, resorting to human rights would seem to be a way of going beyond certain rigidities of the national systems of citizenship, to the advantage of immigrant minorities (Soysal, 1994); multiculturalism theories themselves refer to the framework of political coexistence set by human rights. Likewise, as far as poverty is concerned, they seem to offer a surer basis for political intervention than social rights (Havemann, 2000).

More often than not, there are very good reasons for regarding this new popularity of human rights positively; but there are just as good reasons, I think, for wariness, if only because of the wars now inspired by them. Thus human rights are also seen to represent the rhetoric of the liberated citizen, who should, once and for all, replace all of the collective categories such as classes, women, black people, etc., who were the interpreters of emancipation. Their most enthusiastic defenders, such as David Beetham (1999), see in them the very basis of politics and want them to gain an ever more important place.

Is the logic of human rights really stricter than that of social rights? No-one could doubt their progressive nature from the point of view of the rights of the person; but, as regards social policies, what could render the implementation of these rights more effective than the implementation of social rights? Not to mention the fact that they're regulated by international Charters, which states can adhere to without they're being any obligation to ensure that they are actually respected. Furthermore, how can human rights serve as a basis for the construction of bonds of social solidarity? Human rights carry no project for society, in that they say nothing of how to create or recreate bonds, nor do they speak of the position of people in the social setting. This is why human rights are not a policy, as explained by Marcel Gauchet (2000).

On the other hand, they tend to act as a substitute for both social and political attitudes and they play an important role in the ever more exclusive identification of democracy with law and the juridical. They replace the search for a balance between different social groups and the bases for political coexistence, by the pragmatic correction of injustices that an individual may suffer. Thereby contributing to a fundamental juridical attitude to social life and citizenship, to a purely procedural definition of democracy, to the point of making it devoid of all meaning; they re-propose the idea of an individual freed from the need to make choices as regards collective arrangements, to make ethical choices. This process can only be understood if an effort is made to re-establish the necessary link between the analysis of poverty and the question of citizenship. The strength of the assertions of citizenship (Goodin, 1996) comes from focusing attention on what is common and central, while the response produced by logic of exclusion-inclusion is confined to marginality. If, on the other hand, we take assertion of citizenship seriously, we come to realise that, besides the desocialisation of poverty effected by the new anti-exclusion policies, there is also a process of the desocialisation of rights, the parallel issues of which are still not fully appreciated.

References

Assemblée nationale (1998), *Rapport d'information sur la prévention et la lutte contre les exclusions*, Paris, 1062.

Balibar, É. (1992), 'Inégalités, fractionnement social, exclusion', in J. Affichard and J.B. De Foucauld (éd.), *Justice sociale et inégalités*, Éditions Esprit, Paris.

Beetham, D. (1999), *Democracy and Human Rights*, Polity Press, Cambridge.

Borgetto, M. and Lafore, R. (2000), *La République sociale*, Presses universitaires de France, Paris.

Commission of the European Communities (1998), *Rapport au Conseil sur la mise en œuvre de la recommandation EEC/92/441*.

Commission of the European Communities (1999), *A Concerted Strategy for Modernizing Social Protection.*

Commission of the European Communities (2000a), *Social Trends: Prospects and Challenges.*

Commission of the European Communities (2000b), *Building an Inclusive Europe.*

EAPN (European Anti-Poverty Network) (1999), *Toward a Europe for All.*

Ferrajoli, L. (1994), 'Cittadinanza e diritti fondamentali', in D. Zolo (ed.), *Cittadinanza*, Laterza, Bari.

Gauchet, M. (2000), 'Quand les droits de l'homme deviennent une politique', *Le Débat*, 110.

Goodin, R. (1996), 'La logique exclusion-inclusion', *Archives européennes de sociologie*, Vol. XXXVII(2).

Havemann, P. (2000), 'Social Exclusion, Social Citizenship and the Third Way', Paper presented at the SASE 12th Annual Meeting, LSE, London, 7th – 10th July.

Pioch, R. (1996), 'Basic Income: Social Policy after Full Employment', in A. Erskine (ed.), *Changing Europe*, Avebury, Aldershot.

Procacci, G. (2000), 'Poor Citizens: Social Citizenship versus Individualization of Welfare', in C. Crouch, K. Eder and D. Tambini (eds.), *Citizenship, Markets and the State*, Oxford University Press, Oxford.

Rébérioux, M. (1994), 'Citoyens et travailleurs', *Hommes et Libertés*, 76.

Roche, R. (2000), 'De l'exclusion à l'insertion: problématiques et perspectives', in S. Karsz (éd.), *L'Exclusion, définir pour en finir*, Éditions Dunod, Paris.

Scharpf, F.W. (2000), 'The Viability of Advanced Welfare States in the International Economy: Vulnerabilities and Options', *Journal of European Public Policy*, Vol. 7(2).

Sen, A.K. (1992), *Inequality Reexamined*, Clarendon Press, Oxford.

Sen, A.K. (1996), 'Legal Rights and Moral Rights: Old Questions and New Problems', *Ratio Iuris*, Vol. 9(2).

Sen, A.K. and Nussbaum, M.C. (eds.) (1993), *The Quality of Life*, Clarendon Press, Oxford.

Soysal, Y.N. (1994), *Limits of Citizenship*, University of Chicago Press, Chicago.

Chapter 7

Occupational Precariousness and Political Mobilisation

Serge Paugam

In France, contemporary diverse employment situations are ordered into a hierarchy, not only according to levels of responsibility and power in the workplace, but also, ever increasingly, according to the degree of employment stability and the range of economic and social advantages that the professional activity provides (Paugam, Zoyem and Charbonnel, 1993). Many employees fear the loss of their jobs. The decline of the labour market gives them great cause for concern about the future. Others, whose jobs are not directly threatened, remain dissatisfied with their salary, their working conditions and their promotion prospects. Their professional activity may assure them social status, though this remains precarious as it is not very highly rated, but it cannot, in itself, provide them with the recognition that they expect from their daily efforts.

In a production-oriented society, the modes of integration are based, to a great extent, on professional activity which guarantees individuals material and financial security, social relations, organisation of time and space, a 'work identity'. Émile Durkheim himself put a lot of emphasis on professional groups in the socialisation process. According to him, professional organisation reminds individuals of their social interests and obliges them to a moral discipline which is indispensable to integration within the social system.

> That is why, when individuals who share the same interests come together, their purpose is not simply to safeguard those interests or to secure their development in face of rival associations. It is, rather, just to associate, for the sole pleasure of mixing with their fellows and of no longer feeling lost in the midst of adversaries, as well as for the pleasure of communing together, that, in short, of being to lead their lives with the same moral aim. (Durkheim, 1991, 25)

When the individual is left to himself, he is freed of all social constraints and thus of all moral constraints. Émile Durkheim inferred from this that:

> Accordingly, it can be said that professional ethics will be the more developed, and the more advanced in their operation, the greater the stability and the better the organization of the professional groups themselves. (Durkheim, 1991, 8)

However, it is a fact that, in the present economic circumstances, companies, as professional groups, are subject to external pressures which can threaten their internal functioning and even, in the long run, their survival. The threat of a company closure disrupts its organisation and undermines the integration of its employees because the norms on which this integration is based need a certain level of stability in order to impose themselves upon the employees and to gain their confidence in the regular participation in the productive activity. From the moment when these norms become easy to challenge, they lose their persuasive force and, consequently, threaten the existence of the group itself or, at least oblige it to an adaptation, during the course of which the organisation may still waver.

Thus, precarious situations in a company are, at least partially, the expression of a problem of cohesion of the professional group, itself a source of dissatisfaction for the employees. The latter may, in fact, have the feeling of being outside of the group and so may even feel little concerned by its functioning. When they are in the majority, they may even lose the pleasure of association, as in this case their identity may well be strongly affected by the absence of common projects and of the possibilities of forming any. They may then lose the feeling of being useful to the functioning of the company, in the sense of Émile Durkheim, who observed that:

> The division of labour supposes that the worker, far from remaining bent over his task, does not lose sight of those co-operations with him, but acts upon them and is acted upon by them. He is not therefore a machine who repeats movements the sense of which he does not perceive, but he knows that they are tending in a certain direction, towards a goal that he can conceive of more or less distinctly. He feels that he is of some use. For this he has no need to take in very vast areas of the social horizon; it is enough for him to perceive enough of it to understand that his actions have a goal beyond themselves. Thenceforth, however specialised, however uniform his activity may be, it is that of an intelligent being, for he knows that his activity has a meaning. (Durkheim, 1984, 308)

Continuing in this vein, the hypothesis can be made that employees experiencing insecurity in a company have little chance of being mobilised in political life. This is very much like the questions asked by several sociologists who, in the 1960s, studied the question of political alienation, laying particular emphasis on the subjective dimension of this phenomenon. According to this research, an individual is considered as being politically alienated when he has the feeling of being detached from the society in which he lives, of no longer having any political adherence, of being a stranger vis-à-vis the dictates of the political leaders (Dean, 1960; Thompson and Horton, 1960; Blauner, 1964; Olsen, 1969; Finifter, 1970).

Without resuming here the concept of political alienation, in this chapter I would like to study the effect of precarious forms of occupational integration on political attitudes, by seeking to verify several hypotheses which have been the subject of studies and discussions during this period.[1]

I have retained four hypotheses from these studies, and have adapted them to present economic circumstances and to the problems of job insecurity experienced by today's employees: 1) that of *hostility*: because of the long hours devoted to unrewarding tasks, workers in insecure jobs build up reserves of frustration and of disaffection which find expression in a certain hostility towards, or a certain mistrust of, groups still more disadvantaged than themselves, such as the poor and the unemployed; 2) that of *apathy*: the employees whose occupational integration is insecure have no obvious political orientation at all and remain removed from parties and sociopolitical debates; 3) that of *powerlessness*: insecure occupational integration is no reward for that which is invested in the work process. It is an occasion, par excellence, for withdrawal, and it teaches withdrawal, a lesson that the employee in insecure employment transfers to his political life through his apathy and ignorance of political matters; 4) that of *lack of confidence*: work is an essential aspect of the whole of a person's 'life-chances' and, where it offers little opportunity for the realisation of a person's future, the individual is led to an anomic conception of life. In other words, when the individual is not linked to a job which has meaning, he considers the social order to be less worthy of confidence.

These hypotheses will be tested by the results of a survey carried out in September and October 1995, within the framework of the *Observatoire sociologique du changement*, with a sample of 1036 employees spread over five labour market areas. First of all, I shall try to define occupational integration and its deviant forms, which will then lead to the analysis of the attitudes of employees in insecure jobs to the poor and the unemployed, their political tendencies, their opinions as regards the free market economy and, finally, their level of voter participation.

A Typology of the Forms of Occupational Integration

Defining the ideal type of occupational integration does not mean finding out what, statistically, its majority form is, it means discerning the main features, deliberately simplified, from the historical forms of contemporary societies, which give it meaning.[2] Western societies are both industrial societies and societies of social rights. They are industrial because they are founded on the principle of the technical division of work, the accumulation of capital, economic calculation and the participation of everybody in the collective task of the production of goods and services (Aron, 1962). They are also organised according to the principle of the intervention of the welfare state. All of them have, to varying degrees, defined social rights for their citizens, which corresponds to the process that Gosta Esping-Andersen (1990) qualified as 'decommodification'. This concept refers to the idea of a progressive detachment of individuals vis-à-vis the market logic. In our societies, occupational integration assures individuals recognition of their work, in the sense of their contribution to the productive task, but also, at the same time, recognition of the social rights which are derived from it. In other words,

Coping and Pulling Through

occupational integration does not only mean fulfilment at work, but also incorporation, beyond the world of work, into the basis of elementary protection within the framework of the welfare state system. Each citizen thus becomes something other than just a simple exchangeable commodity. The example of the recent demands of people working in entertainment and show business for better social protection enables us to understand to what degree occupational integration occurs, not only via the affirmation of self in the world of work, but also through the recognition of the rights derived from the protective logic of the welfare state.

In this sense, for employees, the expression 'to have a job' does not only mean having the possibility of finding fulfilment in a productive activity, but also the fact of being in possession of guarantees vis-à-vis the future. Thus, we can define the ideal type of occupational integration as the double assurance of the material and symbolic recognition of work and the social protection which ensues from the job. We can consider the first condition as being fulfilled when employees say that they experience satisfaction at work, satisfaction which may be the remit of *homo faber*, of l'*homo oeconomicus* or of *homo sociologicus* (Paugam, 2000). The second condition will be fulfilled if the job in question is secure, and if it is of a certain duration, in other words if it allows the employee to plan his future.

This ideal type which combines job satisfaction and employment stability can be qualified as *secure integration*. In this case, employees can draw up career projects and invest themselves in the job in order to realise those projects. The satisfaction that they get is the expression of a successful integration in the company, in particular in the relations with their colleagues and their immediate superiors. Starting with this ideal type of occupational integration it is now possible to study its deviations, which will constitute just as many reasons for employee dissatisfaction.

Returning to the two basic aspects, we can distinguish three types of deviation in relation to *secure integration* (see Table 7.1), which we shall respectively call *uncertain integration* (positive relation to job, negative relation to the conditions of employment), *constrained integration* (negative relation to job, positive relation to conditions of employment) and *disqualifying integration* (double negative relation to job and to conditions of employment).

Table 7.1 The ideal type of occupational integration and its deviations

	Job satisfaction	Employment stability
Ideal type:		
Secure integration	+	+
Deviations:		
Uncertain integration	+	-
Constrained integration	-	+
Disqualifying integration	-	-

Uncertain integration corresponds to a more limited form of occupational integration where employment instability is not accompanied by job dissatisfaction. It particularly concerns situations experienced by employees who, while working in good conditions and having good relations with their colleagues and their superiors, nevertheless know that their job is at risk. It may well concern either employees who have a fixed-term contract which will not be renewed, or those employees in companies with an uncertain future. This first type of deviation in relation to *secure integration* may seem marginal. The expectations of employees with regard to stable employment are so high that we may assume that they do not seek to involve themselves too much in a temporary job or in a stable job that they risk losing, thus limiting their possibilities of fulfilment at work. This hypothesis is justified and it should not be dismissed, but it does not fully explain the reality. We can, in fact, just as easily postulate that employees see employment instability as a way of asserting themselves in the world of work, of consolidating their training and of progressively proving themselves, all the more so, because employers sometimes use the precarious employment situation as a workforce selection method.

Constrained integration is a fairly classic form of occupational integration, corresponding to employees who are globally dissatisfied in their work, but whose job is not threatened. Thus, for these employees, their professional activity is not consistent with pleasure as it entails physical suffering, where the working conditions are hard, or moral suffering, where the atmosphere in the company is tense and relations with colleagues and superiors are bad. Thus, occupational integration is not ensured by the work itself, but by the fact that the job is a stable one. These employees may keep hoping for an improvement in their situation in the company and may even organise themselves in order to have their demands met. We may consider this form of integration as being similar to that which characterised the Fordist model during the years of strong economic growth. The affluent workers, whom the British sociologists studied in the 1960s had, for the most part, an instrumental relationship to work and involved themselves in a very limited way in the collective life of the company, the essential being, for them, to improve their daily life outside of the professional world, to be able to settle down with their family in a comfortable house and to have some leisure time. To a certain extent, the only interest in employment that these workers of the post-war boom years had was the salary, as it was the level of this that was the condition for the realisation of all of their projects for the improvement of their living conditions. And the very principle of Fordism was, we know, higher salaries which in turn made mass consumption possible (Boyer and Durand, 1998).

The employees near to *constrained integration* probably have even less chance today of being satisfied with their salary, as companies often limit wage increases, particularly in the sectors of the economy that are seriously threatened by the production of the developing countries. The qualitative survey which we carried out by means of detailed interviews, following on from the questionnaire survey, allowed us to ascertain that, in certain companies, the employees have not had substantial increases in their salary for many years. In these companies, the social ill-being sometimes reaches significant proportions, affecting almost all of the personnel.

This type of occupational integration can also develop in the public services and in state-owned companies. Sometimes, for certain employees, only the nature of the employment contract justifies their being kept in the post. We should here recall the fact that certain state-owned companies or public services practice a kind of sidelining, that is to say the transferring of the 'undesirable' employee or civil servant to subordinate, even useless tasks. In this case, the job and the wage are maintained, but the ordeal is, of course, painful for the people who experience it, as their immediate superiors thus publicly establish their inferiority or their inaptitude. This is more a practice that affects people with the least skills, but this risk of being 'sidelined' can concern intermediate and even superior levels of the hierarchy. When a state employee has been disowned by their department, they are found a secondary task to keep them out of the way, at best temporarily, at worst until they reaches retirement age. This practice comes down, when all is said and done, to purely and simply denying the creative potentialities of the individual in their work. They are thus reduced to being a person who is basically receiving state aid. This practice probably remains fairly extreme, but many public service employees or civil servants experience something similar. They end up feeling a profound repugnance for their work, which their colleagues in the private sector cannot understand, convinced as they are that state employees have got a 'cushy job', and which, in their opinion, means that they have nothing to complain about. Private companies do sometimes end up resorting to this type of practice in certain cases, but they are generally more expeditious in having recourse to compulsory redundancy.

Integration may also become onerous when a company is restructured and employees then notice that their job has been completely transformed in a way that seems to them to be more demeaning. They must then readapt themselves to new duties and are forced to accept what they consider to be a drop in status. This may only be symbolic, but everyone knows that symbols play a considerable role in social relationships. The very idea of a regression or of a refusal of promotion thus becomes unbearable for the employees concerned who see the situation as a non-recognition by others of their professional qualities. Though their job is not threatened, they do not feel any less bitter and their enthusiasm for their work can be profoundly affected.

Finally, *disqualifying integration* is the expression of an occupational integration crisis, as it combines job dissatisfaction and employment instability. It may have the effect of causing relational problems within the company. The employees who experience it have the feeling of belonging to a group within which their identity is threatened, either because their status is clearly inferior to that of the others, or because the group itself is condemned to disappear. Suffering at work is not, in this case, compensated by the hope of an improvement. The social status of these employees is thus more or less called into question. Their situation can be compared to that of unemployed people who have lost their job and who strongly doubt their chances of finding another one.[3]

Some might stress the fact that this type, thus defined, is far removed from the idea of occupational integration. It is, in fact, a question of the most important deviation in relation to *secure integration*. But it is, despite everything, a form of occupational integration as the employees have a job, a work contract and a salary. In reality, these elements only offer the employee an elementary framework for his integration, while at the same time depriving him of everything that could give him meaning, namely recognition, dignity, a means of expression and, finally, stability.

The ideal type of *secure integration* and its three deviations constitute a typology of occupational integration. This typology is not, strictly speaking, a typology of professional identities in the sense of the works of Renaud Sainsaulieu (1977) or of Claude Dubar (1991), but it forms a framework enabling them to be studied. By putting the emphasis, not only on the developments and the sense of the relationship to the job and to employment, which are the historical bases of employee identity, but also on the reasoning through which this is formed within companies, in work relations, but also outside of these relations, with reference to the protective logic of the welfare state, this typology of occupational integration constitutes a tool which tries to reconcile a psychosociological (real-life experience) approach with a 'structural' approach to the economic and social conditions of the development of modern capitalism.[4]

Employee Representations of Poverty and Unemployment

Employees are well aware of this hierarchy of social statuses. They know that as long as they have a job, they cannot be placed in the same category as people who are receiving state aid. That said, the development of professional insecurity undermines, as we have seen, a whole range of employees on the peripheries of employment. The question is thus to know whether the risk of becoming poor or jobless has the effect of making employees in the most insecure jobs distance themselves from, or even become hostile to, those categories which are separate from the wage-earning population or whether, on the contrary, it results in the expression of an attitude of spontaneous solidarity.

Judgement of the Causes of Poverty

To find out what attitudes people have towards the poor, we can, for example, consider the replies to a question focusing on accounting for poverty: 'Why are there people living in need in this country?' Among the possible responses on the questionnaire we used, two suggest causes which, from an ideological point of view, are totally at variance with one another: 'it is because of laziness or a lack of will' 'it is because there is a lot of injustice in our society.' The first can be considered as being the closest to conservative values according to which individuals must take responsibility for themselves. The idea of laziness is opposed to that of courage and implicitly invokes both the ethical dimension of work and a sense of justice based on each and everyone's worth. The second explanation is nearer to progressive values in the sense that it acknowledges the fact that, first and foremost, the poor can be victims of a social system which has put them at an unfair disadvantage. Thus, the acknowledgement of injustice implies, at least indirectly, the defining of redistribution policies in order to reduce poverty.

If employees threatened with the loss of their job explained poverty by laziness, we could see this as being a categorical refusal on their part to identify themselves with a social group that they judge to be of very low status and which they seek to put down all the more, as their own situation might well be a close approximation. This would then be a question of a well-known mechanism of social distinction founded on the principle of social incomparability. Employees in insecure employment could thus say: 'We are fundamentally different because the poor are lazy whereas we earn our wages by the sweat of our brow.' If, on the contrary, these employees experiencing professional difficulties accounted for poverty by the injustice that reigns in our country, this might be construed as being the expression of an attitude of understanding as regards the people affected by this problem. This attitude could then be interpreted as the showing of a certain solidarity with them.

In reality, very few employees took laziness as being the explanation for poverty: less than 3 per cent of the sample. In European opinion polls carried out since the middle of the 1970s on the issues of poverty and deprivation, this explanation has become progressively more marginal, even though there are still some national differences. On the whole, the effects of the economic crisis have led the population to see poverty as a structural mechanism. Nearly half of the employees in our sample explained poverty by injustice.

The results of the analysis enabled us to see that, first of all, unskilled workers explain poverty by injustice a lot less often than the other socio-professional groups (35 per cent against 56 per cent for the skilled workers, for example), which, at first sight, may seem a little surprising. On the other hand, proportionally more of them than of the other categories explain poverty by laziness. We can thus admit that a part of these workers seek to distinguish themselves from other people who, though socially very close to them, are seen as not being likely to make all of the efforts necessary to extricate themselves from their position. As the risk of these worker being considered as belonging to the category of the poor is not nil, the most disadvantaged workers thus seek to create – or to strengthen – a social differentiation, notably by referring to the values of courage and will. This, however, is not a reflection of the attitude observed amongst all of the employees having an insecure occupational integration type. In fact, we can see that, all things being equal, the employees close to *disqualifying integration* explain poverty more often by injustice: the coefficient is 0.53 compared to the employees close to *secure integration* (see Table 7.2).

The result is not significant for employees close to *uncertain integration* and *constrained integration*. Even if unskilled workers have, overall, a more moralising attitude than the other categories when accounting for poverty, this is not the case for employees in a situation of professional insecurity. If we define the explanation of poverty by injustice as being an understanding explanation of a progressive nature, then we must conclude that the employees close to *disqualifying integration* are more progressive than the employees close to *secure integration*. So, for the moment, we cannot validate the thesis of hostility towards marginalised groups that the theorists of political alienation have suggested.

Table 7.2 Specific effects of occupational integration type on the explanation of poverty by injustice (1)

	B	Sig.	%
Integration type			
Secure	*Ref.*		46.6
Uncertain	-.02	n.s.	45.1
Constrained	.26	n.s.	54.6
Disqualifying	.53	***	55.9

(1) Logistic regression model including occupational integration type, gender, age, SEG and type of company. The last column gives the simple difference as a percentage.
Source: OSC Survey 'Emploi salarié et conditions de vie' 1995 (N: 1028).
*: P < .1, **: P < .05, ***: P < .01, ****: P < .001 (n.s.: non-significant).

Opinions on the Rights and Duties of the Unemployed

To test the hypothesis of hostility and complete the analysis, the employees' opinions vis-à-vis the unemployed and unemployment benefit can also be examined and the questionnaire we used included precise questions on this subject. Each question was presented in the form of a ten-point value scale and we asked the people questioned to give their position on this scale (see Table 7.3).

The first scale had the opinion that the unemployed should be obliged to accept any job available or else lose their benefit, at one end, and the opinion that the unemployed should have the right to refuse a job which does not suit them, at the other. The results of the ordered logistic regression, including the integration type, gender, age, socio-professional group and type of company, show that the employees close to *constrained integration* and *disqualifying integration* are significantly more favourable than the employees close to *secure integration* to leaving unemployed people the right to refuse a job that does not suit them: the coefficients are 0.47 and 0.43 respectively. We can thus conclude that the employees whose occupational integration is very uncertain show more lenience towards the unemployed than the employees in stable employment.

The second scale has the opinion that – the benefits paid to the unemployed should be higher – at one end, and the opinion that – benefits are too high – at the other. In this case, the employees close to *uncertain integration* and *constrained integration* think significantly less often than employees close to *secure integration* that the unemployed should receive less benefit. The coefficient obtained for employees close to *disqualifying integration* is comparable, but it is only significant if we take the type of company out of the regression model. We can however see a clearer tendency to defend the benefit rights of the unemployed on the part of employees whose integration is insecure than on the part of the others.

Finally, the third scale has the opinion that associations promoting integration enable people in difficulty to gain access to employment, at one end, and the opinion that these associations create insecurity and not employment, at the other. This question does not specifically concern the unemployed, but it is, however, one of the major questions asked of the integration solutions advocated to help people in difficulty to find a job. We could consider that expressing a critical point of view as regards these integration associations comes down, at least indirectly, to defending unemployed people who refuse to take advantage of the help and actions that they propose. Today, many unemployed people do, in fact, hold very negative views as regards all of these integration measures which do not, in actual fact, lead to a stable job, and they prefer not to have recourse to them. It is striking to note that the employees close to *disqualifying integration* more often consider, and very significantly so, compared to employees close to *secure integration*, that these integration associations create insecurity and not employment (coefficient 0.56). The results are not significant for the employees close to *uncertain integration* and *constrained integration*. We can thus conclude that the more uncertain the integration of the employees, the less ready they are to believe in the integration solutions that are proposed to the unemployed in order to gain access to a job. As the risk of these employees becoming unemployed is high, we can also see this as a sign of disillusion vis-à-vis the future.

The results of the quantitative analysis thus tend towards the showing of greater empathy, even solidarity, on the part of the employees whose occupational integration is uncertain vis-à-vis the disadvantaged groups of the poor and the unemployed. These employees take injustice as accounting for poverty more often than the employees close to *secure integration*. They more often express the opinion that the unemployed should be free to refuse a job that does not suit them. They also more often think that unemployment benefit is not too high, and some of them, in particular the employees close to *disqualifying integration*, are as critical as the unemployed of integration associations. The results do not exactly correspond to those that I obtained within the framework of the qualitative analysis with semi-structured interviews carried out as a continuation of the questionnaire survey. In fact, the interviews enabled us to see that employees in an insecure employment situation, working in companies which offer their staff unattractive pay conditions, often adopt a *distant attitude* and even a hostile attitude towards a minority of the unemployed. Should we see a contradiction therein or, on the contrary, a complementarity of the approaches? It seems that the contradiction is only superficial. The *distant attitude* does not entail hostility towards all unemployed people and does not preclude criticism either of employers or of the free market economy. This is why it is possible to conclude that, though the employees whose occupational integration is very uncertain often seek to distinguish themselves socially from the 'professional' unemployed, they remain, on the whole, more tolerant and more open to the redistribution of income, with regard to the poor and the unemployed in general, than the employees whose integration is assured.

Table 7.3 Specific effects of occupational integration type on opinions (presented in the form of a 10-point scale) regarding the unemployed (1)

	Opinion 1		Opinion 2		Opinion 3	
	B	**Sig.**	**B**	**Sig.**	**B**	**Sig.**
Integration type						
Secure	*Ref.*		*Ref.*		*Ref.*	
Uncertain	.01	n.s.	-.30	*	.14	n.s.
Constrained	.47	***	-.29	*	.10	n.s.
Disqualifying	.43	**	-.23	n.s.(ᵃ)	.56	***

(1) Logistic regression model including integration type, gender, age, SEG and type of company.

Opinion 1: The unemployed should have the choice of refusing a job which does not suit them (as opposed to the radical opinion that the unemployed should be obliged to accept any available job or else lose their benefit).

Opinion 2: The benefit paid to the unemployed is too high (as opposed to the opinion that the benefit paid to the unemployed should be higher).

Opinion 3: Integration associations create uncertainty and not employment (as opposed to the opinion that integration associations enable people in difficulty to gain access to employment).

(ᵃ) The coefficient is approximately the same, but significant when the type of company is not considered in the regression.

Source: OSC Survey 'Emploi salarié et conditions de vie' 1995 (N: 1036).

*: P < .1, **: P < .05, ***: P < .01, ****: P < .001 (n.s.: non-significant).

Towards a Depoliticised Radicalism

Is there a political tendency effect, peculiar to the occupational integration type? One of the hypotheses of the sociologists who have looked into the mechanisms of political alienation was that people who are badly integrated socially and professionally also remain withdrawn in relation to sociopolitical events. Here, we shall try to discover the general political tendency of employees whose occupational integration is insecure and whether they feel close to a particular party.

The Left-Right Split

Whereas the effect of professional insecurity on political tendencies has been the subject of little research works in France, the relation between unemployment and politics has been of more interest to researchers. At the beginning of the 1980s, Dominique Schnapper (1982) acknowledged that this relation was still not well known, but with the support of various research conducted both in France and abroad, she hypothesised that the direct effect of unemployment on political activism or on electoral behaviour was weak, but that the indirect effect led to a slight shifting of the vote to the left, this being due rather to the behaviour of people who were not unemployed but who were very much aware of the employment crisis. A few years later, Annick Percheron and Béatrice Roy (1988) were able to study the impact of unemployment on political behaviour more precisely by using surveys of representative samples. They were able to note both an attitude of political withdrawal and indecisiveness that was more widespread among white-collar workers than among managers and blue-collar workers, a phenomenon of radicalisation in favour of the left, and, among long-term unemployed blue-collar workers, stronger political involvement and increased support for the French Communist Party. Finally, in the CEVIPOF survey of March 1995, Jacques Capdevielle (1999) observed, among unemployed blue-collar workers, both an attitude of political withdrawal and an indictment of the political community.

All of these results suggest that unemployment reinforces a tendency to left-wing radicalism, but can also have the effect, at least if we base ourselves on the last survey, of a certain disillusion with regard to political life in general. What about the effect of insecure occupational integration? Since the employees who deviate from *secure integration* more often take injustice to explain poverty, we might assume that they are more left-wing than right. This question implicitly comes back to the idea that wealth redistribution policies are necessary for the restoration of greater social justice, traditionally a demand supported by the parties of the left. To discover the political tendencies of the employees, we used a ten-point scale on which we asked them to give their position. If we group together the first two levels of the scale which are situated more to the left, we obtain about 7 per cent for the employees close to *secure integration*, between 16 and 17 per cent for the employees close to *uncertain integration* and *constrained integration* and, finally, 24 per cent for the employees close to *disqualifying integration*. Thus this graduation marks a clear tendency in favour of the left for the employees whose occupational integration is insecure. This is moreover verified by the results of the ordered logistic regression which takes all of the positions of the scale and includes all of the usual variables (see Table 7.4).

The least integrated employees are thus, overall, more attached to the ideological world of the left. An additional analysis allowed us to confirm that the employees close to *constrained integration* and to *disqualifying integration* are also, other things being equal, clearly more in favour of the opinion that 'the entire organisation of society must be changed by revolutionary action' (Paugam, 1999) than the employees close to *secure integration*. Given that we were able to ascertain a very strong correlation between left-wing political positioning and a revolutionary attitude,[5] we can thus conclude that insecure occupational integration has an effect on left-wing radicalism. This is along similar lines to the results that Annick Percheron and Béatrice Roy established on the subject of the effect of unemployment.

Table 7.4 On the subject of politics, people talk of left and right. Generally speaking, where do you situate yourself on this scale (from 1 for left-wing to 10 for right-wing)? (1)

	B	Sig.	%
Integration type			
Secure	*Ref.*		6.7
Uncertain	-.51	***	16.0
Constrained	-.46	***	16.9
Disqualifying	-.75	****	24.2

(1) Ordered logistic regression model including occupational integration type, gender, age, SEG and type of company. The last column shows the simple difference as a percentage for the first two levels, situated furthest to the left, taken together.
Note: A positive coefficient signifies closer proximity to the right, a negative coefficient closer proximity to the left.
Source: OSC Survey 'Emploi salarié et conditions de vie' 1995 (N: 956).
*: $P < .1$, **: $P < .05$, ***: $P < .01$, ****: $P < .001$ (n.s.: non-significant).

However, this does not mean that the employees who are less integrated professionally have a personal commitment to political life or even that they are interested in it. Their radical attitude vis-à-vis the transformation of society may correspond to a certain despair. Feeling close to the left does not necessarily mean trusting the parties that represent it. It may be more a question of bitterness towards employers and the economic policies supported by the right rather than massive support for the political leaders of the left. To clarify this, we need to examine attitudes towards the political parties more closely.

Disillusion vis-à-vis Political Parties and Feeling of Powerlessness

The question of proximity to political parties is not commonly asked in the big statistical surveys in France, in particular when the subject of the surveys does not specifically focus on politics. Some people see this issue as being a question belonging to the private sphere and prefer not to reply. Among the employees questioned, 33 per cent replied that they do not feel close to any party. This seems a high proportion (see Table 7.5). It may be that some people preferred not to reply, not because they do not have a political opinion, but simply because they do not feel sufficiently implicated by a political party. It is striking to note that 61 per cent of the employees having declared no political proximity positioned themselves exactly in the middle of the left-right scale.[6]

Most of the employees indicated that they feel closest to the parties of the left, in particular to the *Parti socialiste* (37 per cent). Among the right-wing parties, the *Union démocratique française* was preferred about 8 per cent of the time and the *Rassemblement pour la République* 10 per cent. Very few of the employees indicated a proximity to the National Front. They were also very few to express their preference for the extreme left. If the employees close to *uncertain integration* to *constrained integration* and to *disqualifying integration* define themselves as being more left-wing than employees close to *secure integration*, it would be logical that they also feel closer to the parties of the left. Table 7.5 shows a strong correlation between political proximity and occupational integration type, but this needed to be verified with the help of a logistical regression model as it is not impossible that this is simply a consequence of the structure. Once the effect of gender, age, the socio-professional group and type of company had been checked, it effectively appears that the employees whose occupational integration deviates from *secure integration* do not have, other things being equal, a significant affinity to a left-wing political party, whether this be to the *Parti socialiste*, the French Communist Party or the Greens (see Table 7.6).

Table 7.5 Which party do you feel the closest to?

in %

	None	Extr-Left	Greens	PCF	PS	UDF	RPR	NF
Integration type								
Secure	27.8	1.2	4.0	4.0	37.2	11.3	13.2	1.4
Uncertain	40.1	0.6	3.9	6.6	33.5	3.3	10.4	1.7
Constrained	30.1	0.0	4.4	7.4	43.4	7.4	7.4	0.0
Disqualifying	40.7	1.5	4.0	9.1	33.7	4.5	4.5	2.0
Total	33.0	0.9	4.0	6.1	37.1	7.7	9.8	1.3
N	333	9	41	62	374	78	99	13

Source: OSC Survey 'Emploi salarié et conditions de vie' 1995 (N: 1009).
Chi2 (21) = 53.4944, Pr = 0.000.

Thus we arrive at a paradox: employees whose occupational integration is insecure feel more attached to the ideological world of the left than the employees whose occupational integration is assured. However, this does not make them closer to the political parties that represent the traditional values to which they hold. This paradox can be explained by the feelings of frustration and of disillusion that they experience. The gap between their aspirations and reality causes them to feel a certain disillusion. As I was able to note in the detailed interviews, many among them have lost any hope of seeing their situation improve. Consequently, the response of the political parties seems to them to be derisory and the expressions: 'they are all the same', 'they only think of themselves', 'they are all rotten'...

laconic as they are, are actually the expression of a malaise and a feeling of powerlessness vis-à-vis a future which is threatened.

Table 7.6 Specific effects of occupational integration type on proximity to left-wing political parties (1)

	Greens		PCF		PS	
	B	**Sig.**	**B**	**Sig.**	**B**	**Sig.**
Integration type						
Secure	*Ref.*		*Ref.*		*Ref.*	
Uncertain	.14	n.s.	.49	n.s.	.12	n.s.
Constrained	.51	n.s.	.01	n.s.	.30	n.s.
Disqualifying	.57	n.s.	.41	n.s.	.07	n.s.

(1) Logistic regression model including integration type, gender, age, SEG and type of company.
Source: OSC Survey 'Emploi salarié et conditions de vie' 1995.
*: $P < .1$, **: $P < .05$, ***: $P < .01$, ****: $P < .001$ (n.s.: non-significant).

In this disillusion as regards the political parties, we must also see a more general disillusion with regard to the functioning of the free market economy and the competition which reigns there. We were able to ascertain, for example, that the employees close to *disqualifying integration* approved more often than the others the opinion that 'competition is dangerous and leads to bringing out the worst in people' (see Table 7.7).

Table 7.7 Specific effects of occupational integration type on disillusion with respect to the free market economy (1)

	B	**Sig.**	**%**
Integration type			
Secure	*Ref.*		5.6
Uncertain	.05	n.s.	10.5
Constrained	.20	n.s.	9.9
Disqualifying	.73	****	19.8

(1) Ordered logistic regression model. The responses are ordered into 10 positions according to whether the employees were more or less in agreement with the proposition: 'Competition is dangerous. It leads to bringing out the worst in people'. This model includes occupational integration type, gender, age, SEG and type of company. The last column gives the simple difference as a percentage for the people the most in agreement with the proposition.
Source: OSC Survey 'Emploi salarié et conditions de vie' 1995 (N: 1036).
*: $P < .1$, **: $P < .05$, ***: $P < .01$, ****: $P < .001$ (n.s.: non-significant).

It is true that those political parties which are likely to govern support the principle of the free market. Even if the left-wing parties still mean to regulate the market through state intervention, they remain relatively powerless in the face of economic constraints when they are in power. The employees who risk losing their job point out that redundancies continue at a high rate whichever political party is in government. So, when they see that powerful companies plan to make a, sometimes large, part of their staff redundant, though their financial results are positive, they do not understand why the authorities do not oppose this. Hence, they have the feeling that nothing is done to stop this process and that they are the designated victims of it. Consequently, the left-wing radicalism which still characterises their attitude leads to a political void in terms of a party.

The fall of the Berlin wall in November 1989 and the ineluctable decline of the French Communist Party explain these disillusions to a large extent.[7] By more or less agreeing to lend their support to free-market economic tendencies and to participate in a 'left coalition' government, the French Communist Party probably reassured the electorate of the moderate left, but it certainly disappointed the employees whose occupational integration is the most insecure. These people expected it to offer clearer opposition. Since then, they have felt abandoned, vulnerable to the ups and downs of the market and without hope.

Thus, what may appear to be a condemnation of a system which leads to their rejection does not translate into a political commitment on their part, but, on the contrary, into a strong disillusion. This phenomenon confirms then the hypothesis of political powerlessness, analysed by the sociologists specialising in alienation.

Professional Insecurity and Abstention from Voting

The feeling of powerlessness vis-à-vis the future can also be linked to a lack of confidence in the institutions which regulate political life. Voter participation is a good indicator of the interest that individuals have for political life and for the parties involved in it, but, above all, it is an indicator of social integration in the sense that it involves the individual in the exercise of his citizenship. It is possible not to be interested in politics and to be integrated into social life, but not going to vote is a manifest sign of withdrawal with regard to the functioning of national institutions. It expresses a refusal to take part in public affairs and, on a large scale, it constitutes one of the elementary forms of the erosion of social cohesion. The question is thus to find out whether the disillusion seen vis-à-vis the parties when occupational integration is insecure, is also accompanied by a renouncement of one's vote.

We must, of course, distinguish between registration on the electoral roll and abstention. At the time of the presidential election of 1995, 9 per cent of French people were not registered on the lists and 11 per cent abstained from voting in both rounds: thus one elector in five remained completely removed from the election (Héran and Rouault, 1995a). The analyses of the electoral roll registrations have shown that, for the socially well-integrated categories, registration appears to be a behaviour norm independent of the politicisation of the individuals. On the other hand, for the geographically less stable categories, young people and tenants, employees in the private sector and those having renounced Catholicism, registration on the rolls appears more to be a choice dependent upon political conscience (Bréchon and Cautrès, 1987). If we group those not registered and those abstaining, recent studies have enabled us to see that the French people who remained the most removed from the last presidential election do not form a homogenous category (Héran and Rouault, 1995b). It is more a question of a continuum between two poles: the first, strongly attached to the vote, is made up of rural communities which include dignitaries, farmers, and intellectuals such as mangers and teachers; the second groups the big urban areas where unskilled white and blue-collar workers live. The factors of voter participation are thus diverse: the level of education, place of residence, but also family stability and union culture, particularly in the industrial world. François Héran and Dominique Rouault also ascertained the effect of the nature of the work contract and of unemployment. Whereas 17 per cent of employees in a stable job remained removed from this election, this phenomenon of exclusion concerned 32 per cent of employees in an insecure job and 31 per cent of unemployed people. It is worth noting that these authors followed the same process to study participation in the municipal elections which were held in June 1995, i.e. approximately a month after the presidential election. The people who systematically remained apart from the electoral scene of this spring 1995 represent nearly 30 per cent of unemployed people and employees in temporary jobs, with employees in a stable job representing less than 15 per cent. In the opinion of the authors, unemployment and professional insecurity may well leave their mark on the political conscience.

In our survey, approximately 93 per cent of employees of French nationality indicated that they went to vote. The question asked did not require a difference to be made between the types of election. The question must thus be understood in a general sense. This high voting rate is however explained, at least partially, by the date of the survey which was carried out a few months after the 1995 presidential election. This is the type of election which arouses the most interest. It is thus probable that the people questioned replied as a function of this particular election.

The results of the analysis enabled us to see that the employees close to *disqualifying integration* have, other things being equal, a more distant attitude with regard to voting than the employees close to *secure integration* (coefficient - 1.32, see Table 7.8). In other words, the occupational integration type of the most insecure employees is the only one to have a significant effect on voter participation.

This must be seen as the expression of indifference on the part of these employees as regards electoral issues.[8] It is, in a way, a question of detachment vis-à-vis elementary forms of participation in collective life. Not only is the occupational integration of these employees threatened, but it also brings them so little job satisfaction that their social identity is affected. They no longer have any hope of seeing an improvement in their situation and no longer expect anything of the elections. In actual fact, even before they have lost their job, they already have

Coping and Pulling Through

the attitude of those unemployed people who withdraw into themselves. The relationship that they maintain with others and with the world around them is distant because they feel that they have lost their place, or have never succeeded in acquiring one.

Table 7.8 Specific effects of occupational integration type on voter participation (1)

	B	Sig.	%
Integration type			
Secure	*Ref.*		96.1
Uncertain	-.19	n.s.	96.1
Constrained	-.03	n.s.	96.6
Disqualifying	-1.32	***	90.4

(1) Logistic regression model including occupational integration type, gender, age, SPG and type of company. The last column shows the simple difference as a percentage.
Source: OSC Survey 'Emploi salarié et conditions de vie' 1995 (N: 999).
*: P < .1, **: P < .05, ***: P < .01, ****: P < .001 (n.s.: non-significant).

The employees close to *disqualifying integration* who prefer to abstain expect to lose, whoever wins the election, as they reckon that none of the candidates will defend their interests.[9] Though they judge themselves to be more left-wing and often express, as we have seen, a radical opinion regarding the transformation of society, they no longer trust the political parties. In fact, they consider that the victory of a left-wing candidate will not change their situation any more than the victory of a right-wing one. This indifference is not the expression of a lack of political socialisation or of a lack of knowledge on the subject, the people surveyed replied to the questions they were asked in a coherent way, and nor, in the detailed interviews, did we come across any employees who were badly informed of the differences between the political parties. The tendency to abstain from voting is thus better explained by a process of disillusion. The lack of confidence of these employees in the political community is linked, it is true, to the difficulty the large parties have in bringing concrete solutions to professional insecurity and to unemployment. Since their interests are not defended in the way that they would like them to be, we might be led to think that the present-day system of political representation is, in part, unsuitable. In a way, it is a question of a void that the political parties cannot manage to – or do not seek to – fill.

However, it is not advisable to generalise. In fact, not all of the employees in a situation of insecurity adopt, to a significant extent, a more distant attitude with regard to voting, only a minority of the most disqualified among them.

The forms of occupational integration do affect political behaviour. The hypothesis according to which employees who are badly integrated in the professional world are the most hostile towards certain marginalised categories of the population was not proved. These employees show, on the whole, more tolerance towards the poor and the unemployed in general, and are also more favourable to the maintenance of the level of unemployment benefit and to the redistribution of income in favour of these groups than the employees close to *secure integration*. The analysis of political tendencies enabled us to see a stronger left-wing tendency among the employees in a position of insecurity, but no significant attachment to a party incarnating these political values. Finally, the analysis of opinion vis-à-vis the market and voter participation led me to emphasise the disillusion of the employees close to *disqualifying integration*. In other words, the hypotheses of apathy, powerlessness and lack of confidence were confirmed in this research. In the face of this process, the political parties must ask themselves some questions about the long-term risk of democracy leaving a minority of voters a prey to despair.

Notes

1   Amongst all of these authors, Melvin Seeman (1967), for example, sought specifically to study the political consequences of alienation in work. This approach was influenced by the neo-Marxist thought of the 1960s which postulated that the mechanisms of domination in work had direct effects on the conditions of social and political life.

2   We should be clear about the term 'idéal' which, to Max Weber, did not mean that the objective of the intellectual procedure was a normative one. The more exact term as Dominique Schnapper (1999) reminded us recently, would be 'idéel' which would have the advantage of avoiding confusion by stressing that the method refers to the construction of an idea or a point of view, i.e. the conscious and reasoned schematisation of reality in order to better understand it. But it must be admitted that since the first translations of the work of Max Weber into French, the term 'type idéal' has imposed itself, which now makes it difficult not to adopt it.

3   The term 'disqualifying integration' refers to the concept of social disqualification. The integration is disqualifying because it is the beginning of an identity crisis process which may lead to the accumulation of handicaps (Paugam, 1991).

4   An empirical verification was undertaken notably by making a factor analysis of multiple relations which enabled us to highlight the two axes (job satisfaction and employment stability) which form the two dimensions of the typology and the variables which contributed to their definition (Paugam, 2000, 103-120).

5   Out of 95 employees in favour of the opinion that the organisation of our society must be changed by revolutionary action, about 70 per cent of them positioned themselves on the first four levels to the furthest left of the ten-position scale, 25 per cent on level 5 and the rest on level 6.

6   Of the other employees who did not give a political party preference, 18 per cent chose a left-wing position (inferior to or equal to 4 on the scale) and 21 per cent a right-wing position (superior to or equal to 6 on the scale).

7   The decline of the French Communist Party was previous to the fall of the Berlin wall. Political analysts consider its electoral fragility to date from the end of the 1960s. However, it is unquestionable that it continued to play a role in the political socialisation of the working class, even though the latter has also gradually become weaker (Ranger, 1986).

8   Indifference is one of the three reasons for electoral abstention according to Alain Lancelot. The other two are perplexity and hostility (Lancelot, 1968).

9   This also refers to the analysis of certain American political experts who conclude that people feel alienated, powerless, cynical, deceived and even potentially disloyal when,

in their eyes, there is no longer any party at all which defends their interests (Levin and Eden, 1962).

References

Aron, R. (1962), *Dix-huit leçons sur la société industrielle*, Éditions Gallimard, Paris.

Blauner, R. (1964), *Alienation and Freedom. The Factory Worker and his Industry*, University of Chicago Press, Chicago.

Boyer, R. and Durand, J.P. (1998), *L'Après fordisme*, Éditions Syros, Paris.

Bréchon, P. and Cautrès, B. (1987), 'L'inscription sur les listes électorales: indicateur de socialisation ou de politisation?', *Revue française de science politique*, Vol. 37(4).

Capdevielle, J. (1999), *Les Opinions et les comportements politiques des ouvriers: une évolution inévitable? irrésistible?*, Cahier du CEVIPOF, 21.

Dean, D.G. (1960), 'Alienation and Political Apathy', *Social Forces*, Vol. 38(3).

Dubar, C. (1991), *La Socialisation. Construction des identités sociales et professionnelles*, Éditions Armand Colin, Paris.

Durkheim, É. (1984), *The Division of Labour in Society*, translated by W.D. Halls with an introduction by Lewis Coser, Macmillan Publishers Ltd, London.

Durkheim, É. (1991), *Professional Ethics and Civic Morals*, Routledge, London.

Esping-Andersen, G. (1990), *The Three Worlds of Welfare Capitalism*, Polity Press, London.

Finifter, A.W. (1970), 'Dimensions of Political Alienation', *The American Political Science Review*, Vol. 64(2).

Héran, F. and Rouault, D. (1995a), 'La présidentielle à contre-jour: abstentionnistes et non-inscrits', *INSEE Première*, 397.

Héran, F. and Rouault, D. (1995b), 'La double élection de 1995: exclusion sociale et stratégie d'abstention', *INSEE Première*, 414.

Lancelot, A. (1968), *L'Abstentionnisme électoral en France*, Presses de la Fondation nationale des sciences politiques, Paris.

Levin, M.B. and Eden, M. (1962), 'Political Strategy of the Alienated Voter', *Public Opinion Quarterly*, Vol. 26.

Olsen, M.E. (1969), 'Two Categories of Political Alienation', *Social Forces*, Vol. 47(3).

Paugam, S. (1991), *La Disqualification sociale. Essai sur la nouvelle pauvreté*, Presses universitaires de France, Paris.

Paugam, S. (1999), 'Formes d'intégration professionnelle et attitudes syndicales et politiques', *Revue française de sociologie*, Vol. XL(4).

Paugam, S. (2000), *Le Salarié de la précarité. Les nouvelles formes de l'intégration professionnelle*, Presses universitaires de France, Paris.

Paugam, S., Zoyem, J.P. and Charbonnel, J.M. (1993), *Précarité et risque d'exclusion en France*, La Documentation française, Paris.

Percheron, A. and Roy, B. (1988), 'Chômage et politique', *Cahiers du CEVIPOF*, 2.

Ranger, J. (1986), 'Le déclin du Parti communiste français', *Revue française de science politique*, Vol. 36(1).

Sainsaulieu, R. (1977), *L'Identité au travail. Les effets culturels de l'organisation*, Presses de la Fondation nationale des sciences politiques, Paris.

Schnapper, D. (1982), 'Chômage et politique: une relation mal connue', *Revue française de science politique*, Vol. 32(4-5).

Schnapper, D. (1999), *La Compréhension sociologique. Démarche de l'analyse typologique*, Presses universitaires de France, Paris.

Seeman, M. (1967), 'Les conséquences de l'aliénation dans le travail', *Sociologie du travail*, 2.

Thompson, W.E. and Horton, J.E. (1960), 'Political Alienation as a Force in Political Action', *Social Forces*, Vol. 38(3).

Chapter 8

Continuity of Identity and Survival

Danièle Laberge and Shirley Roy

This chapter will deal with continuity of identity or identity crises in situations of survival, in particular in the situations facing itinerant or homeless people, who indisputably find themselves in an extremely vulnerable position and are confronted with survival on a daily basis. The guiding premise of this entire reflection is that objective living conditions contribute to the maintenance, transformation or strengthening of individual identities.

The reflection will be approached from three angles which are considered to be important to both the identity debate and the homeless identity debate: the recognition of skills, the role of social institutions and the discourse of social workers. Before starting this analysis, it is important to first recall the concrete living conditions of the majority of homeless people and look at the effects that categorisation has on the 'itinerant' identity.

Itinerant Living Conditions and Self-image

One of the most striking realities of the itinerant experience concerns the lack of residential security. The absence of sufficient financial resources, in addition to uncertain personal conditions makes permanent access to housing extremely difficult. Even though some of these people live in small hotels, supervised accommodation, inner-city lodgings, others take refuge in places lacking security: disused tenement or commercial buildings, the corridors or tracks of underground railways, train or bus stations, car parks, waste grounds, public conveniences, etc. Residential instability, the frequenting of unhealthy and dangerous 'non-places' significantly undermines individuals (Power, French, Connelly and al., 1999).

The difficulty of gaining access to private spaces forces homeless people into public or semi-public spaces where they are more easily subject to confrontation, rejection or repression. The daily lives of the homeless consist of risks: the risk of being attacked, of having no money, of being without shelter, of being hungry, of being short of drugs, of being alone, of not experiencing any physical pleasure, of being deprived of love and affection, of being excluded from the last place of belonging. The fear of these dangers necessitates the use of various protection measures and even these can sometimes turn out to be harmful for the person. For example, the need to have one's 'fix' may mean having recourse to illicit activities;

the absence of safe places for the night incites homeless people to gather in squats or to sleep during the day (Anderson, 1996); the need for money forces some homeless people into prostitution, etc. Numerous studies seem to show that despite their efforts to protect themselves, these people are subjected to frequent physical and sexual assaults (Brassard and Cousineau, 2000; Novac, Brown and Gallant, 1999).[1]

Problems of mental health and drug addiction (Novac, Brown and Gallant, 1999; Mercier, 1993) are the common fate of many itinerant people.[2] Personal disorganisation, the refusal of treatment, the difficulties involved in identifying possible sources of help are all factors which serve to increase the vulnerability of the homeless (Tolomiczenko and Goering, 1998; Drogoul, 1996). These problems also make homeless people all the more visible because of their atypical or seemingly threatening behaviour. These dynamics are not unrelated to an increase in the criminal repression of the homeless: victimisation (Novac, Brown and Gallant, 1999), judicial measures (Landreville, Laberge and Morin, 1998), repeated periods of imprisonment. But prison only favours the deterioration of both their psychological and physical state.[3] The setting in motion of such dynamics affects their psychological ill-being (anxiety, stress, depression, etc.), and reduces their feelings of security and their survival capabilities.

Residential instability and the lack of access to private spaces oblige itinerant people to live their sexuality in conditions which are often harmful to their health and their psychological equilibrium (Jurgens and Gilmore, 1994). In fact, contrary to a very commonly held prejudice, itinerant people do have a sex life, but it takes place in a clandestine world, of denial, of violence, of prohibitions and of segregation (the streets, prison, shelters, etc.). As Michael Pollak (1990) recalled, sexual and emotional needs endure even in extreme situations. Moreover, for some, sexual activity is a means of survival, marked by the need to obtain goods or money.

Although homeless people see themselves as not being in good health, they almost always only resort to the relevant services in times of crisis (Marks, Taylor, Burrows and al., 2000; Stein, Andersen, Koegel and Gelbert, 2000; Ambrosio, Baker, Crowe and Hardill, 1992). They are distrustful of the health services and of the mental health services in particular. Numerous experiences may go some way to explaining these negative conceptions: consultation in an emergency situation, involuntary psychiatric hospitalisation in a refusal of treatment context, the imposition of treatment within the framework of legal proceedings, the threat or withdrawal of support by social workers. These forms of care have real practical consequences: loss of one's room, one's place or one's goods during a hospitalisation for example; loss of the custody of one's children, etc. Such experiences determine perceptions and subsequent behaviour.

Living on the street or within the 'street outreach system' (shelters, day centres, soup kitchens, etc.), the length of time spent there and the associated conditions of existence cause important, even radical changes to the representations of inter-individual, social (Boydell, Goering and Morrell-Bellai, 2000; Desjarlais, 1999;

Snow and Anderson, 1987) and institutional relationships. Here, as elsewhere, these representations are complex constructions which are developed from information which is more or less correct, perceptions which are more or less justified and experiences which are more or less well understood. Nevertheless, they are always at the root of the decision to act. Homeless people make use of certain mechanisms to escape stigma and its consequences; symbolic distancing of themselves from homelessness being the most well known (Farrington and Robinson, 1999). Besides these mechanisms, homelessness feeds negative self-images and affects the perception of one's own value and one's personal ability to act (Boydell, Goering and Morrell-Bellai, 2000; Desjarlais, 1999).

The Opinion of Others in the Constitution of a Homeless Social Identity

Within the attributed part of identity (identity for others), several writers insist on the importance of institutional designations in the identification process. In fact, the forming of specific recognised categories may make identification possible and can set the process of negotiation of personal identity (identity for oneself) in motion. These designations confer a

> special legitimacy to these categories and thus to the social spheres from which they are constructed and reconstructed. (Dubar, 1995, 118)

Such a thesis is not new and proves to be true in the case of the homeless. However, the objective living conditions of these people, and the many forms homelessness takes, give rise to variations of this thesis. On the one hand, the homeless or itinerant category has taken a stronger and stronger substantive form over the years. For example, in France homelessness has become an administrative category, allowing individuals to be classified within the framework of the 'Revenu minimum d'insertion' (income support) law. In Quebec and in Canada, despite the lack of an administrative category, itinerancy has been pinpointed as a priority for governmental intervention. Over the last 15 years, a community help network for itinerant people has been built up (a network which is subsidised and supported by the state) and research programmes addressing the issue of homelessness have been developed. These elements contribute, through a specific designation, to the construction of an itinerant identity at different levels. Thus, homeless people see their situations named, recognised and potentially taken care of: their actual existence is acknowledged through places, policies, services, all kinds of measures.

On the other hand, notwithstanding this recognition, the position of homeless people is charged with negativity and the associated stigma is powerful. Depending on their profiles and their various life experiences, these people adopt different strategies which take account of the effect of the label. Some consider the term homeless to be entirely unacceptable, even though they display the outward signs and regularly use the services responsible for providing them with help and support. They do not see themselves as homeless and seek to distance themselves from this description by proposing an alternative interpretation of their situation. In this way they attempt to limit the negative effects of being described as homeless.[4] Others, on the contrary, actively lay claim to the term and accentuate the corresponding behaviour, lifestyle, symbols and discourse.

The way that homeless people choose to speak about themselves shows how they see themselves and the image that they wish to project. A series of needs is thus identified, a certain form of help is demanded, a lifestyle is asserted and, at the same time, the reference points of this world are established. Resorting to a variety of descriptions whilst living on the street also shows a range of survival methods and action strategies.

Recognition of Skills in the Construction of Identity

A wealth of literature on the subject of professional identity (Dubar, 1999; Sainsaulieu, 1987) insists on the role and the importance of work in the definition of social and personal identity, and on the need to develop specific skills allowing identity to be established and changes in the social organisation to be adapted to. These skills are varied and correspond to the carrying out of activities which are positively invested. Thus, the competence of a good mother will be recognised by how well her children are educated, their politeness, their good school results, etc.; the competence of a worker will be recognised by his or her punctuality, initiative, ability to solve concrete problems, etc.; the competence, however modest, of a sportsman or sportswoman will be recognised by his or her devotion to training, precision, quality of movement, sense of discipline and honour, etc. The abilities described above, suppose the mastering of skills, the gaining of knowledge, the exercising of judgement, the ability to act in accordance with set expectations, etc.

It could be argued that there are two dimensions to the idea of competence: a social dimension, which corresponds to conformity to norms and expectations and which can be called normative skill, and a performative dimension, which can be defined as the appropriateness between the goals aimed for and the means implemented in the deployment of the action. More often than not, these two dimensions are confused and the performative element is put into the same category as the normative element, as in the examples mentioned above. Our hypothesis requires these two dimensions to be considered separately.

Hence, for the analysis of the situation of itinerant people, we think that it is important to distinguish between conformity to norms and activities relating to survival, thus enabling a better understanding of the meaning of competence. Generally, homeless people do not have specific professional skills, they do not have regular work. Those who are still in some kind of paid employment have temporary, non-specialised and, for the most part, menial jobs. Furthermore, interpersonal relations are poor, even non-existent. So, at first sight, homeless people lack competence in the most socially prestigious fields: work, family, leisure and, more broadly, consumption.

This is not a question of a demonstration of a different lifestyle, of reference to another normative system. It could be argued that a life of wandering does not constitute a choice for the majority of people who live it. It is not a question of the expression of an alternative type of philosophy (hippy, ecological, voluntary simplicity, etc.) which would suppose normative and performative behaviour situated on another level and could have meaning in such a system. An itinerant life is, on the contrary, a situation which is directly related to the constraints of existence in our contemporary societies.

If this absence of normative and performative competence seems to correspond to objective criteria, acknowledgement of one's own lack of competence is not easily done and really means that one's identity is at stake. To account for these difficulties, David A. Snow and Léon Anderson (1987) have identified three broad categories of personal strategies which aim to bridge the gap between the perceived identity and the identity actually lived: recourse to mythical narratives, aloofness, elevation of the itinerant life.

However, normative social expectations are not confined to only positive aspects. Although it is rarely expressed in such a way, survival is a powerful social norm, nobody expects homeless people to commit suicide or let themselves die of hunger or cold. Thus there are infra-perceptual norms with regard to the preservation of one's own life. In certain extreme situations the respect of these norms demands real exploits from the performative point of view: finding accommodation or shelter for the night or the week ahead; begging and managing to convince different types of people to give money; satisfying one's needs for alcohol or drugs; avoiding the cold, police arrest, verbal or physical abuse. Success in each of these situations requires skills, knowledge, judgement, in short, competence and this is the condition upon which the survival of these people depends.

Homeless people constantly find themselves in paradoxical situations: the skills that they use to live and survive on a daily basis are judged to be transgressive from the point of view of explicit social norms, yet they must resort to them to survive. Though the behaviour of homeless people seems to be subject to a certain unanimity as regards the way it is seen from the outside, the way the people themselves view their situations and the demands imposed by the need to survive is not monolithic. For example, for some, soliciting money is a definite performative skill, a sign of resourcefulness and autonomy in relation to the system, while others see it only as a sign of laziness.

The Place of the Street Outreach System in the Construction of the Homeless Identity

There is a broad consensus in social science about the fundamental role of social institutions in the construction of social and personal identities. However, this role can take various forms and contribute to the production of a plurality of identities for the social actors. Reflection on the role of institutions in the production of identity must also take into account the fact that not all of these identities are socially prestigious or aspired to, that they are potentially oppositional and that they are capable of leading to negative personal consequences. Thus, the street outreach system as a producer of identity cannot be compared to other social systems or institutions, not because it does not contribute to the production of social effects, but rather because its specificity shapes the people to whom it is addressed in a very particular way.

The Quebec street outreach system is made up of a range of community organisations assisting homeless people.[5] For the most part, these organisations base their work on an adapted model of social support, structured around the stabilisation, reassurance and socialisation of the homeless (Roy, Rozier and Langlois, 1998). Regular hours, the possibility of meeting people you know, the reforming of habits, the permanency of the centres and of the teams of social workers and ease of access constitute different aspects of the stabilisation objective. This response to essential needs (food, clothing, shelter, care, etc.), should make homeless people feel more secure and protected both from the uncertainties of a life of deprivation and from a certain level violence related to life on the street. The frequentation of the community organisations should put a stop to isolation by the development of interpersonal ties both between the homeless people themselves and the social workers. The community organisations seek to play a role in both primary and secondary socialisation through support activities and also through recreational activities (visits to the cinema, billiards, bowling, summer camps, dances).

Through their interventionist approach (stabilisation, reassurance, socialisation), the community organisations constitute important anchorage points for the homeless. So paradoxically, though the aim is social and professional reinsertion, autonomy and the taking of responsibility for oneself on the physical and psychological level, with the very existence of the network creating the conditions for insertion, the environment is one which is closed in on itself, that of the community services, and identification with the homeless figure is encouraged.

Identity: Proximity and Distance in the Discourse of Social Workers

Finally, it is important to look at the discourse used by the social workers of these community organisations and examine the role it plays in the identity construction process of homeless people. Roughly speaking, the philosophy advanced is expressed by a holistic type of approach to the person. This approach leaves much room for adaptability, flexibility, informality, and adopts a particular form depending on the specific characteristics of the people met. Thus, it is the intervention method, which must adapt to the needs, individual rhythms and the demands of the homeless people and not the reverse. Respect for others, the according of status to the capabilities of the individual and the search for how a person's potential can be used, are expounded as being central elements of the intervention process. The social workers wish to establish a reciprocal relationship with the people they receive and seek to portray themselves as an available resource person rather than as someone in a position of authority. The ability to establish a relationship of trust is an element unanimously maintained by the various services and the social workers. The latter find themselves, or are placed, in a position which offers up a figure for identification, a significant other image of father, sister, friend, etc.

These choices, with regard to the intervention philosophy, are coherent with a social support approach, but lead to several questions and contradictions. The desire to establish a reciprocal relationship and the fact of coming to represent an identification figure cause a discrepancy to be introduced between the message broadcast and the message received. The humanist approach, the wish to recognise people in their totality demands the highlighting of similarities and the playing down of differences between the social worker and the homeless person. Through empathy with the homeless, and because it is thought that a reciprocal relationship requires discourse to be on an egalitarian level, social workers can be heard to say to homeless people: 'we are all alike'; 'I can understand your distress because we have all experienced this'; 'the stakes and issues of life are the same for everybody'. Because they are seeking to ease the sufferings of the homeless and to restore their confidence, social workers accord the homeless lifestyle status. The skills developed by homeless people are recognised by a positive evaluation of the strategies that they use to survive.

The hypothesis could be made that this intervention approach disturbs the points of reference of the homeless person's identity. Firstly, the confusion of roles and the role of identification that represents the social worker as a friend, father, etc., is, to say the least, problematic: if all positions and roles are interchangeable, why is it that 'it is me rather than the social worker who is on the street'? Next, through the explicit wish to respect the other and his or her choices, the conferring of prestige to life on the street, and to the system of ingenuity that this supposes, is perceived by the homeless person as an encouragement to remain there. In fact, several social workers do not permit themselves to influence homeless people in their life courses because they are convinced that the ways of getting off the street (local authority housing, shelters, small, inner-city hotels) are not real alternatives, or because they do not accept that they have the legitimacy to do such a thing. Many social workers see themselves as someone who accompanies, whose function is to minimise the risks and the consequences of homelessness, and they reject the model of the professional social worker. Finally, the discourse developed by social workers can lead to the belief that living conditions are of little importance, once people adopt a positive and proactive attitude; in short, that they are not central to the definition, transformation and maintenance of individual identities.

The combination of these elements (the confusion of roles, the conferring of status on the itinerant lifestyle, negation of objective living conditions) creates a marked disjunction in the homeless person. He or she is effectively grappling with contradictory messages, making a coherent definition of self difficult. Paradoxically, the messages sent reinforce the individual responsibility of homeless people by recognising them as actors in their own lives, though they do not have the means to realise or assume their choices. If we are alike, and identification with the social worker occurs positively, why persist in the street outreach system? In this scenario, homeless people experience even more strongly the feeling of failure at being where they are, as they do not have the power to change their lives nor the means at their disposal to live any other way. Their life perspective is limited to the homeless network, with a confused status-conferring discourse coming from the subject of identification (the social worker) and a denigrating, even stigmatising discourse coming from various authorities of normative production.

Continuity of Identities and Survival?

It can be stated that, and all writers agree on this matter, identity is not constructed definitively, but it is redefined at various stages in life and that our identities are multiple. The identity issue, having fuelled scientific literature for decades, shows particular specificities in the case of homeless people because of their objective living conditions. Though they mark transformations and reconstructions of identity, they do not have a homogenous effect, moreover, not more than for any other group or population. Various strategies are used by homeless people and various meanings given to life on the street.

Within the scope of this text we have considered the process of the construction of a homeless identity from some of the factors contributing to the renegotiation of such an identity: objective living conditions, categorisation, the development of skills, the role of social institutions, the discourse of people offering their help.

This is not an exhaustive list, but examination of these factors has enabled some of the effective mechanisms to be understood. However, we need to continue this reflection and to try to identify still more precisely the critical points or stages at which partial and temporary adaptation, because of the special situation of survival, is transformed into a new identity, which then tends to become fixed. In this respect, one of the important elements of identification with the itinerant way of life is the duration: the more time that is spent living on the streets, the stronger the homeless identity becomes (Snow and Anderson, 1987).

A radical change in living conditions and fast and effective action to help homeless people off the street are the conditions necessary to avoid the institution of a process of identity transformation. Although not sufficient in itself, getting off the street and away from an objective survival situation is the essential basis for the fostering of the idea of integration and for the renegotiation of an 'identity for oneself' and an 'identity for others', thereby disposing of the homeless identity.

Notes

1   In the study of the health of itinerant people in the city of Toronto, it is reported that 40% of the people interviewed had been victims of a physical assault during the course of the last year (Ambrosio, Baker, Crowe and Hardill, 1992). American work also shows a high incidence of rape among itinerant people (St-Lawrence and Brasfield, 1995).

2   It is generally acknowledged that this is an important phenomenon though research results vary regarding the extent of these problems amongst the itinerant population.

3   In the latter case, it is known that imprisonment with its strict rules of behaviour and numerous restrictions is the very reason for the increased risk of the transmission of HIV/Aids and of hepatitis (unprotected sexual practices associated with the need for money and drugs, as well as intravenous drug use). (Feldman and Miller, 1998; Ministère de la santé et des services sociaux, 1997; Jurgens and Gilmore, 1994).

4   During the various interviews that we conducted we heard people describe themselves as: 'borderline', emotionally dependent, manic-depressive, bulimic-anorexic, drug-addicted or 'hooked', as 'junkies', squatters, dancers, nomads, artists, etc.

5   In the greater Montreal area alone, there are more than 120 organisations dedicated to helping homeless people. Each of these organisations offers a range of services to a different clientele (young people, women, men, etc.) and addresses a different problem (alcoholism, drug abuse, mental health, etc.). See the *Répertoire des ressources communautaires pour personnes itinérantes dans le Grand Montréal*, 2000, published by the Centre de référence du Grand Montréal et la Régie régionale des services de santé et services sociaux de Montréal-Centre.

References

Ambrosio, E., Baker, D., Crowe, C. and Hardill, K. (1992), *The Street Health Report: A Study of the Health Status and Barriers to Health Care of Homeless Women and Men in the City of Toronto*, Street Health, Toronto.

Anderson, R. (1996), 'Homeless Violence and the Informal Rules of Street Life', *Journal of Social Distress and the Homeless*, Vol. 5(4).

Boydell, K.M., Goering, P. and Morrell-Bellai, T.L. (2000), 'Narrative of Identity: Re-presentation of Self in People Who are Homeless', *Qualitative Health Research*, Vol. 10(1).

Brassard, R. and Cousineau, M.M. (2000), 'Victimisation et prise en charge des itinérants. Entre aide et contrôle', in D. Laberge (éd.), *L'Errance urbaine*, Éditions MultiMondes, Sainte-Foy.

Desjarlais, R. (1999), 'The Makings of Personhood in a Shelter for People Considered Homeless and Mentally Ill', *Ethos*, Vol. 27(4).

Drogoul, F. (1996), 'Psychiatrie de la précarité et de la misère', *La revue du praticien*, 46.

Dubar, C. (1995), *La Socialisation. Construction des identités sociales et professionnelles*, Éditions Armand Colin, Paris.

Dubar, C. (1999), *La Crise des identités. L'interprétation d'une mutation*, Presses universitaires de France, Paris.

Farrington, A. and Robinson, P.W. (1999), 'Homelessness and Strategies of Identity Maintenance: A Participant Observation Study', *Journal of Community and Applied Social Psychology*, Vol. 9(3).

Feldman, D.A. and Miller, J.W. (eds) (1998), *The Aids Crisis: A Documentary History*, Greenwood Press, Westport.

Jurgens, R. and Gilmore, N. (1994), 'Prisons et divulgation des renseignements médicaux. Analyse juridique et éthique', *Criminologie*, Vol. XXVII(2).

Landreville, P., Laberge, D. and Morin, D. (1998), 'La criminalisation et l'incarcération des personnes itinérantes', *Nouvelles pratiques sociales*, Vol. 11(1).

Marks, S.M., Taylor, Z., Burrows, N.R. and al. (2000), 'Hospitalization of Homeless Persons with Tuberculosis in the United States', *American Journal of Public Health*, Vol. 90(3).

Mercier, C. (1993), *Toxicomanie et itinérance. Recension des écrits*, RISQ, Montréal.

Ministère de la santé et des services sociaux (1997), *Des priorités nationales de santé publique 1997-2002*, Gouvernement du Québec, Québec.

Novac, S., Brown, J. and Gallant, G. (1999), *Perdues dans la jungle de la rue. Une décennie de changements pour les femmes sans abri à long terme*, SCHL, Ottawa.

Pollak, M. (1990), *L'Expérience concentrationnaire. Essai sur le maintien de l'identité sociale*, Éditions Métailié, Paris.

Power, R., French, R., Connelly, J. and al. (1999), 'Health, Health Promotion, and Homelessness', *British Medical Journal*, Vol. 318.

Roy, S., Rozier, M. and Langlois, P. (1998), 'Les interventions des centres de jour. Des pratiques diversifiées d'un modèle spécifique d'accompagnement social', *Nouvelles pratiques sociales*, Vol. 11(1).

Sainsaulieu, R. (1987), *Identité et relation de travail*, Éditions Privat, Toulouse.

Snow, D.A. & Anderson, L. (1987), 'Identity Work among Homeless: The Verbal Construction and Avowal of Personal Identities', *American Journal of Sociology*, Vol. 92 (6).

Stein, J.A., Andersen, R., Koegel, P. and Gelbert, L. (2000), 'Predicting Health Services Utilization among Homeless Adults: A Prospective Analysis', *Journal for Health Care for the Poor and Underserved*, Vol. 11(2).

St-Lawrence, J.S. and Brasfield, T.L. (1995), 'HIV Risk Behavior among Homeless Adults', *AIDS Education and Prevention*, Vol. 7(1).

Tolomiczenko, G.S. and Goering, P.N. (1998), 'Pathways into Homelessness: Broadening the Perspective', *Psychiatry Rounds*, Vol. 2(8).

Chapter 9

Social Action and Domination

Franz Schultheis

Even though the issue of domination in the social relationship to vulnerability has been raised many times in theoretical approaches and historical analyses of social politics, it has rarely been the object of systematic empirical analyses. The little input that has taken place has mostly been inspired by interactionism or phenomenology, and the notion itself of domination too often remains locked into the idea of methodological individualism. Two individuals are brought together – a vulnerable person and someone who is supposed to help – in a situation of direct communication and negotiation, whilst the institutional setting, the political and ideological issues of the measures deployed, the specific strategies, social and cultural characteristics of those seeking help, are widely disregarded, though they all play a part in the production of the effects of the social action.

This chapter will try then to provide some theoretical reflections on the theme proposed by this book, with a sort of thematic highlighting of a piece of research centring on the German social security system's taking charge of poor, vulnerable people at risk (Schultheis, 1999). This research was of a pluri-methodological nature and included, among other things, ethnographic fieldwork over a period of several months in the form of practical work experience in a Social Security Office in a town in southern Germany. This enabled us to follow closely all sorts of exchanges – linguistic, material, symbolic – between those seeking help and the professional actors of the office.

The Catch-All Character of the Categories of Social Law

What was striking from the first day was the miscellaneous nature of the forms taken by what we here call vulnerability: stepping behind a counter-window in such an institution enables you to see, in just one morning, a procession of subjects, or clients with such varying circumstances and life courses, for whom suffering and misery take such different forms and, above all, have such different causes, that the only common denominator appears to be the fact that they find themselves in a juridical-administrative definition of being on the poverty line. Everyone sitting on the waiting room benches has come to claim the help due to those whose disposable income is situated below this poverty line – the cause, the origins, etc. of this situation are only of indirect interest. Hence, we are confronted with a non-causal and non-categorical conception of poverty, or of vulnerability, with a catch-all logic. The sociological observer, who shares this social universe by standing behind the counter of an institution such as this, comes face to face with an extremely differentiated population. In a single morning, we saw a long-term unemployed person, a physically handicapped person in her wheelchair, a father who was the head of a large family and whose salary was insufficient to support the family, an elderly lady with an inadequate pension, a young person with psychiatric problems who had just been discharged from a psychiatric hospital, a young girl of 18 wanting to leave the family home and set up on her own, without having the necessary resources, a businessman who had gone bankrupt, a young doctoral student without a grant, who came to ask for help with her upkeep to be able to finish her thesis, a young drug addict, a young woman, head of a single-parent household with her baby in her arms, and finally, a homeless person who came to get his daily allowance of 15 marks.

In short, each person had an individual destiny and a personal biography which was apparently irreducible, unique and incomparable to others and, despite everything, they all shared a common fate: a lack of financial resources, economic insecurity, an absence of adequate individual resources, or primary solidarity to be able to deal with their fragile situation, and they had all resorted to social security, with all of the stigma and symbolic sufferings involved in such a step.

Amongst this population, gathered together in a single juridical-bureaucratic, catch-all category, we came across a group of people who seemed particularly interesting, given that they were the target of a global, not to say total, social care programme. They were pregnant women in a 'conflict of pregnancy' situation, whose specific vulnerability seemed to be of very particular interest to the political decision-makers.

A Special Programme to Combat a Particular Form of Vulnerability

The model called 'Mother and Child' was set up in 1975, following the conclusions of a piece of research carried out by a group of scientific experts consisting of psychologists, ethologists, educationalists and paediatricians. These experts were charged with the scientific supervision of a sociopolitical experiment in Waldshut, a small town in the south of Germany.

A report, written by one of its proponents on the occasion of the tenth anniversary of the creation of this allowance, stresses the 'scientific' character of this sociopolitical measure and praises a 'philanthropic' couple who greatly contributed to the success of the model – Mr Hassenstein, a paediatrician from Freiburg, and his wife. According to this report, Mr and Mrs Hassenstein had not only supplied the basic theoretical model of this original measure, but had also supervised its implementation.

Having had access to this report, these comments aroused our curiosity and, after a bibliographic search, we found a publication by the two main authors of the

'Programm Mutter und Kind' which bore the title *What Children Are Owed*. This work proved to be very significant, as it explained the philosophy and the logic of a new type of political control of family life. On the basis of the dyad 'mother and child' as an 'irreplaceable anthropological constant', the two authors explain that the delegation of the maternal functions to a third party, even if this means the child's grandmother, must be avoided at all costs. Even the mother's part-time absence can result in 'psychological deprivation' for the child and have disastrous consequences (juvenile delinquency, delays in psychological development, etc.). Which is why they present their 'mother and child' model as a sociopolitical approach, all the more operative to avoid such risks because it addresses a family type which is 'deficient' and 'incomplete', leading to a special kind of socioeducational supervision.

Thus, from the beginning, this programme was conceived as an institutional measure capable of, at least partially, restoring the classic family order endangered by the advent of women wage earners, and the drift towards a socialisation of the work of reproduction, judged 'disastrous' by the two authors. The model implemented thus made a public guarantee of a minimum income for pregnant women agreeing to participate in this experimentation for a period of three years after the birth of their child. Moreover, they would have to devote themselves uniquely to their educational tasks and give up any employment they may have had outside the home.

The absence of any concern with the return of the beneficiaries to the world of work is characteristic of the sociopolitical practice, and the ideological finality of the 'programme'. Furthermore, it included socioeducational measures, aiming to promote 'the best possible' educational practice of the participants, thanks to systematic supervision by midwives, paediatricians, social workers and psychologists. Participation in this educational programme was obligatory and aimed, as its scientific promoters stressed, to avert the negative social effects of the deficient educational competence, characteristic of single mothers. The model 'Mutter und Kind', created at the very same time as the liberalisation of abortion in the Federal Republic of Germany, also explicitly aimed to motivate 'lone' pregnant women to 'choose the child', and to abandon the idea of an abortion thanks to the possibility of being taken care of financially for a period of three years.

Here, we are faced with a very special form of state intervention in family affairs: the welfare state offers a guaranteed family income to pregnant women deciding against a termination of pregnancy, and declaring themselves ready to limit themselves exclusively and continually to work within the family.

Thus, the sociopolitical care programme implemented in the Land of Baden-Württemberg made provision for state benefits to be paid over a period of three years to mothers-to-be who decided against an abortion, on condition that they live alone, or more precisely, without a spouse, that they give up any professional activity they may have had, and that they also agree to participate in a sociopsychological care programme. Through a sociohistorical reconstruction of how this was implemented, by analysing oral sources (informants) and written sources (political and administrative documents), we saw that the promoters of this sociopolitical action model seemed to be thinking of, and planning for, a form of pluri-dimensional vulnerability, functioning rather like a kaleidoscope: each turn gave another configuration, another definition of the social problem being targeted.

At one point those who invented the measure seemed to be concerned with the potential termination of pregnancy under the social clause (distress), and thus the vulnerability of the foetus; at another it was the sociopsychological fragility of the women, as mothers-to-be in a conflict of pregnancy situation; at another it was the material insecurity of the future single-parent family (no male breadwinner) that seemed to be the focus of the social issue or, at yet another it was a matter of worrying about the vulnerability of the child to be born into a single-parent family, a family-type openly shown to be deficient by the scientific promoters of the programme.

The Social Invention of a Particular Model to Combat a Particular Form of Vulnerability

The model was drawn up by a group of psychologists, psychoanalysts, educationalists and social workers, mandated by the government of the Land of Baden-Württemberg, and it claimed to offer systematic and scientifically-based care for the forms of vulnerability outlined above. This makes the measure particularly interesting for a critical analysis of the construction process for a particular social problem. According to our hypothesis, social intervention in a situation of vulnerability, which omits, not to say suppresses, the issue of domination with a well-meaning, but stereotyped conception of the clientele targeted, gives rise to a whole series of unplanned, unwanted and uncontrolled effects. These unplanned effects result from the juxtaposition in the programme of the imposition of a way of being in a sort of supervisory hothouse (comfortable form of social domination as regards material living conditions, but burdensome as regards the day-to-day life of the women obliged to agree to remain 'alone', and with a considerable effect on their life projects and biographies) on the one hand, and on the other, the strategies of the clients who, as we were able to see, often very actively contributed to the production and reinforcement of the effects of the domination that they were then subjected to, apparently in a purely passive way. We are thus looking, not at the psychology, but at the sociology of 'victims', and the idea dear to Max Weber and Pierre Bourdieu, according to which people who are dominated contribute to their own domination by their acceptance of a dominant vision of the social world.

The Many Hidden Facets of a Falsely Homogenous Category of Vulnerability

The systematic study of the files of the social services Youth Department showed that this social action programme concerned lone mothers from the least privileged social strata (46%, with an average age of 21), but also women having been employed in jobs requiring a certain level of skill (46%, with an average age of 26), and also a relatively important group of women having a university diploma (8%, with an average age of 29). The social heterogeneousness of this population ran counter to the 'figure of misery' stereotype that the promoters of this 'programme' had in mind. This reminds us of the uncertain character of the definition of a 'social problem', accompanying all measures of this type. Above all, this specific situation constitutes a real experiment of the strategies that social actors use when faced with measures aiming to simultaneously control and help them.

All of the mothers, and particularly those with a high cultural capital, spontaneously criticised themselves for their 'excessive fixation' on their child. They all claimed to be psychologically 'overwhelmed' by the family tasks as they had been imposed on them, even though they were their sole occupation. At the same time, all of them insisted on the incompatibility of the education of a child and a professional occupation, even part-time. Thus, the definition of the maternal role as 'total social role', to use Erving Goffman's phrase, and as imposed by the programme, goes hand in hand with an internalisation of the educational model, and of the familial philosophy inherent to this type of social intervention. All of the women interviewed showed this type of 'moral and logical conformism' as expressed by Émile Durkheim (1975), and everything happens as if the sociopolitical supervision were as effective as masculine domination in the relationships of couples under the conditions of traditional family life, producing and reproducing a certain conception of the place of women in the social world. These women told us at length about their feelings of inadequacy and guilt with regard to their child, whilst insisting on the fact that the latter was the exclusive focus of their preoccupations and occupations. Even towards the end of the third year, the mothers interviewed told us that they had not taken any steps at all to find work. They appeared anxious, even panic-stricken as soon as the interview focused on this question. The conditions of existence in this type of laboratory, imposing the exclusivity of a dyadic relationship with the child, the loss of all social contact with the outside world, plus the global care programme led to a sort of systematic repression of everything that could happen afterwards; and in actual fact, a very large number of the recipients became dependent on social security: for the women without qualifications and those with a university diploma, the rate was even almost 50%. Those with an 'average' level of professional skill fared better.

**The Presuppositions and Unconsidered Aspects of the Sociopolitical
Programme Aimed for**

Looking at the social consequences of this sociopolitical programme, it must be
remembered that they are not simply the result of a sort of dysfunctioning of a
measure which just needs a better 'running in' period and a few adaptations. On the
contrary, they seem to be a part of the presuppositions and preconstructions which
are at the root of this type of social action in the face of vulnerability. Amongst
these presuppositions, it is possible to pick out:

- The erroneous idea of the isolation of vulnerable women created by the
  meeting at the social security office window. As a paradigmatic configuration
  of an individualising vision of vulnerability, the encounter at the window runs
  the risk of losing sight of the forms of domination 'before protection', in
  relation to which public assistance can constitute a resource for liberating
  action. Many of the women questioned admitted to us that they had seen the
  programme as an unsuspected opportunity to escape, to free themselves from a
  suffocating marital life. It is these forms of masculine domination, endured by
  these women at their moment of greatest vulnerability, which pushed them into
  the arms of the promoters of the programme analysed.
- The illusion of purely passive entitlement, very frequent in social politics in
  general, and in social action dealing with vulnerability in particular, seems to
  have made a not inconsiderable contribution to the unleashing of the strategies
  deployed by the future clients of the programme who, depending on their
  circumstances and social profile, seemed to see very different opportunities in
  the offer they were made, and tried to use these opportunities to best advantage
  their respective future projects, even though the latter would too often prove to
  be illusory.
- Together with the two preceding presuppositions, a falsely coherent and
  unitary idea of the social profile of the clients contributed, as we were able to
  see, to the unawareness of the very strategic use made of the measures. Instead
  of representing a coherent social category, as the very idea of vulnerability and
  insecurity seems to suggest, the clientele we met showed great sociostructural
  differences and, depending on their social profile, a beneficiary of the
  programme could develop very particular strategies, and thus contribute to the
  production of effects which were difficult to foresee.
- Finally, we saw that different forms of omission, characteristic of the social
  action model analysed, were accompanied by a quasi-mechanical conception of
  the results to be produced by the sociopolitical intervention implemented. The
  contents of the official reports produced by the promoters of the programme
  made it clear that they were in a state of almost total ignorance, or misappraisal
  of the day-to-day life of the women supervised by their model, and of which
  they vaunted the benefits, leaving aside all of the contradictions, sufferings and
  harmful effects that we encountered in the stories of the women to whom we
  spoke.

In short, it seems that this is a specific example of the recurrence of the social risks that this type of care engenders. The strategies of the women in the face of this measure differed according to their social profile. Whilst the women from the more modest environments saw the measure as a substantial material help, those who been employed in a skilled job seemed to see it more as a good opportunity to obtain a prolonged maternity leave, and as an easier way of realising their family project. But it is in the women with university diplomas that the most important biographical changes can be observed. All of them claimed to have lived with a spouse until their entry into the programme, and that this relationship had been unsatisfactory, even intolerable. These women had perceived the 'programme' as an escape route, enabling them to 'make a fresh start', despite the risk of finding themselves in a situation of long-term dependence on social services. Though Émile Durkheim (1975) was certainly right when he declared in his lecture on 'La famille conjugale' that the state was going to become a factor with an ever more direct role to play in domestic life, he was only thinking of the constitutional state, which by a whole series of changes to family rights has, in effect, helped to radically transform family relationships by removing the institutional bases of the patriarchal and authoritarian family model, and by granting all family members the status of autonomous holders of rights. He could not have foreseen to what extent the modern state, in its more and more accomplished form of welfare state, would play such a role a century later. Though, for the most part, the two forms of state intervention in family affairs take the form of greater equality and a reduction of masculine and paternal domination, they can, as we have tried to show, be paid for at the price of the establishment of new forms of dependence and domination.

References

Durkheim, É. (1975), 'La famille conjugale', in É. Durkheim, *Textes III*, Presses universitaires de France, Paris.
Schultheis, F. (1999), *Familien und Politik*, Universitätsverlag Konstanz, Konstanz.

Chapter 10

Facing Social Vulnerability and Coming Through: Towards a Theory of Weak Acting

Marc-Henry Soulet

This concluding text aims to think through the idea of weak acting and to add a dual reflection, carried out together with Vivianne Châtel, on the notions of facing things and coming through, after having had the way prepared by the preceding chapters. More precisely, this first outline of a theorisation of weak acting, despite the risks of incompleteness and weakness hidden in such an exercise, seeks to examine the existence of specific forms of acting in a context of vulnerability. In other words, how does a situation of vulnerability influence the nature of the acting? What forms does acting actually take when the conditions of 'ordinary' acting are disturbed? In short, what is acting in a situation of important material and symbolic deprivation where even the possibility of acting is difficult?[1]

In order to provide answers to such questions and to draw the outlines of acting in a situation of vulnerability, we shall endeavour to delineate the typical frameworks of acting and to indicate the ways in which weak acting both borrows and distances itself from other forms of acting, before trying to depict the forms of this particular kind of acting.

False Starts and a True Enigma

But, first and foremost, it is important to explain the premises on which this examination is based. This will also provide the opportunity to stress what this text does not pretend to explain, to highlight the key notions that it takes in its support by distinguishing them from other approaches and uses, and to better formulate the problem in order to isolate the enigma around which it is built.

1. First of all, the word weak in the term 'weak acting' does not describe the result of the action, but the nature of the action, which is supposedly altered because of a particular context. That an action is understood to be weak because it does not achieve its goal or because the results obtained are of little importance or interest does not of concern here. Moreover, the fact that it is the nature of the action which is being focused upon explains the

substantive use of the verb, acting, rather than the substantive action which could risk overshadowing the essence of the process in favour of evaluation of the result. The descriptive weak thus is then intended to qualify particular characteristics related to the actual unfolding of the action.

2. Similarly, the action of coming through does not refer to any kind of substance of the person acting. So, it is not a question of seeking, or of postulating, an essential quality that a person who has come through is actually in possession of, such as a notion like resilience would suggest (Cyrulnik, 1999; Manciaux, 2001), this capability of a person to not let themselves be demoralised and to overcome difficult ordeals. In other words, whatever the differences between the actors, in terms of skills, motivations, psychological resources..., it is important to be interested in something other than just the qualities possessed by the actors. Not only because of the risks of reification of the fact of having successfully coped with the situation in the consequently naturalised 'strength' of the actor – 'Only the strong make it through' – but also, and especially, because it is the ways of acting in a situation of vulnerability that are at the centre of this examination, rather than the reasons that explain the fact of having managed to successfully deal with such a situation.

3. Here, reference to the action does not refer to some sort of a minimalist dimension of a reaction to an order which is imposed, to an action so constrained that its only affect would be an adaptation to the situation. There is no corrective dimension involved in the idea of weak acting. Quite the contrary, it must be borne in mind that it is not qualified by the result, and that the point is that the result can be 'strong'. It is not so much a question of providing a normative connotation of positivity, in the opinion an outside observer, or of satisfaction, in the opinion of the actor him / herself, but much rather of stressing that what interests us here is the fact that the acting in question can be transforming. In other words, as it is not the result itself which is the object of this examination, the reasoning must be pushed to its extremes and we must not only say that it may be that the result obtained, despite the 'weak' character of the action, may change the situation in which the acting originated, but also that it is heuristic to think of the terms weak and transforming as being coexistent. It thus becomes, in a logic of thinking to the extremes, pertinent to postulate that the nature of weak acting can be all the better seen because the result of it is strong, i.e. it leads to a transformation of whatever was making the situation lived a vulnerable one.

4. At the same time, it is not at all a question of twisting things semantically in order to vindicate weakness, to make it into a more or less strategic weapon, nor is this a tactic to invert stigma and still less an exhortation that the weak should surpass themselves (Jollien, 1999). If we can easily imagine the importance of the production of meaning in the overcoming of ordeals of suffering (insubstitutability and incommunicability), the fact

remains that, in the analysis of what concerns us here, we must beware of falling into feeling sorrowful and of taking weakness as a resource. This option would, in fact, amount to essentializing the action in the will born of adversity, even to making failure and suffering a condition of redemption. Nevertheless, we must draw upon this surpassing of the reduction in the power of acting, which is born of suffering, for one of the acting conditions, because of the working upon oneself that takes place, the working upon the definition of the situation in which one finds oneself and on one's relation to the world. Summed up magnificently by the expression of Jacques Roux 'Make suffering a place of acting' (Roux, 1997).

5. Coming through is not a reference to some imaginary transition from an undignified or unacceptable condition to an idealised or socially recognised status, to the idea of becoming a figure who is no longer marginalised and who then enters into ordinary social relationships. Without wishing to deny the interest of the work which has taken this as its subject (Castel, 1999; Bergier, 1996), and even acknowledging how much this theorisation outline owes to it, it must, however, be recognised that such work has had too great a tendency to lead to an interpretation of exceptionality. Like it or not, we are obliged to admit that a heroic image is often conveyed in the background. These paths to a way out, because they are seen as being movements in the direction of a return (to normal?), as journeys of re-integration, as obstacle courses, suppose, in order to be observable and analysable, starting with extreme cases. In a way, the theoretical-political examination rejoins the methodology procedure to root the act of coming through in situations which are extreme (where it is necessary to have touched rock bottom, or almost), but which are limited by definition. What is aimed at here is, on the contrary, to try to use the recourse to the notion of coming through for less extraordinary situations, situations which, all in all, are more banal, though problematic for the individual caught up in them.

6. The expression situation or context of vulnerability is based on a broad conception of this term. However, the notion will not be extended so far as to lose all of its heuristic character, i.e. up to and including our vulnerable condition of being, that is, because we are human and therefore mortal, we are essentially vulnerable, or because we are supposed to be autonomous, we are exposed to risk. Likewise, vulnerability will not be limited here to spheres of poverty, of material or symbolic deprivation. The focus is not the person who – or the social category which – has been made vulnerable. This is certainly to avoid any exaggerated compassion, but especially, on a more basic level, to signify a fundamentally different analytical approach. By mobilising the notion of vulnerability, we do not wish to stress, as is most often done, the possibility of a particular group being affected by some risk, thus becoming a group at risk and, if the group is then affected by that risk, becoming a group which has been made vulnerable, reified in a

particular status of established fragility.[2] In such a schema, the emphasis is placed on variables which are exogenous or endogenous to the group, qualifying it as being exposed to a risk and therefore vulnerable (as represented archetypally the category of single-parent families), thus contributing to the reification of vulnerability as a state, even to the incorporation of a status of a vulnerable person, when it is not purely and simply a question of identifying individual psycho-biological capabilities, by stating the inequalities of individuals vis-à-vis risk, which enables certain child psychiatrists to distinguish hyper-vulnerable, pseudo-vulnerable, invulnerable and non-vulnerable children (Anthony, 1987).

7.   Similarly, despite its interest, a problematisation such as that of Robert Castel, which categorises vulnerability as an intermediate state between integration and disaffiliation, understood as an 'area of turbulence (...) which is characterised (...) by precariousness in the relationship to work and by a fragility of relational supports' (Castel, 1992), is removed from what serves as a basis for the analysis outlined here. *A contrario* to what the title might let us suppose, in this work by Robert Castel, vulnerability is understood as an area between integration and exclusion, the importance of which is on the increase because of the weakening of systems of social protection. The resurgence of vulnerability conveys, in this theoretical construction, a new condition linked to the 'destabilisation of the stable' which is characteristic of contemporary societies. Remarkably conducted as this analysis is, the notion of vulnerability therein is more indicative of a state of being undermined and weakened, explicative of the problems of contemporary societies, than of the typical situation of the weakening of the frameworks that we shall here try to identify as a place for a possibly different mode of action.

8.   The vulnerability on which our attempt to clarify weak acting is based is to be thought of in a relational sense, connecting an individual having particular characteristics and circumstances which in turn have their own particular characteristics. It is a question of an interactional and relative notion. Vulnerability in itself does not exist, no more than does being vulnerable in oneself, but individuals are vulnerable vis-à-vis certain circumstances, in certain conditions. Obviously, it is not a matter of naively thinking that all things are equal. The 'chances' of one day finding oneself in a position of vulnerability are not the same for everyone. A structural dimension is involved, related to the position of individuals in the social structure as regards some of its characteristic sectors, such as present-day work or education, for example. Lode Walgrave (1992) undertook the analysis of the consequences of this unequal exposure of individuals to social institutions. This resulted in his forming the notion of societal vulnerability to account for the fact that, structurally, the inequalities accumulated and led to making these individuals profoundly vulnerable, not only by not permitting them to benefit from the positive side of social

institutions, but also by confronting them with discriminatory reasoning and control. But however important this inequality may be, vis-à-vis the risks of being made vulnerable, because of the very functioning of society, or of some of its principal institutions, it does not help us to understand what the peculiarity of the fact of being made vulnerable is.

9. Vulnerability is used here less as an objet, *a fortiori* as a state, than as a context of action, as a situation presenting singular characteristics that affect the individuals who find themselves involved in them. A situation of vulnerability is in this sense to be understood as marked by a weakening of the ordinary, stable structures of action, as if hit by a faltering of the normative frameworks on the basis of which the previous and regular, in a word, normal, action resources had been built.[3] To put it another way, in our opinion, vulnerability designates a context in which the rules of the game are no longer clear and the social norms no longer coherent. Neither the one nor the other are actually clear to the actors, nor are they sufficiently present in the minds of the individuals, to take an expression of Émile Durkheim, because they are no longer congruent with the situation, because they are obsolete, invalidated or simply foreign, non communal, non shared. In a way, this type of situation nears what Raymond Boudon (1974) calls structures of interdependence in which a system of roles regulating the relations between individuals does not exist, unlike structures of interaction which are codified and signposted by roles making the mutual and reciprocal actions of the actors predictable. Such a situation can be fundamentally identified as a breaking of routines, these regular, quasi-automatic actions, these means of organising, in a stabilised way, interactions between men and their human and material environment (Conein, 1998). However, this must not lead us to deduce that weak acting is be identified with a simple restoration of routines, characterising a capability of acting according to summaries of experience, exempting the actors of all planning or deliberation and allowing them to save themselves cognitive and physical effort. And this, quite simply, because the precise role of the routines is to render the interaction between man and his environment unproblematic. At best, they can be the result of weak acting, not its method, as the distinctive feature of weak acting is that it works in a problematic context. This rupture of regularities, in essence problematic because it makes the rules opaque, creates two major consequences. On the one hand, it produces unpredictability and uncertainty. As determination by the rules becomes less marked, it becomes difficult to foresee both the result of one's action and the return action of Others. But also, it proves difficult to attribute credit to other actors and to attribute an indubitable meaning to one's own will to act. In this sense, weak acting is 'a response of the actors to an uncertain and indeterminate situation' (Felouzis, 2001).[4] On the other hand, the resources so far possessed are no longer relevant to the situation; they become inadequate in relation to this new context. A

situation of vulnerability is marked by a deficit of resources, making the action risky so far as its results are concerned. More precisely, the problematic character of such a situation invalidates the previous resources, or reveals an absence of resources, making the possibility of acting difficult.[5] It is thus not so much a matter of charting a weakness or an absence of resources on the structural level, but rather of highlighting this weakness or this absence at a given moment, in a precise context. This is then how vulnerability must be understood, as being, above all, situational. This is the way in which the United States found itself in a situation of vulnerability following the attack of 11 September 2001 on the World Trade Center. Its fire-power was impressive, but it was turned towards an air attack from abroad. The kamikaze hijacking of airliners on American soil to attack ultra-protected targets invalidated all of the anti-missile batteries despite their being 'within rifle range' of these flying bombs. So, the American army, still largely based on the ideas of the cold war model, also found itself momentarily powerless, even though it was and still is the most powerful army on the planet, in the absence of a clearly identifiable enemy.

In view of this attempt at conceptual clarification, it is now possible to reformulate the main issue around which our attempt is structured. Is it possible to imagine a way of acting, i.e. one which transforms the situation and, is thus reflexive, which is not strategic due to a context which makes the work of projection impossible because of the uncertainty of the goals, the lack of durability of the norms and of the action frameworks, and the irrelevance of the resources?

Contextualising and Describing Weak Acting

To try to reply to the above, and thus to clarify what weak acting encompasses, it is important to start with the assumption made by Erhard Friedberg (1997) according to which action as a process cannot be thought of without setting it in a context which gives it meaning.[6] The action is in fact always mediated by a more or less coherent whole and given structure by games, the rules of which organise the interaction processes and, therefore, define it.

Typical Action Frameworks

Postulating that particular forms of acting may exist in a particular context, notably one marked by uncertainty of the rules and instability of the structures, implies, logically, admitting the existence of other contexts having other particular and distinct properties which would also affect the nature of the acting taking place within them. It is thus important, at this point of our attempt to clarify weak acting, to try to identify and to characterise the formal action frameworks which qualify the forms of acting. To do this, we can turn our thinking around and go back to the works of Émile Durkheim (1951), taking his logic of the societal configurations of excess and deficit of rules in his descriptions of forms of suicide, which he then used quasi-explicitly, to identify a normal societal model. For our part, and more modestly, we shall here seek to identify an action framework where normal rules are present and an action framework having an excess of rules, so that by contrast we can then describe an action framework with a rule deficit, and for each we shall try to highlight the specific forms of action.

1. The framework of normality, that of the sufficient, but not excessive presence, of norms and structures, the in-between model used by Émile Durkheim, can be designated the model of unstable stability. It presents itself as a reliable framework, allowing a minimum of predictability but sufficiently flexible to be able to evolve in accordance with the unfolding of the action, i.e. able to integrate the effects of the action and in a position to give a meaning to the very fact of acting. Risk, if it exists, is controlled; it is in fact related to the capability of acting on the world. The action is uncertain in its results, but it unfolds within a reassuring framework for the person acting. This framework is characterised by three main dimensions, which also constitute as many available resources, even if they are not always identified as such by the actors: 1) an ontological security, to use the expression of Anthony Giddens (1990), based on the feeling of the continuity of self and on the consciousness of the stability of the environment; 2) a supposition of autonomy of the actors, leading to imputation of responsibility, enabling the consequences of the actions undertaken to be assumed and recognition to be attributed; 3) a weak interdependence of the spheres of action, allowing a degree of balancing to take place as a function of the results of the actions, and allowing the actor not to be totally involved in his actions. Inside this action framework which resembles a near stationary equilibrium, the action must be reflexive. As the uncertainty is relative, i.e. it only concerns the result of the action, acting supposes working with risk while trying to control it. We are at the heart of a model where confidence appears central, confidence in the stability of the framework, confidence in the possibility of developing an action which will bring results, confidence in one's resources, but also where confidence is coupled with risk, as the latter is intimately linked to the capability of acting. The paradox of this middle-of-the-road framework, which could be considered normal in the statistical sense of the word, is that for acting to be possible there is a combination of a need for both stability and instability. For risk to be controllable, it is important for it to be set in a reliable framework, allowing a minimum of predictability. Consequently, acting can only take the form of a calculation, of a weighing up of what is possible as regards what is probable, as it will inescapably lead to a modification of the stability/instability relationship, strengthening certain spheres of everyday life and weakening others.

2. Paradoxically, the framework of excess, that of excessive constraints, can be described as structural stability. It is characterised by a large degree of routine, by a surfeit of rules in the organisation of everyday life, together with the unwavering continuity of the material and human environment, though this does not however exclude the possibility of being confronted by the arbitrariness of the rules or of the ways in which they are applied. Here we find ourselves, to use an expression of Émile Durkheim, in a fatalist configuration[7] which we can imagine as having either a negative connotation, for example a prison with rules that are too burdensome, or a positive connotation, such as some kind of Eden filled with an assured beatitude and thoughtless peace of mind (as found in sects). In these contexts of structural stability, the levers of action actually seem relatively limited or unusable, despite the existence of possible resources, insofar as action appears to be in vain vis-à-vis the stability of the context.[8] In this faith model, marked by the certainty that everything is stable, acting supposes the circumvention of certainty and consequently takes, first and foremost, the form of dissidence, implying breaking with the rules of the game and the changing of the action framework, or the steering of a delicate course, based on the diversion of the rules inside of the action framework imposed.[9] The total institution analysed by Erving Goffman (1961) very well illustrates both the framework of excess of constraint and the forms of action which result from it. An institution which takes responsibility for the totality of the dimensions of human life sees itself exposed to de-individualisation and to relational functionalism, the consequence of which is the creation of a parallel world by the people secluded in it, a world supported by antithetical values of personification and humanisation of relations.[10]

3. The deficit framework, that of the absence of rules giving rise to a lack of regulation, can be called structural instability. Uncertainty reigns supreme, and is in fact the only thing that is certain. The problem, in a way, is that of the certainty of the risk of the action frameworks breaking or being non-existent for the stabilising of the action, like the university, described as a weak institution by Georges Felouzis, or the organised anarchy of Erhard Friedberg (1997). Everything is shifting in the absence of explicit and durable norms. In the face of the arbitrariness of the situations, it consequently becomes difficult to make forecasts, to put forward activity sequences. This context of mistrust, characterised by the certainty that everything is uncertain and by an extreme lability of the codes and of the framework, can limit a person to resignation (acting becomes adapting oneself, making do) or else lead to a form of acting having at its centre the reduction of uncertainty, the reintroduction of predictability and the establishment of confidence in relationships to Others and to the institutions. Confidence thus resembles as much a goal as a means of acting. The problem, however, resides in the interdependence of the

spheres of action of the individuals placed in such circumstances. It is the whole of their person which is at stake in each action undertaken. This total intersecting of the spheres of action obviously makes the fact of acting very costly, but, paradoxically, can sometimes intensify the acting capability. Like the outcast analysed by Isabelle Taboada-Leonetti,[11] a surfeit of constraints, causing both the evanescence of ordinary points of reference and total uncertainty as to what tomorrow may bring because it reduces the objective possibilities and the scope of action, may push the individual to intensify his action capability. It is not a question here of listing the reserves of resistance that individuals are capable of mobilising in an inhuman context, but of emphasising the obligation of the actionalist strengthening of the action. The part of the actor, as it were, is increased in the individual when the constraints are such, be they too strong or totally non-existent, that the individual finds himself totally caught up in the interaction, wholly a part of the situation.[12] Consequently, the observable radicalisation of the action becomes a question of survival, or at least of the maintenance of the previous, vital commitments. When the individual is totally caught up in the game, when there is no escape, when there is nowhere left to move to seek other resources, his only alternatives are to abandon the game or to intensify his action capabilities.[13] However, contrary to the analysis made by Isabelle Taboada-Leonetti, strictly speaking, it is not possible to consider this type of action as resembling a strategic activity.[14] Clear evaluation of the constraints, formal identification of the resources and, even more so, the affirmation of explicit ends are quite simply not conceivable because of the very uncertainty of the context and because of the instability of the rules that prevail.

The typological characterisation of the action frameworks summarised in the table below is not sufficient in itself to enable us to understand all that the notion of weak acting entails. It merely helps to specify action contexts and to deduce the typical action categories from them. So now it is a question of trying to describe weak acting. By taking other forms of acting in their relation to certain action contexts and by borrowing from and distancing ourselves from these forms, we shall try to outline the possibility of a weak form of acting from questions born of its relationship to these other forms of acting. Our recourse to the latter does not mean that we intend to make an exhaustive survey, but rather that we intend to extract the main themes that characterise them in order to be able to examine the form of acting which takes place in a situation of vulnerability.

Table 10.1 Typical action frameworks

	Structural instability	Unstable stability	Structural stability
Context status	Certainty that everything is un-certain: mistrust	Relative uncertainty: confidence	Certainty that everything is stable: faith
Nature of the action	Acting supposes reducing the guaranteed un-certainty	Acting supposes working with risk while trying to control it	Acting supposes getting around certainty

Acting Categories

Strategic acting. This form of action, archetypical of the action framework of unstable stability, is based on a relationship of strength between two composed entities, which are identifiable and conscious of themselves and of the resources that they have at their disposal. To use the expression of Michel de Certeau (1984), they suppose 'an isolable subject of will and ability' of Another, but above all it imposes the forming of an own place for the gathering (or the capitalising) of resources for their subsequent re-use (or reinvestment). Working with space, as it isolates the places of the context, with time, as it supposes the withdrawal of the means from the context for their subsequent mobilisation elsewhere, strategic acting is carried by a goal independent of the circumstances, even transcending them. Strategic acting is projection and is thus not limited to the circumstances. In this sense, it is in essence not only transforming, as it is called upon to convert elements drawn from a past or present situation in a future situation, but also reflexive as this conversion supposes the conception of one's action and the appreciation of its partial effects under way. Hence, strategic acting asks of weak acting whether *it is possible to have a goal without strategy.*

Tactical acting. Complementary opposite of strategy for Michel de Certeau, tactical acting is expressly a part of the here and now, incapable as it is of constituting a place of its own or of isolating Another. Without any possibility at all of capitalising advantages, it consumes everything in the moment and is therefore strongly dependant on the circumstances. It is the situation which forms the whole of the action framework. Tactical acting cannot extend beyond the situation in which it takes place, it is 'knotted up in the context and cannot be detached from it' and is 'indissociable from the present instant, from particular circumstances and from a *way of doing*' (De Certeau, 1984).[15] All in all, it expresses a whole series of actions available to the weak person as there is no other place besides the place of the Other. It characterises a calculated action essentially determined by the absence of an own place. Georges Felouzis (2001) characterises tactical acting with four points: 1) It is exercised in a situation of great indeterminacy (the choices are thus dependent on the situation); 2) It is constructed as a function of the means and not of the ends; 3) It is the implementation of a practical imagination; 4) It is pre-strategic in the sense that the actors seek to construct objectives.[16] Tactical acting asks of weak acting whether a *transforming action can be rooted in circumstances.*

Makeshift. Characterises working with material or resources borrowed from a third party. It is first a question of acting by using, understood as a production, a way of employing products imposed by a dominant order, meaning making something out of something else. Subverting, not by rejecting, but by using for ends, and according to references foreign to the system that one cannot escape, with which one must compromise.[17] Makeshift in this sense means having to put together expedient materials, i.e. materials which one does not control and which thus make it unthinkable and impossible to effectively programme the action. This 'science of the concrete', close to the intuition spoken of by Claude Lévi-Strauss (1966), which attaches more importance to the event than to the structure, is born of the impossibility of foresight. And if there is creativity, it is imposed by the action context. In this sense, doing regularly takes the form of composition as it is, above all, a question of an adaptation to the situations lived. The need to compose and to adapt entails a great deal of flexibility and especially a capability to work on the event beyond the project.[18] Makeshift asks of weak acting whether *an action can be transforming when it is based on an absence of own resources, or rather, when the action takes its strength from resources which are foreign to the actor.*

Cunning. In this type of acting, the actor is a hypocrite (in the Greek sense of the word). He functions on another level, by metaphorizing a dominant order, by twisting the meaning, but without leaving the situation in which he actually finds himself. 'Cunning consists of corroding from the inside that which does not seem able to be attacked head on' (Balandier, 1977). Cunning echoes the Greek *Métis*, a form of intelligence and thought totally committed to the practical which 'is applies to situations which are transient, shifting, disconcerting and ambiguous, situations which do not lend themselves to precise measurement, exact calculation or rigorous logic' (Détienne and Vernant, 1991, 3-4). It is a way of knowing, a mental attitude and an intellectual behaviour, based on intuition, resourcefulness and a sense of opportunity. *Métis* knows how to recognise the favourable moment (*kairos*), seizing on a unique situation which will never again arise. It is based on the idea of scoring a success and is the opposite of *logos* and its pure rationality. Consisting of wiliness and trickery, it does not have its own place, it is 'the opportunity that makes the thief'. It draws its power from the gap between appearances and the social reality. It becomes a trap to deceive someone stronger (like Goupil does Isengrin). Thus it supposes a stronger other who is caught from within. Art of the weak, neither illegality, nor delinquency (Autès, 1999), it characterises an operating model which borrows from two registers: the facts, on the one hand, symbolic relationships on the other. Cunning asks of weak acting whether *a work of transformation can be based on a symbolic level without isolating Another.*

Rage. Characterised by the absence of a dominant to whom one can put a face, by the absence of an opponent, this form of acting does not have a situation-transforming dimension. It is precisely the absence of meaning of the situation lived which defines the actors, the impossibility of finding an explanation that refers to a defined social relationship or to a particular intentionality of society. Rage resembles an act of destruction, but especially an action on oneself, as destruction of self (Dubet, 1987). Rage asks of weak acting whether, *an action which has no opponent and which does not become destruction of self can be transforming.*

Resistance. This form of acting supposes an opponent against whom one can engage in a struggle. The civic disobedience of Gandhi, or the creative disobedience of Pierre-André Taguieff (2001, 11), resistance is always thought of in reference to an alternative. 'As there is no resistance or revolt without the regulating idea of the humanity or the society that is desirable.' Refusal and affirmation of a collective identity are in this sense indissociable. Resistance describes both a passive form of refusal (maintenance of the previous modes of expression and action) and an active form of creation of new social relationships (Soulet, 1980). It always concerns a way of acting of those dominated who, because of an identity through situations lived, become aware of a communal identity and thus develop a communal action. Resistance asks of weak acting whether, *an action can go beyond a situation by means of the dual capability of taking a stand and producing a new identity which is individually produced without the existence of an outside opponent.*

Thinking through Weak Acting

As we have tried to show in the introductory part of this text, our attempt at a theoretical construction is not meant to resemble an ontology of the person, whether resilient or otherwise, but a pragmatic examination of a way of acting constrained by the characteristics specific to situations of vulnerability. It is not a question of seeking an essential quality, a natural virtue, which could be attributed to this weak form of acting, but of looking at forms of doing which undergo a materialisation that can easily be specified.

The Outlines of Weak Acting

What is acting when it is confronted with indeterminacy as regards the ends and uncertainty as regards the means, when it concerns any member of society the moment that he finds himself placed in a situation having particular characteristics for him: a weakening of the frameworks and an evanescence of the resources, when he experiences:

contexts that appear to be tests to which the actors must respond rather than situations bound by a series of causes. (Dubet and Vérétout, 2001, 430-431)

When the situation does not allow for predictability, when the agent does not have relevant resources that can be mobilised, when he does not have the possibility of transforming the context of the situation in which he finds himself, the only way of acting that he has at his disposal in order to achieve a transformation is to act on the definition of the situation, i.e. to act on himself. Georges Felouzis (2001, 104) clearly illustrates the link between this form of acting and the absence of resources which can be mobilised:

> ... having given up on changing the world in which they move, the students are obliged to change themselves or to change institutes.

Changing the situation presupposes then a change of disposition. The agent can act on the world because it acts on him. 'Emergence from a crisis, sometimes long and often difficult, is also a "transformation of self"' (Dubar, 2000, 171). This acting centring on the definition of self occurs via a reorganisation of the way of life, it leads to a reconstitution of identity and imposes a symbolic calculation. In this sense, 'the process of making an object of one's self and the process of role taking' (Biernacki, 1986, 20) are essential to understanding this form of acting.[19] This work cannot be dissociated from subjective control of one's own existence occurring inevitably through a work of elaboration of meaning.

But this investment in everyday life is not in itself sufficient, it is not only the filling of a temporal vacuum (even if this is not insignificant), it is not the addition of activities nor just the pursuit of new or newly rediscovered interests which can account for the form of acting engaged in. It is, in fact, indispensable that the dimensions, preoccupations, behaviours and actions link up in a way that makes sense, that they form, through a process of reorganisation and interpretation, an action-image, to take an expression of Christian Lalive d'Épinay (1983, 170) 'this mechanism organising a range of practices' of everyday life. This co-ordinator of the action system, both organising principle of everyday life and regulating principle of the event, unlike habitus which is formed more on a collective basis making it a quasi-invariant for the individual, evolves and is transformed because it 'does not suppose any other mediator between meaning and practice besides the actor himself'. This lack of influence of the group and of the social structures, although somewhat a-sociological *a priori*, is interesting here for the very reason that it accounts for the individualised procedure of the production of this acting and, consubstantially, of the fragility of this production even if it is quite obviously out of the question to imagine an 'individual socialisation', though individualised forms of 'imaginary socialisation' may exist.

Alexandre Jollien (1999) illustrates very well the logic of this voluntary and anticipatory socialisation. More than the functionalist idea of the reference group with which one identifies, one has to see in one's little book all of the methodical work which the renegade must do, so many ethnomethods that need to be mastered, all of the codes that need to be assimilated though one is a total stranger to them. It is in this sense that this voluntary socialisation can be described as explicit action, for want of being able to speak of strategy. It is not so much the fact that the world is saturated with constraints – which would call for contingent rationality – but particularly that it is uncertain and unpredictable, creating a contextual situation of vulnerability, which can be so long-term as to become structural.

This 'invention' of practical norms is symbolic and eminently social, which Jean-Claude Kaufmann (2001, 161) reminds us of in his last work:

> Egocephalocentric ideology proposes its customary interpretation model: the individual himself develops a reflexivity susceptible to changing the course of the action... More precisely (as in other phases of individualisation), the reflexive process is triggered by the contradictions internal to the social issues.

Any production of meaning can only be social despite the outward appearance of an individualisation. In fact, the agent draws from the pool of collective values to attribute a normal meaning to his practice. However, what is profoundly individual and original is this 'symbolic calculation' which, through a reconceptualisation of experience (Ogien, 1995), leads to a reorganisation of the biographical threads of the agents.[20] This process obviously supposes the reduction of the importance, both symbolically and practically, of the biographical thread which proved to be weakening in the situation of vulnerability, as compared to other existing or nascent threads.

The question which now arises focuses then on the how of this process and not on the why, aiming more to understand what makes some people become part of a logic of adaptation whilst others take themselves as the object to be worked upon and redefined, and consequently reorganise their relationship to the world. Hence, it is important, after having revised exactly what is at the heart of weak acting, to describe the praxeological components.

Facing Things and Coming Through: Reflexivity and Capabilities of Transformation. To try to reveal the first of these components, it might be helpful to go back to the vernacular meaning of facing things (*faire face*) by comparing it to other related symbolisations. Facing things is not the same as making a stand (*faire front*) which refers to the fact of resisting, of not backing off, with a dual dimension of passive refusal and active creation of an alternative previously thought of. It is also different to making do (*faire avec*) which means adapting oneself to the circumstances, to making little compromises with the constraints, doing what one thinks is best (*faire au mieux*).[21] Facing things, comparatively, is not only the development of an activity of the management of discredit and of the diversion or neutralisation of stigma, but also and especially the engaging of a reflexive process leading to recognition of the problematic nature of the situation lived. The common denominator, and the main theme of facing things is the idea of a problematic situation being recognised as such, of the making of a connection between what I am and what I could/should have been.

Coming through, getting out of this situation recognised as being problematical, thus consists in reducing the uncertainty, in reintroducing predictability into one's relationships with Others and the environment by working on the definition of the situation. Acting subjectively by trying to give a meaning to the world in order to be able to objectively transform the world. This sense of weak acting is based on the distinction between the operating capability and the action capability, the first presupposes only the assumption of the obligations of the role that one occupies at a given moment, the second supposes a work of reflexivity involving a disengagement from self, an auto-objectivation, a distancing from oneself, entailing, at least potentially, an unlearning of habits, a disincorporation of habitus, a work of disconnection with certain roles.

> Reflexivity, which must not be confused with the activity of calculating thought, implies the possibility of an appraisal of oneself, (...) of taking oneself as object and thus (...) of calling oneself into question. (Legrand, 1993, 31)[22]

Here the importance must be stressed of reflexivity on the journey already made in order to develop the capability of projecting and acting, it is at the basis of the process of accentuation of the power of being able to act upon one's life (René, Turcotte and Blais, 2002).

Thus, if coming through can constitute a form of acting that transforms the problematic situation lived, this is possible, precisely because of the absence of sufficient resources to be able to act on the framework of the situation, by action taken as regards the definition of the situation. The core hypothesis on which our attempt to define acting in a situation of vulnerability is based, can be formulated as follows: a transformation of the situation is initially symbolic, i.e. it is a question of working on a putting into words and of constructing a narrative account, the work of an author, only made possible by seeking the support of a history from which resources can be drawn.

Acting in a Situation of Vulnerability: Making Oneself Another. To further explain this idea of working on oneself, we can turn to René Descartes who, in setting out the maxims of his moral doctrine in the third part of the *Discours*, calls, in the third maxim, for the conquering of oneself rather than of the world.

> My third maxim was to try always to conquer rather myself than fortune, and to change rather my desires than the order of the world; and generally, to accustom myself to believe that there is nothing that be entirely within our power but our thoughts... (Descartes, 1994, 43)

He refers implicitly to the Stoics and particularly to the Manual of Epictetus distinguishing between the things which depend on us (our thoughts, our judgements, our tendencies...) and the things which do not depend on us (our bodies, wealth, power...). Rather than reforming the world, it is more effective to reform one's thoughts. The existentialist approach of Jean-Paul Sartre also helps to better understand this idea of the taking of self as the object of an action when, taking the Heideggerian concept of abandonment to qualify the fact that, since God does not exist, we can do as we please, he points out that the range of what is possible is unlimited and man, not finding 'anything to depend upon either within or outside himself', is condemned to be free. Without values or order legitimating his conduct, he is therefore condemned to be what he does, thus to become, in fine, the matter of his own action (Sartre, 1973, 34).

But this symbolic action rests on a first principle: making of oneself Another.[23] Constructing oneself as one's own subject of will and ability in relation to Another, but a particular Other who does not have exteriority. For there to be a transforming action, it is important to construct a defaulting otherness. But where is this other to be found when there is no opponent? In the construction of another self that one is seeking to dispose oneself of. Consequently, the condition of coming through entails an action of self on self. As so well formulated by Bertrand Bergier (1996), 'I interpellates the you', 'Others drive me to a face-to-face with myself', these expressions describe a form of relational management of self[24] where what is important is to succeed in constituting an otherness, be this within oneself, in order to then take it as a support for the reconstitution of an own place from which to take or mobilise resources, to capitalise them so as to be able to manage them in the action, which, of course, is more difficult within the framework of an open world traversed by a plurality of values and possibilities.[25] The basis of weak acting consists, in this sense, in transforming a problematic situation into a situation which is problematised allowing the identification of an opponent who is no other than oneself.

Projecting without Prior Strategy: Converting Resources and Constructing an Interest. By definition, the situation of vulnerability supposes the absence of own resources which can be instantaneously mobilised prior to the action, or at least the absence of resources which are relevant, adequate, adapted to the new context. Reducing the uncertainty to enable the action thus consists in 'formulating' the contingencies, in organising them in a world of sense.

> Each new contingency, whatever the importance may be, implies the choice of alternative lines of action, capable of holding the trajectory in an order which is as controllable as possible, that is to say of maintaining a gyroscopic schema for the trajectory which is as favourable as possible. (Strauss, 1992, 170)[26]

The resources are elaborated during the action, the means are constructed on the way, using different methods derived from cunning (diversion, use of others' resources as support for one's own action[27]), makeshift (composition of external resources and instrumentation) from ingenuity (resourcefulness consisting of showing ingenuity with the means available) (Villechaise-Dupont, 2002)... Though these registers of constitution and mobilisation of resources are undeniably present in weak acting, they nevertheless pose a major problem: all of these resources are used up in the situation. They are totally exhausted and thus no capitalisation is possible. In fact, the only thing that can be capitalised is experience (obviously of varying richness but still accessible to everyone). Fundamentally then, reflexive experience proves to be the principle method for the production of resources for weak acting, It is given concrete expression by resource conversion procedures, i.e. 1) a revitalisation of dormant resources so far unexploited; 2) a rehabilitation of discredited and thus unused resources; 3) an actualisation of previous resources which take on another meaning in a new context. It is not, however, a question of denying the importance of external resources, whether provided by an institution or available socially, thus avoiding a retreat into oneself and enabling attention to be given to the identification of the action frameworks which are the most favourable for the deployment of the acting skills. Rather it is simply a question of recalling that recourse to these external resources is only possible because of this unique working on one's own being-in-the-world.

> Working on his history enriches the strategic capability of the actor. By gradually becoming aware of the way in which his 'choices' are pre-oriented, the individual can modify them. But let us not fool ourselves, the cards dealt (social, economic, cultural) do not change, the actor simply better perceives the field of possibilities and optimises his game. (Bergier, 2002)

It is, in any case, a question of an inscription of the experience lived in another structure of interpretation of the world, enabling it to be understood that the resources and the skills can be acquired in the actual situation and that they can be reviewed in the interactive acting dynamic. In a way, conversion reminds us that the problem did not reside in the absence of resources (who is really totally devoid of resources, even if possession of them varies fundamentally, structurally speaking, in scope and variety from one agent to another?), but in the absence of the possibility of capitalising resources. A resource is an element at the disposition of the agent which he takes and transforms (converts) into a means to support a capability of acting in a given situation. It is thus of utmost importance that the agent finds the conversion principle which will change his resources, however weak they may be, from inoperative to useful, and this resides in the working upon himself, allowing him to reconstitute, beyond the objective of coming through, another way of occupying a place in the world.

Consequently, we should take into account that one of the basic components of weak acting lies in the construction of an interest and its management. Here we can take the categories highlighted by Luca Pattaroni (2002) to describe this process of the simultaneous definition of the goals and the use of the means to attain this objective: 1) choice as a manifestation of an own will; 2) commitment as the fact of setting down an act as subject; 3) management referring to the maintenance of the commitment in the long-term and the keeping of the role, implying the capability to submit to outside expectations to guarantee the management. In other words, what this typology shows is the fact that clear awareness of the intricacies of the acting is not given at the beginning of the action.

The parallel with the notion of deliberation, contrary to the general will, helps us to explain this idea of the formation of an interest or a goal during the action. What is special about deliberation is the fact of coming to a non pre-determined decision by and during a discussion (Manin, 1985).[28] We have incomplete preferences and it is in the process of interior deliberation and dialogue with others that the decision is formed and not through the existence of a will that is already determined before the action is begun. The action is in this sense the method of definition of the goal of the action, just as the formation of will is not a product of a fact *a priori*, but of a specific deliberation process. Likewise, deliberation differs here from the calculation of the rational actor who is equipped with a coherent body of preferences and a known state of constraints, enabling him to choose the optimal solution.

Acting is both a means of attaining a goal and an operation of the construction of a goal, to take the idea of Georges Felouzis (2001) which makes acting within a weak institution, in the sense of an institution which weakly structures the action, a form of pre-strategic acting, i.e. working on the construction and on the definition of the goals of the action. In fact here we need to distinguish between two goal levels: 1) coming through, i.e. the goal is inscribed in the problematical situation, it does not go beyond it, it is merely a question of getting over the problematic character of the situation; 2) going somewhere because it is not a matter of a simple return to normal, going beyond the situation calls for something else at the same time as being something else which is attainable. Hence the need to construct an interest which will eventually constitute a goal in itself, disconnectable and disconnected from the problematical situation, able to be pursued after this has been overcome, but which owes everything to the situation, as it can only be attained through the fact of having gone beyond the situation, and because it was formed in the work involved in this. It is in this sense that this form of acting is transforming, situation transforming and transforming because it is the producer of something other than just the enclosing connection in the situation. We should thus distinguish between the goal related to the actual situation, rooted in the going beyond of this, i.e. indetachable from the context, and the strategic goal, which is a goal that transcends the situation and is linked to the rules of functioning, to the normative and normalised action framework, as typically illustrated by the strategic action par excellence entailed in a game of chess. This distinction is the principle, I think, of the difference in opinion between our characterisation of weak acting and that of the tactical action of Georges Felouzis,[29] though both are rooted in a common action context, that of uncertainty and unpredictability. This 'disagreement' then rests on the fact that the indeterminacy of the expected ends in the framework of a weak institution, at the heart of the analysis of the student condition, is not found in the situation of vulnerability that we have tried to model, as the point is that the goal, even if we have to go on to differentiate between several goal levels, is clear: to get out of the situation. Furthermore, the problem, if we are to consider weak acting as a pre-strategic action, resides in the fact that there is not each time a definitive translation into a long-term project, into a goal, which is independent of the circumstances, of the problematical situation. In fact, it has to be admitted that weak acting may contain elements of strategic acting,. particularly the transforming dimension, without however being a form of strategic acting and without guaranteeing that this is what it will become.

Transforming the Situation: Working in a Non-Linear Temporality. Weak acting needs time. This process cannot take place in a temporality which is too limited. It is a question of an important symbolic effort, and time is a non-negligible condition for its accomplishment. In fact, the duration creates the conditions for its elaboration and the putting to the test of a judgement of one's situation. In this sense the relationship to time is fundamentally different to that which prevails in strategic acting where time is broken up into consecutive periods which are chronologically and causally linked, enabling the casting of oneself forward (projection) and the casting of oneself in advance (anticipation), or in tactical acting where time is broken up into disjointed periods, which are successive but not chronologically or causally linked, establishing the force of the event and its inclusion in the here and now. In weak acting, the progression, understood as a change of nature from one stage to another does not actually make sense, but at the same time everything does not happen immediately. The individuals advance, go a little way along the road, rearm themselves in the face of their history and their future; they take on depth and density, enabling them to rediscover a projection capability. But literally, there is no progression in the sense of a step having been taken. The modification is in essence qualitative and subjective. It is the result of the resources mobilised by the actor and by a modification of his view of himself, very often supported by the environment; it is not an increase in value in an objective space sanctioning dispositions or aptitudes. This evolution is not primarily somehow orientated towards something, but is, above all, focused on self.

The efficiency of the experiential disposition is in fact slow-release. It is based on the variable of time which enables an accumulation of real-life experience and a questioning of self, of one's trajectory and one's place in the world, which will condition the discovery of an interest and/or will give (back) assurance and enable forgotten means to be rediscovered to assume a re-enrolment in a world partially different. However this activation cannot be timed. The setting in motion cannot be easily predicted and is even uncertain; it cannot be operationalised. Facing things and coming through resembles in this sense a game of Snakes and Ladders with moves that hasten or hinder one's progression. Some people move forward more quickly and climb all the ladders, others take more time. Some move backwards, even back to square one, before beginning again; others slither down a snake or miss a turn and have to wait a while before being able to continue. In this sense the relapses can also be a way of participating in the game of resource conversion. In fact, rather than speaking of forwards and backwards movements, we should be speaking in terms of fluctuations: in risk taking, in self-confidence, in attachment to the present situation and detachment from it in order to go on towards a new world. This fluctuation is in fact the expression of a production and reproduction of indecisiveness to take a decision, to project, whilst running as few risks as possible (Blanc, 1999). It characterises the multiple transactions that the actors in a situation of vulnerability make with the worlds of integration (employment, family, institutions...) and with the various dimensions of life (private, social, public, work, friends...) enabling enclosure in a unique status and the previous negativity of interactions to be overcome, leading to a phenomenon of emancipation from the situation of vulnerability.

The Conditions of Weak Acting

Characterisation of the outlines of weak acting allows, with the undeniable risk of a simplistic interpretation, the formal conditions which make it possible to be pointed out. These conditions are both socially produced, supported and conveyed and individually borne, developed and met. Because although it can be said that weak acting is an eminently individual process, supported by the actor's working upon the definition of the situation that he is living,[30] this work draws its resources and its forces from within a social context that gives meaning and legitimacy to what he does. In other words, if weak acting presupposes reflexive conditions, if the human being is a being who interprets and interprets each of his actions, the meaning that he gives them is not a totally individual production; to do this he draws the symbols which are necessary to produce this meaning from his social environment and from a stock of socially available practical and symbolical knowledge.[31]

A Break with Obviousness. One of the elements which is often used to account for radical modifications of the social inclusion of individuals and particularly for phenomena of identity conversion resides in the presence of trigger events which have the effect of upsetting the ordinary progress of existence and of creating an exceptional situation causing considerable disruption on the individual and relational levels. In other words, these events cause a break in routine – but also a break in commitment, in the sense given to this term by Howard S. Becker (1963) – and introduce a problematical relationship to everyday life. By provoking a rereading of the past, they allow a reconceptualisation of previous experience and a search for new alliances with society. But these trigger events can only be considered as such because they occur at an opportune moment, that is to say with the progressive appearance of a feeling of weariness regarding the situation which is finally apprehended as being tiresome and costly (Molo, 2000).[32]

This problematic situation is born of a contradiction between what one is and what one would like to be, of an identity discord between what one is socially supposed to be at a certain age and what one effectively is at this moment in one's life. This work of problematisation supposes the deconstruction of the previous experience and a questioning of its signification, often resting on an interpretation in terms of the cost/benefit ratio, as much symbolic as practical. This appreciative logic supposes reference to another system of norms and values than the one previously in force and, thus, a work of comparison between the present way of life and a way of life which serves as a reference, very often constructed from an interpreted form of conventionality. This comparison is conveyed to the awareness of individuals by existential tensions implying the need for them to be managed.[33] And, in this sense, paradoxically, it is the requirement of the management of these tensions which produces individualisation and action.

It remains to be understood how this process of the realisation of existential tensions works. Rather than seeking a first principle, an originating moment,[34] perhaps we should consider the fact that the problematisation, rather than being what triggers the entering into action, is only one of the conditions for this. Problematisation should then be understood only as the recognition of the fact that the situation lived does not sit with the socially normed objective of self-fulfilment. And that without this reflexive relation, the problematical nature of the situation remains only a non-usable force. Consequently the supports of the problematisation are more prosaically rooted in a phenomenon of weariness vis-à-vis a way of life, the existential contradiction of which appears more and more flagrant. But furthermore, just as for deviance (Matza and Sykes, 1957), the problematisation of situations of vulnerability is subject to the onslaughts of technical, institutional or symbolic procedures of neutralisation. These neutralisations must in fact themselves be neutralised for the problematisation to produce a work of the questioning of self, of one's being-in-the-world and the meaning of the situation lived.

The working upon oneself, at the heart of this process, supposes the presence of symbolic resources as a framework of interpretation of self and of the world, the action-images of Christian Lalive d'Épinay, and as a repertoire of behaviour in the world. It is thanks to them that at a certain moment the situation lived can be envisaged as being unsatisfactory and demand reconsideration that other dimensions of existence can be valued and invested in and that another life project can be redrawn. This type of resources comes back to the unique history of each person and to the incorporations made during the course of an individual, multi-contoured social trajectory. It is rooted in an experiential patrimony, forming, on the one hand, a reference framework allowing the interpretation of one's own experience and one's relationship to the world, and constituting on the other, a repertoire of action models and codes of conduct learnt and internalised during the course of one's biography.[35] But, above all, these symbolic resources are the first principles of the conversion of the invalidated or unusable resources possessed by the agent, so that they can serve as supports to get out of a situation for which they were of no use. The presence of interlocutors thus becomes invaluable to help and to confirm this operation of conversion of resources. Here, the key idea, developed by Peter Berger and Thomas Luckmann (1984), appears of a conversation apparatus, but, examined from the point of view of the resources, this comes down to pinpointing the existence of people available to help reflect on the problematical situation lived, to evaluate it, to recognise the links between the present and the past, to find explanations, to identify the consequences...

> 'Normal-Smith' refers to the persons whose perception, orientation to, and interaction with deviants facilitate the transition, that is to say who a) establish cognitive congruence for pivotally normals; b) blur the distinction between deviants and normals; c) organize and orchestrate transition ceremonies; d) facilitate entry to normal places and roles by supplying hardware and resources for entry. (Giesbrecht, 1983, 301-302)

These interlocutors constitute not only a reserve of practical and symbolic means upon which to draw, but also an opportunity for maieutical work supporting the reflexive process of the individual on the situation of vulnerability that he is living.

A Unique Accessibility. This critical examination of the meaning of the situation lived causes a break, setting in motion a working upon oneself and upon one's environment, along the lines of an acceptance of a redefinition of one's inscription in the world and the desire for a re-socialisation into areas of society that one does not master. This then means that the actor in a situation of vulnerability must focus his sustained attention on the potentialities and the aspects of his integrity which are intact. Whichever road is followed, it presupposes, as Peter Berger and Thomas Luckmann call it, the existence of a transformation space enabling progressive experimentation with a new identity and the testing of its feasibility.

Retaking control of one's own destiny, in this sense, in this idea of unique accessibility, is not merely supported by reversal leading to rejection of the gains that consummation could bring. These critical moments are thus occasions of formation and expression of a will for social affiliation, correlative to the refusal to activate safety clauses, to the feeling of having exhausted the relevance of the neutralisation techniques, of the pretence (Goffman, 1963), and of the perception of the uselessness of making compromises with oneself and with others. This procedure of rearmement of the judgement of oneself implies, for the individual, the modification of the opinion that he has of the activities that he carries out. All of the force of the logic of internalisation is encountered here, as responsibility of oneself and for oneself and as a prerequisite to the very existence of the transformation of one's situation (Le Poultier, 1986). Through the acquisition of this norm, the individual can no longer think of himself as the object of events, but interprets himself as responsible for the situation in which he finds himself. The acquisition of the norm of internalisation consists in turning the problem around to the only object that can be worked upon for itself, i.e. oneself. The responsibility is no longer transferred to an exterior entity, but is incorporated thanks to an effort of comprehension of one's own biography. In this sense, coming through is firstly a working upon oneself, even if it is also, and to a great extent, a working with others.[36]

Abandoning the relational management of self, the logic of accommodation, the actor in a situation of vulnerability mobilises then a logic of distancing of oneself, implying the ability to distance oneself from oneself, to objectivise, to disengage, to un-involve oneself (Bajoit, 1997). Bertrand Bergier greatly insists on the importance of an egocentred attitude, the principle of an experiential disposition enabling one to 'conjugate life', to put the present back in its context in a succession of facts, to make it a part of a history.

> The experiential disposition invites this reflexive attention and this evaluation of oneself. Let us recall that the issue does not reside in some form of controlling of the situation but in a pursuit of personal unity. It is necessary to understand oneself. (Bergier, 1996, 95)

Unique accessibility must therefore be seen as an authorisation, inducing the facing of oneself and, therefore, as an opening up to oneself, allowing the interrogation of one's participation in one's history. We should probably see in this relationship to past and future history the key to this acquisition of a norm of internalisation. This examination of the past is a part of the obligatory points of access to self and to the reorientation of one's perception of the world. But to be able to do this, a work of recollection is supposed, very often accompanied by a reconceptualisation of previous experience:

> This supposes first knowing one's history, then accepting it so as to recognise oneself in it, thus perhaps requiring an effort to find again what has been lost through having being eclipsed or through having being forgotten. (Boulte, 1995, 127)

But above all, one social condition must be met to enable this unique work to be set in motion: the existence of a social basis serving as a laboratory, mediated by significant others, who come to physically and symbolically support this activation of self, so that this process of subjectivation is fostered.

A Social Confirmation: To be an author is to publicly commit to a responsibility vis-à-vis oneself. Commitment is the giving of a guarantee, it is an operation of accreditation as testified by Jacques Ion and Michel Peroni (1997) and particularly the interest that they give to the fact that 'publicising is the practical organisation of the mechanisms of exposure through which personalisation can be made'.

Unique accessibility opens the way to a rearmement of self which, in fact, supposes a social confirmation, by the so-called ordinary milieu and by the institutional procedures, of a personal value or a specific individual skill that is socially valued.[37] This selection is akin to a mechanism of restoration of an isonomy, to a principle of affirmation and reconstitution of a formal equality vis-à-vis the world, thus cancelling out the former vulnerability.

> To retain confidence that he is indeed who he thinks he is, the individual requires not only the implicit confirmation of this identity that even casual everyday contacts will supply, but the explicit and emotionally charged confirmation that his significant others bestow on him. (Berger and Luckmann, 1984, 170)

Here, it is in fact a question of recognition of the conditions of acceptability of this back-to-front moral career. The identity transaction procedures between these people and their environment are also regularly convoked. Individual mobilisation, condition of an access to the possibility of being able to better influence one's own future, is in fact only possible in connection with resources offered by specialised services or by elements of the milieu. Though here we must emphasise the ambiguity of the reference to external support. On the one hand, this is indispensable as confirmation of the will for and the reality of the identity transformation. On the other hand, it constitutes an obstacle. In fact, a double motion of detachment on the one hand, and of support on the other must be considered regarding these forms of social help and support. The example of associations for ex-alcoholics, ex-drug addicts, battered women... is a patent illustration. Identification with a group of people who are like oneself is an important element of disengagement from a problematical situation. At the same time, the problem is the getting away from the condition of ex-something and from this victimological identification model, thereby freeing oneself of this image which is also stigmatising. This connection to institutional services and the environment is, in this sense, to be conceived as a continual transaction, in the way that Jean Remy and Liliane Voyé (1991) understand it,[38] leading to successive relational and identity adjustments.

According to Peter Berger and Thomas Luckmann there is a dual condition for this work of social confirmation to be able to come to the support of the alternation process: a conversation apparatus, allowing the individual who is undergoing a conversion of identity to experience a new way of categorising his world and to argue the identity which is being acquired on the one hand, and a plausibility structure, enabling this new identity to be affirmed in the private sphere with significant others, and in the public space with generalised Others, on the other. In a way, it is a question of a confirmation structure based on symbolic procedures of gradation.[39] In other words, it is important that the actor is convincing in order to work the passage from a virtual identity which is asserted, to a real, recognised identity, to take the analysis categories of Erving Goffman (1963).[40] The key issue then is making plausible both the transformation of the individual relationship to the problematical situation lived and that of the social relationship to others, which presupposes, in the latter case, individual experimentation, within the action, of methods of resuming one's ties to Others, as well as the availability of forms of social regulation and of spaces for the bringing of oneself into play. For this fact of coming through to be effective in reality, it is important to have at one's disposal socially proven perspectives which support the experimentation, the interpretation and which validate the setting in motion of self, i.e. to be able to lean on elements of explanations, official or spontaneous, that allow the way that has been taken to be understood and to be given meaning and credit from a social point of view. It is then easy to see the importance of being able to benefit from informal or professional interlocutors able to provide such explanatory theories, as well the need for spaces, institutional or not, for the elaboration, expression and the bringing into play of new forms of being in the world, all part of the remit of a narrative identity which must not only allow a person to tell their story, but also create the conviction in each and everybody that the way taken heralds a 'good life'.[41] Testimony here is of capital importance (Roux, 2002).[42] Saying, but also explaining through experience after having put – or in order to put – a certain distance between oneself and the experience, in order to better understand it and to make it better understood; stating, but also reminding oneself and, hence, reflecting on oneself; telling, but also finding the posture of an actor through the act of an author (Bergier, 1996).

In this respect, the role of the conversation apparatus is nodal as it conditions the possibility of speaking differently of oneself and of putting into words that are identity related the subjective reality that the agent is seeking to make real. As facing things and coming through is no more than a sum of expertise, it is important to present, in practical acts, but also in verbal interactions, this new way of being. This involves a 'patching up' of the past via, among other things, the continuation of an association, mostly on a different basis, with previously significant people or groups and for whom this alchemy is anything but obvious, as Peter Berger and Thomas Luckmann (1984, 181) remind us.

> They continue to be around, are likely to protest too fanciful reinterpretations, and must themselves be convinced that such transformations as have taken place are plausible.

Trust, Condition of Felicity for Weak Acting

To conclude this attempt at the conceptualisation of weak acting, it is important to go beyond just the revision of its minimum conditions and to seek to show what exactly constitutes the crux of its happening. And it is not in the least paradoxical to say that this condition of felicity[43] is to be sought in trust.

In a way, one of the essential characteristics of weak acting is the fact that it is stamped through with risk. It is risky because what is undertaken may not prove to be conclusive, risky because what is undertaken may prove to be conclusive, and therefore a new world must be confronted, with norms and ways of behaving that are socially different from the ones that the actors had been used to. It is also marked by the uncertainty of the admissibility of one's undertaking of transformation by Others, one's preferred interlocutors and the whole of society. Consequently, we must remember that the question of trust runs through the entire process begun by the agent for the durable transformation of his situation. Risk and trust are in fact indissociable, the latter serving as it does to contain the dangers and uncertainty inherent to certain activities. In fact, risks emerge only as the results of decision and of action, i.e. they do not really exist in themselves, while trust is based on a circular relationship between risk and action. It presupposes a relationship to the world which maintains a dialectical relationship between objective risk and blind delegation to a third party (an individual or an institution), between uncertainty of the consequences of one's activity and faith (*fides*) in Others. It proves to be essential both to establishing stable social relations and to reducing the complexity of the social systems; it is a way for the social actors to face the uncertainty and the vulnerability inherent to social relations (Barber, 1986). And for the actor in a situation of vulnerability, the issue of trust is of increased importance.

The Restoration of Peace of Mind

Trust always supposes a certain degree of uncertainty.[44] The only reason that there is action is because there is risk. The reference to risk enables the consequences of social activities and individual actions, by nature uncertain in their results, to be recognised and accepted. But, at the same time, taking risks into account also supposes a certain stability which gives a feeling of security (Ème and Laville, 2000). Trust, as both a controlled relationship and blindness to risk, can only be attained within a familiar world which reinstates events within the limits of the known and certain world, as Niklas Luhmann (1988) explains.[45] Peace of mind, understood as a feeling of confidence in the continuity of the world of objects and in the constance of social activity, represents an important element of a maintained inclusion in the world. It

> characterises a state of tranquillity, of peace, of serenity, an absence of worry which is
> an essential aspect of the feeling of security... It characterises situations of everyday life
> where sufficient familiarity with our environment, with the systems that we use
> (housing, transport, food, work...) means that we do not have to worry about them (do
> not have to take direct responsibility for them) and we are thus able to attend to our own
> affairs. Peace of mind is an inescapable aspect of living together. (Hérard-Dubreuil,
> 2000, 1)

Even though the forms of peace of mind (individual and social) have a dimension of fragility, paradoxically, they nevertheless constitute an important element of weak acting. In fact, peace of mind acts as a counterbalance to the need for a continual reaffirmation of the work of problematisation by offering, in parallel, the guarantee of a respite in the working upon oneself. Reflexivity, at the heart of weak acting, is, in this sense, only supported by a relationship to the world which in other respects is stamped with familiarity, just as basic security only has meaning, for the agent in a situation of vulnerability, in the maintaining of the awareness of risk. The basis of peace of mind is inscribed first and foremost in the creation of common routines which chart both the field of possibilities and our interpretations of the actions of others (there is a continuity of things, of events, of actions which occurs without our realising it). But, at the same time, as far as weak acting is concerned, because of the situation of vulnerability in which it is rooted, peace of mind cannot only be based on routines; much more than that it supposes a reflexive practice, a practical conscience, aware of, and questioning, conducts, rules and frameworks, enabling both the action undertaken to be given a meaning in relation to a chosen way of life and to make it commonplace, in order to reintroduce it into the familiar part of the symbolic world of the actor.

Restoration of Credibility

Wanting to come through and go beyond a situation of vulnerability consists, fundamentally, in having to prove one's reliability, in making one's conduct predictable, thus enabling the others with whom one interacts to anticipate one's behaviour. And we know to what extent the predictability of behaviour is at the heart of the organisation of social relations; it constitutes one of the vernacular, but vital forms of social control (Mendras, 1976).[46] The key issue then, becomes the obligation to produce the conditions of acceptability, for oneself and for others, of the path one takes to come through and of one's break with the situation of vulnerability, so as to regain reliability in one's relationship to others, so as to (once more) become a person worthy of trust. In fact, the restoration of credibility, combines two aspects: 1) Social trust is mobilised in situations of fragility or uncertainty and, in particular, in situations where one is dependent on other people as regards one's future. To a certain extent, seeking to have oneself recognised as being credible comes down to putting oneself in a situation which comprises risks inherent to the fact of trusting oneself to another/others on whom this recognition is going to depend; 2) Credibility comprises reference to predictability. It implies the expectation that the partners of the interaction are going to assume their responsibilities and their obligations, some of which exceed their own interests.

To the extent that the process of weak acting is inscribed in a context of vulnerability, one of the essential workings of trust, i.e. here the attribution of credibility, is immediately invalidated. The trust of attachment, this trust which is based on a thoughtless way of putting faith in people and in their words, this intuitive and, in a way, completely naive trust like that of a child in its parents, has been burdened by the weight of uncertainty. Only interpretative trust can then serve as a support for the regaining of credibility, submitting the acts and the words of the actor to the (inevitably critical and reserved, at least initially) assessment of others (Petitat, 1998).[47] He has to, in a way, make others want to take a bet, on the basis of a risk which is measured by the giving of practical guarantees (carrying out one's work correctly, being on time for appointments, managing one's affairs properly, matching one's acts to one's words...). To establish this trust through interpretation, we fragment the areas of confidence.

> Someone may be greatly trusted for his discretion, but that does not mean that the same level of trust is put in his strategic capabilities, his honest management of the cashbox, the transparency of his decisions or his respect of other people's territory. This differentiation goes with sectional exchanges, which only call upon certain skills and qualities of the partners. This tendency to fragmentation limits the risks and becomes more pronounced with the division of labour. (Petitat, 1998, 209)

In this sense, the restoration of credibility is via symbolic and discursive work which aims to make acceptable both the problematic situation lived and the path taken to attain the projected condition. All of the past must be interpreted in order to confirm the present and to see what may be presaged for the future. In this sense, the setting of the problematical situation lived into a narrative becomes a key element of the production of this credibility[48] both by its content, as it indicates a radical modification of thinking one's being in the world, and by its very performance since, as an elaboration procedure of a narrative identity, it allows the agent to present himself (again) as the subject of his history and thus to (re)access the ownership of self. Of course, this reconceptualisation will be all the more sincere and more admissible socially if it is supported by acts and is translated into specific ways of behaving. But this idea of discursive production must not be understood strictly as strategy, with the intentionality and calculation that this supposes. At the very least these cannot be visible, otherwise they would risk being seen as mere stratagems and, consequently, lose all effectiveness. Just as fundamentally, this reconstruction of one's history cannot be feigned, it must be sincere, as Jacques T. Godbout (2000, 168) explains on the subject of talent.

> Now, to establish this reputation, it must be sincerely believed. Because is not possible to play the game long-term, the person is going to lack the motivation... In short, talent is realistic because there is a return, but it exists because, for there to be a return, this must not be why it is done.[49]

Conclusion

At the end of this attempt at a conceptual clarification of acting in a situation of vulnerability, there is a great risk of making a moral approach to the person and to the maintenance of self the basis of the development of a capability of acting, be this a weak form of acting, and the danger is also very real of seeing this type of analysis likened to a dissimulation and to a legitimation of existing social relationships, the very generators of the vulnerable dimension of the situation in which the agent finds himself. Therefore, in order to remove all risk of misunderstanding, we need to insist on the need to link this sociologico-phenomenological analysis of weak acting to a socio-structural analysis of social determinism which reminds us that the distribution of resources and risks being socially unequal, the propensity to being exposed to situations of vulnerability is not the same for everybody, and nor especially are the chances of being locked into weak acting on a long-term basis. We are well aware of the difficulty of making the two things hold, but it is the challenge posed by the form of conceptualisation of weak acting that has been attempted in the above text.

Notes

1   Or, to take the very fine expression of Spyros Frianguiadakis (2002): What is 'acting when individuals find themselves at the limit of actability?'

2   Moreover, this interpretation of vulnerability very often corresponds to categories that are first and foremost administrative.

3   In some ways this configuration resembles that brought to light by William Thomas and Florian Znaniecki (1996) – social disorganisation, personal disorganisation, demoralisation – revealing how much the breaking or the obsolescence of stable and explicit social frameworks could be the cause of the destructuration of the action channels. Georges Felouzis (2001, 47) takes up a similar argument to explain the disorientation of students on their arrival at university. 'This means that the "roles", in the sense of the "organised models of behaviour", that the students have learned in secondary school are no longer congruent with the new action context in which they are moving. This discovery is thus also a "reality shock", insofar as the rules of school are no longer current, whilst the new rules are not yet really known.'

4   In this sense we share the premises of the analysis of Georges Felouzis (2001), but not its development, particularly when he characterises the type of action which occurs in such a context of uncertainty and vagueness as a tactical action. We shall try to explain later on how falling back on the notion of tactical action does not seem to us to do justice to something that acutely describes a way of acting deployed in such circumstances.

5   See the very convincing analysis made by Jean-Émile Charlier and Frédéric Moëns (2002) of the paradoxical situation of priests in a situation of symbolic exclusion without material exclusion. Their situation has lost all legitimacy because of a modification of the position of the Church and because of the strategy of the latter to face up to this and they see that all of their previous resources are unusable, the credibility of them undermined.

6   Georges Felouzis uses similar reasoning to understand the adaptation to University of new students. He thus connects the action context, the university as a weak institution, a system which does not impose 'clear collective goals' on its members 'and in which the means to be implemented remain vague', and the nature of the tactical action developed as a reaction by the students (Felouzis, 2001).

7   Fatalism characterises the fourth form of suicide distinguished by Émile Durkheim. Unlike the first three, it is not the subject of a specific chapter but simply appears in a footnote. If Émile Durkheim gave it so little attention, this is probably the result of his focusing on the weakening of the rule as one of the ills of modern society as suggested by Bernard Lacroix (1973).

8   'In any case, I am obliged to give it' was all an elderly lady could reply when the appointed guardian and an accompanying visitor asked for her permission to open certain drawers during a first visit following a court decision to take tutelary measures to protect her personal assets and finances as she had been judged incapable of doing it herself (Séraphin, 2001).

9   Here, we do not agree with the analyses – such as that of Gilles Séraphin – according to which, in a context of an excess of constraints or of strong domination, the acting developed is of a tactical nature. Tactical acting is subject to all the powerfulness of the time and the place in the absence of any other isolable thing for the orientation of one's

action. It is precisely the absence of visible and clearly identifiable domination which establishes the strength of the here and now in which tactical acting can be deployed.

10 In this extreme experience, the existence of this parallel world is a condition of adaptation and survival, a condition of the maintenance of identity and of the affirmation of the permanence of the status of human being (Pollack, 1990).

11 'Whilst we had been expecting to see a docile, discreet, self-effacing person on welfare, the actor suddenly appeared, obstinate, maladjusted, awkward... The stronger the constraints, the more the individuals seem involved in the establishing and the reinforcement of the process itself (that of becoming a social outcast)' (Taboada-Leonetti, 1994, 221).

12 Which Jean-Claude Kaufmann (2001, 202) explains in another way. 'The more open the social space, non defined *a priori* by frameworks of constraint, the more intense is the work of normative elaboration.'

13 Illustrated repeatedly by the case of Agnès, a transsexual studied by Harold Garfinkel (Garfinkel, 1984; Hess, 1986). Biologically a man, Agnès, before her operation, already appeared and lived as a woman. And in order to keep this secret, she always had to be one step ahead, always obliged to construct an anticipatory action to avoid an awkward situation which could make her run the risk of being discovered, and all this in the absence of resources as she had not been socialised into a feminine way of being. Her entire problem resided in the fact of having to behave as a woman whilst never having learnt to be a woman, and in a context where any lapse would have meant the end of her being thought of as a woman. Agnès thus had to continually and voluntarily create her feminine being in the body of a man with the obligation of maintaining, in everyday life, in every interaction, in each situation, this constructed femininity. She had to learn to be a woman whilst showing that she was already a woman. For example, she did not know how to cook though every young woman in the USA in the 1950s was obliged to know. So, she asked the mother of her boyfriend, who was Indonesian, to teach her to cook Indonesian dishes, a legitimate request, thereby hoping to acquire the basics of cookery without revealing her general lack of cookery skills.

14 'The strategies of responding to a difficult social situation simply describe individual or collective ways of behaving, conscious or unconscious, suitable or unsuitable, implemented to attain certain ends. These ends are defined by the individuals as a function of their evaluation of the situation of interaction, that is to say, as a function of the importance of outside constraints and of their own action capabilities' (Taboada-Leonetti, 1994, 183).

15 Though the meanings of tactics (the art of organising one's forces to win a battle) and of strategy (the art of organising battles to win the war) of Karl von Clausewitz (1968) are very different from those used here and borrowed from Michel de Certeau, one point unites them: tactics are used in the here and now of a particular context, strategy is part of the long-term and the management of one's forces in time and in space.

16 The analysis of Georges Felouzis (2001) takes formal aspects which are relatively close to those that we are trying to develop here, however, there is a central element which is different, the fact that the actors in a situation of vulnerability have a precise goal (even if it is a short-term one and despite the fact that whatever lies beyond it cannot be foreseen): to get out of their situation.

17 One of the finest examples, given by Maurice Godelier (1972), remains the use of the iron axe instead of the stone axe as imposed by the missionaries on the Trobriand Islanders and which resulted, not in greater productivity, but in a reduction in the time spent working and an increase in the time spent waging war on neighbours and enemies.

18 See the example of social intervention as a form of professional activity fundamentally based on this way of doing things, particularly because of the lability of the clientele.

19 Cf. on a completely different issue, but in a very similar perspective, the work of Jean-Claude Kaufmann (1995) on role taking in his analysis of the exposure of bare breasts on the beach.

20 'To the good reasons of instrumental rationality, we must add, and often contrast, the good ethical reasons, those that bring into play the relationship of the subject to himself' (Dubet and Vérétout, 2001, 429).

21 '...essentially this is to be understood as the idea of that which escapes us and which brings us to make all of the compromises that are necessary to maintain the existing circumstances, all of those little betrayals of ideality which are merely the product of the ferocious principle of reality. 'Making do' is relinquishing a little in order to be able to do something anyway, even though one of course acts with a full awareness of one's limits' (Le Gall, Martin and Soulet, 1986, 7).

22 Claude Lefort (1988) emphasised the institution and the maintenance of democracy in the dissolution of the points of reference of certainty and its government by the reflexive capability, i.e. by a constant examination and revision of social and institutional practices. In this sense, reflexivity partakes of the reproduction of the system, reproduction which is broadened and displaced by the very fact that thought and action are refracted. Advanced modernity today sanctions the extension of this reflexivity to the individual so that he establishes, maintains and governs himself as a subject in a context where there is also indeterminacy of the final ends and the obligation of giving a meaning to one's own course. In this sense the individual is here at least as uncertain as the uncertainty. 'The reflexive subject must construct the experience of self and the relational management of self. That which defines the subject, is precisely this incessant work which allows him to link the different dimensions of his experience and to structure relations with others' (Fransen, 1997, 29).

23 This attempt to define weak acting as the symbolic working upon oneself is poles apart from the behavioural control of self, developed by the psychological behaviourist theories (Van Rillaer, 1992).

24 In this relational management of self Guy Bajoit distinguishes a duality in this working on the subject, which is complementary and opposite, that of individuation constructing the individual on the basis of the who am I, and that of realisation constructing the actor on the basis of what do I want, resulting from the attachment of the individual to his expectations and from his commitment to himself to realise them among others. 'I call "relational management of self" the process by which the individual is subject, that is to say, manages the existential tensions between others' expectations of him and his own expectations of himself' (Bajoit, 1997, 117).

25 We are in fact close to what Anselm Strauss (1959) calls identity transformation and Peter Berger and Thomas Luckmann alternation (1984). Anselm Strauss however focuses his attention essentially on changes of status (particularly on organised changes such as initiation) and thus on the identity transformations which ensue.

26 Taking medicine as an example, Anselm Strauss (1992) explains this phenomenon by the way that doctors seek to both sequence the medical trajectory of the patient and to keep the options open for as long as possible.

27 Example of the tennis player subjected to the power of his opponent but who, by seizing upon the ball very quickly after the rebound, captures this force and returns the ball, making use of speed and his return capability.

28 'Law *is the result of general deliberation,* not *the expression of the general will*' (Manin, 1985, 84, author's italics). The analysis of Bernard Manin applies to the formation of the general will, but, basically, fully coincides with our idea that the goals do not completely precede the action but are, for some at least, formed in the action, at least as far as weak acting is concerned.

29 Georges Felouzis (2001, 108) defines the relationship of tactical acting to the goals in the following way: 'Their action is in fact 'tactical' in the sense that nothing or almost nothing is defined at the outset, and in that the objectives and the means are only constructed as the degree course develops, as a function of the particular study context.'

30 It seems right, in fact, to consider that it is a question of a work of individuation, different from the repetition of an incorporated habitus and from the expression of a collective identity.

31 Alfred Schütz (1964) effectively highlighted the existence of cognitive and practical backgrounds to the action, non specific to a given situation, but serving as a support, as a general behaviour repertoire, to the action.

32 This logic of disengagement from a way of life judged to be unsatisfactory feeds a subjective condition of non-belonging, of a *no man's land* which is encountered in types of career inversions and identity transformations such as ceasing to be homeless. Progressively, the actor seeks to disengage from an experience which no longer satisfies him as the initial attraction is no longer there and, at the same time, he seeks to break with a social world which, though it previously enabled him to give a meaning to his practice, shows itself to be discordant with the new interpretation that he makes of his past experience (Molo, 2000).

33 Guy Bajoit (2000) insists on the importance of the structural tensions, this gap between what institutions give to hope and the possibilities of the realisation of identity that are truly offered, as a support to the obligation of managing.

34 Thus, the argument of having hit rock bottom does not seem to be fully satisfactory in this sense as it does not in any way allow us to account for all those who live this situation but who do not try to escape from.

35 'Man in daily life, as I have said, finds at any given moment a stock of knowledge at hand that serves him as a scheme of interpretation of his past and present experiences and also determines his anticipations of things to come' (Schütz, 1964, 283).

36 'This involves a reinterpretation of past biography *in toto*, following the formula, "Then I *thought*... now I *know*"... Pre-alternation biography is typically nihilated *in toto* by subsuming it under a negative category...' (Berger and Luckmann, 1984, 179)

37 'The most important conceptual requirement for alternation is the availability of a legitimating apparatus for the whole sequence of transformation' (Berger and Luckmann, 1984, 179).

38 At a symposium on the concept of social transaction and its sociological relevance, Jean Remy tried to differentiate between transaction and negotiation: 'Transaction is a lot less formalised. It is diffuse, it is continuous. It is possible for it not to be explicitly seen as a moment of confrontation and discord. The partners may not be clearly positioned. It is the same for the problems to be solved. The game has varying scenes, as the number of actors may change according to the circumstances' (Remy, 1992, 87).

39 These operations are the opposite of the ceremonies of degradation analysed by Harold Garfinkel (1986).

40 See the distinction made by Luca Fumagalli (2002) between subjective-virtual and objective-symbolic insertion.

41 Claude Dubar (2000), taking the work of Paul Ricœur linking account and action in support, also emphasises the great importance of the narrative work in the process of going beyond identity crises.

42 Thus leaving a trace can, in a situation of great vulnerability, resemble a test of validation of being alive.

43 Analogous to the way that Erving Goffman (1983) highlighted 'the condition of felicity' of verbal interactions, that which allows mutual understanding in the exchange (i.e. the

presupposition that makes us judge the verbal acts of an individual as not being a manifestation of strangeness).

44 Weak acting also comes up against the uncertainty of one's own effectiveness; it is constantly referred back to its intrinsic fragility. For the actor, it is a question of convincing himself and especially of convincing his immediate social and institutional environment of his will to come through. Confidence in the strength of his resolution rests first and foremost on the maintenance of the problematical character of the situation that one wishes to escape (Caiata-Zufferey, 2002).

45 'We can live within a familiar world because we can, using symbols, reintroduce the unfamiliar into the familiar' (Luhmann, 1988, 95).

46 In his own way, Diego Gambetta (1988, 217) takes the idea of predictability as being intimately linked to trust. 'Trust (or, symmetrically, distrust) is a particular level of the subjective probability with which an agent assesses that another agent or group of agents will perform a particular action, both *before* he can monitor such action (or independently of his capacity ever to be able to monitor it) *and* in a context in which it affects *his own* action.'

47 Louis Karpik (1996) distinguishes two components in the mechanisms of trust: the mechanisms of judgement which enable the reduction of ignorance, founded on personal trust (network) or impersonal trust (classifications, designations, guides) and the mechanisms of promise enabling the risks of opportunism to be countered (encompassing the quality of the people, the network or the normative wholes).

48 Isabelle Astier (1997) has already stressed the importance of the putting into narrative, more particularly of the passage from the private account to the civil account, as a way of accrediting the situation lived (situations of deprivation and need in the case studied), with a view to attribution of resources by the authorities. The recitative procedure thus possesses a moral force enabling the gaining of approval.

49 The distinction between intention and result may allow this apparent paradox to be accounted for and according to which it may be profitable not to seek one's own interest, on condition that this is done sincerely.

References

Anthony, E.J. (1987), 'Risk, Vulnerability, and Resilience: An Overview', in E.J. Anthony and B.J. Cohler, *The Invulnerable Child*, Guilford Press, New York.

Astier, I. (1997), *Revenu minimum et souci d'insertion*, Éditions Desclée de Brouwer, Paris.

Autès, M. (1999), *Les Paradoxes du travail social*, Éditions Dunod, Paris.

Bajoit, G. (1997), 'Qu'est-ce que le sujet?', in G. Bajoit and E. Belin (éd.), *Contribution à une sociologie du sujet*, Éditions L'Harmattan, Paris.

Bajoit, G. (2000), 'Qu'est-ce que la socialisation?', in G. Bajoit, F. Digneffe, J.M. Jaspard and Q. Nallet de Brouwere (éd.), *Jeunesse et société. La socialisation des jeunes dans un monde en mutation*, Éditions Desclée de Brouwer, Bruxelles.

Balandier, G. (1977), 'Ruse et politique', in Cause commune, *La Ruse*, Union générale d'éditions, Paris.

Barber, B. (1986), *The Logic of Trust*, Rutgers University Press, New Brunswick.

Becker, H.S. (1963), *Outsiders. Studies in the Sociology of Deviance*, Free Press of Glencoe, London.

Berger, P. and Luckmann, T. (1984), *The Social Construction of Reality: A Treatise in the Sociology of Knowledge*, Pelican Books, London.

Bergier, B. (1996), *Les Affranchis. Parcours de réinsertion*, Éditions Desclée de Brouwer, Paris.

Bergier, B. (2002), 'Le concept d'auteur dans la problématique de l'affranchissement', in V. Châtel and M.H. Soulet (éd.), *Faire face et s'en sortir*, Éditions universitaires, Fribourg.

Biernacki, P. (1986), *Pathways from Heroin Addiction Recovery without Treatment*, Temple University Press, Philadephia, 1986.

Blanc, C. (1999), *Longs accueils pour sans abri. Exclusion, urgence et identité indécidable. Analyse des processus de prolongement des séjours au sein d'abris pour sans abri*, Mémoire de Licence de la Faculté des Lettres, Fribourg.

Boudon, R. (1974), *The Logic of Sociological Explanation*, translated by Tom Burns, Penguin Education, Harmondsworth.

Boulte, P. (1995), *Individus en friche*, Éditions Desclée de Brouwer, Paris.

Caiata-Zufferey, M. (2002), 'Sortir de la toxicomanie: une question de confiance', in V. Châtel and M.H. Soulet (éd.), *Faire face et s'en sortir*, Éditions universitaires, Fribourg.

Castel, R. (1992), 'De l'exclusion comme état à la vulnérabilité comme processus', in J. Affichard and J.B. De Foucauld (éd.), *Justice sociale et inégalités*, Éditions Esprit, Paris.

Castel, R. (s/s la dir. de) (1999), *Les Sorties de la toxicomanie*, Éditions universitaires, Fribourg.

Certeau, M. de (1984), *The Practice of Everyday Life*, translated by Steven Rendall, University of California Press, Berkeley.

Charlier, J.É. and Moëns, F. (2002), 'Face à la disqualification. Identité altérée des prêtres. Les ruses de l'exclusion symbolique', in V. Châtel and M.H. Soulet (éd.), *Faire face et s'en sortir*, Éditions universitaires, Fribourg.

Clausewitz, K. von (1968), *On War*, edited with an introduction by Anatol Rapoport, Penguin Books, Baltimore.

Conein, B. (1998), 'La notion de routine: problèmes de définition', *Sociologie du travail*, 4.

Cyrulnik, B. (1999), *Un Merveilleux malheur*, Éditions Odile Jacob, Paris.

Descartes, R. (1994), *Discourses on the Method*, University of Notre Dame Press, Notre Dame.

Détienne, M. and Vernant, J.P. (1991), *Cunning Intelligence in Greek Culture and Society*, translated by Janet Lloyd, Humanities Press, Atlantic Highlands.

Dubar, C. (2000), *La Crise des identités. L'interprétation d'une mutation*, Presses universitaires de France, Paris.

Dubet, F. (1987), *La Galère. Jeunes en survie*, Éditions Fayard, Paris.

Dubet, F. and Vérétout, A. (2001), 'Pourquoi sortir du RMI? Une 'réduction' de la rationalité de l'acteur', *Revue française de sociologie*, Vol. 42(3).

Durkheim, É. (1951), *Suicide. A Study in sociology*, Free Press, Glencoe.

Ème, B. and Laville, J.L. (2000), 'L'enjeu de la confiance dans les services relationnels', in R. Laufer and M. Orillard (éd.), *La Confiance en question*, Éditions L'Harmattan, Paris.

Felouzis, G. (2001), *La Condition étudiante. Sociologie des étudiants et de l'université*, Presses universitaires de France, Paris.

Fransen, A. (1997), 'Balises et écueils d'une sociologie du sujet', in G. Bajoit and E. Belin (éd.), *Contribution à une sociologie du sujet*, Éditions L'Harmattan, Paris.

Frianguiadakis, S. (2002), 'Au bord de la rupture ou faire face sans s'en sortir', in V. Châtel and M.H. Soulet (éd.), *Faire face et s'en sortir*, Éditions universitaires, Fribourg.

Friedberg, E. (1997), *Local Orders: Dynamics of Organized Action*, translated by Emoretta Yang, Jai Press, Greenwich.

Fumagalli, L. (2002), *L'Insertion en sursis. Analyse du parcours post-carcéral d'anciens détenus*, Éditions universitaires, Fribourg.

Gambetta, D. (1988), 'Can we trust Trust?', in D. Gambetta (ed.), *Making and Breaking Cooperative Relations*, Blackwell, Oxford.

Garfinkel, H. (1984), *Studies in Ethnomethodology*, Prentice Hall, Englewood Cliffs.

Garfinkel, H. (1986), 'Du bon usage de la dégradation', *Sociétés*, 11.

Giddens, A. (1990), *The Consequences of Modernity*, Polity Press, Cambridge.

Giesbrecht, N. (1983), 'Stakes in Conformity and the 'Normalization' of Deviants: Accounts by Former and Current Skid Row Inebriates', *Journal of Drug Issues*, Vol. 13(1).

Godbout, J.T. (2000), *Le Don, la dette et l'identité. Homo donator versus Homo oeconomicus*, Éditions La Découverte, Paris.

Godelier, M. (1972), *Rationality and Irrationality in Economics*, translated by Brian Pearce, NLB, London.

Goffman, E. (1961), *Asylums. Essays on the Social Situation of Mental Patients and Other Inmates*, Anchor Books, New York.

Goffman, E. (1963), *Stigma. Notes on the Management of Spoiled Identity*, Prentice Hall, Englewood Cliffs.

Goffman, E. (1983), 'The Condition of Felicity', *American Journal of Sociology*, Vol. 89(1).

Hérard-Dubreuil, G. (2000), 'Risque et temps. Vers une refondation de la quiétude', Paper at the interdisciplinary seminar on urgency organised at the University of Fribourg on 31 March and 1 April 2000.

Hess, R. (1986), 'Quel corps? pour Agnès', *Quel corps?*, 32-33.

Ion, J. and Peroni, M. (1997), 'Avant-propos', in J. Ion and M. Peroni (éd.), *Engagement public et exposition de la personne*, Éditions de l'Aube, La Tour d'Aigues.

Jollien, A. (1999), *Éloge de la faiblesse*, Éditions du Cerf, Paris.

Karpik, L. (1996), 'Dispositifs de confiance et engagements crédibles', *Sociologie du travail*, 1.

Kaufmann, J.C. (1995), *Corps de femmes, regards d'hommes. Sociologie des seins nus*, Éditions Nathan, Paris.

Kaufmann, J.C. (2001), *Ego. Pour une sociologie de l'individu*, Éditions Nathan, Paris.

Lacroix, B. (1973), 'Régulation et anomie selon Durkheim', *Cahiers internationaux de sociologie*, 20.

Lalive d'Épinay, C. (1983), 'Récits de vie et quotidienneté', *Revue suisse de sociologie*, 1.

Le Gall, D., Martin, C. and Soulet, M.H. (1986), 'Éditorial', *Les Cahiers de la recherche sur le travail social*, 'Faire Avec', 10.

Le Poultier, F. (1986), *Travail social, inadaptation sociale et processus cognitifs*, Éditions du Centre technique national de recherche sur les handicaps et les inadaptations, Paris.

Lefort, C. (1988), *Democracy and Political Theory*, University of Minnesota Press, Minneapolis.

Legrand, M. (1993), *L'Approche biographique*, Éditions Desclée de Brouwer, Paris.

Lévi-Strauss, C. (1966), *The Savage Mind*, University of Chicago Press, Chicago.

Luhmann, N. (1988), 'Familiarity, Confidence, Trust: Problems and Alternatives', in D. Gambetta (ed.), *Making and Breaking Cooperative Relations*, Blackwell, Oxford.

Manciaux, M. (éd.) (2001), *La Résilience. Concepts, applications*, Éditions Médecine et Hygiène, Genève.

Coping and Pulling Through

Manin, B. (1985), 'Volonté générale ou délibération', *Le Débat*, 33.

Matza, D. and Sykes, G. (1957), 'Techniques of Neutralization: A Theory of Delinquency', *American Sociological Review*, Vol. 22.

Mendras, H. (1976), *Sociétés paysannes. Éléments pour une théorie de la paysannerie*, Éditions Armand Colin, Paris.

Molo, C. (2000), *À contre-courant. Analyse des processus individuels d'adoption d'un mode de vie ordinaire*, Mémoire de Licence de la Faculté des Lettres, Fribourg.

Ogien, A. (1995), *Sociologie de la déviance*, Éditions Armand Colin, Paris.

Pattaroni, L. (2002), 'Les compétences de l'individu: travail social et responsabilisation', in V. Châtel and M.H. Soulet (éd.), *Faire face et s'en sortir*, Éditions universitaires, Fribourg.

Petitat, A. (1998), *Secret et formes sociales*, Presses universitaires de France, Paris.

Pollack, M. (1990), *L'Expérience concentrationnaire. Essai sur le maintien de l'identité sociale*, Éditions Métailié, Paris.

Remy, J. (1992), 'La vie quotidienne et les transactions sociales: perspectives micro ou macro-sociologiques', in M. Blanc (éd.), *Pour une sociologie de la transaction sociale*, Éditions L'Harmattan, Paris.

Remy, J., Voyé, L. and Servais, É. (1991), *Produire ou reproduire*, De Boeck Université, Bruxelles.

René, J.F., Turcotte, G. and Blais, M.F. (2002), '*L'Empowerment*, balises pour un véritable pouvoir d'agir', in V. Châtel and M.H. Soulet (éd.), *Faire face et s'en sortir*, Éditions universitaires, Fribourg.

Rillaer, J. van (1992), *La Gestion de soi*, Éditions Mardaga, Bruxelles.

Roux, J. (1997), 'Mettre son corps en cause: la grève de la faim, une forme d'engagement public', in J. Ion and M. Peroni (éd.), *Engagement public et exposition de la personne*, Éditions de l'Aube, La Tour d'Aigues.

Roux, J. (2002), 'Faire trace. Les épreuves indiciaires de soi dans le roman 'Joseph sous la pluie' de Mano Solo', in V. Châtel and M.H. Soulet (éd.), *Faire face et s'en sortir*, Éditions universitaires, Fribourg.

Sartre, J.P. (1973), *Existentialism and Humanism*, translation and introduction by Philip Mairet, Eyre Methuen, London.

Schütz, A. (1964), 'Tiresias or our Knowledge of Future Events', in A. Schütz, *Collected Papers II*, Martinus Nijhoff, The Hague.

Séraphin, G. (2001), *Agir sous contrainte. Être 'sous' tutelle ou curatelle dans la France contemporaine*, Éditions L'Harmattan, Paris.

Soulet, M.H. (1980), 'Identités collectives, résistance au changement et rapports de sociabilité', in P. Tap, *Identités collectives et changements sociaux*, Éditions Privat, Toulouse.

Strauss, A. (1959), *Mirrors and Masks; the Search for Identity*, Free Press, Glencoe.

Strauss, A. (1992), *La Trame de la négociation. Sociologie qualitative et interactionnisme*, Éditions L'Harmattan, Paris.

Taboada-Leonetti, I. (1994), 'Contraintes sociales et stratégies individuelles: la place de l'acteur', in V. De Gaulejac and I. Taboada-Leonetti (éd.), *La Lutte des places. Insertion et désinsertion*, Éditions Hommes et organisations, Marseille.

Taguieff, P.A. (2001), *Résister au bougisme. Démocratie forte contre mondialisation techno-marchande*, Éditions mille et une nuits, Paris.

Thomas, W. and Znaniecki, F. (1996), *The Polish Peasant in Europe and America: A Classic Work in Immigration History*, University of Illinois Press, Urbana.

Villechaise-Dupont, A. (2002), 'La résistance des acteurs en situation précarisée: ressource et défi pour l'intégration', in V. Châtel and M.H. Soulet (éd.), *Faire face et s'en sortir*, Éditions universitaires, Fribourg.

Walgrave, L. (1992), *Délinquance systématisée des jeunes et vulnérabilité sociétale*, Éditions Droz, Genève.

Index

For Product Safety Concerns and Information please contact our EU
representative GPSR@taylorandfrancis.com
Taylor & Francis Verlag GmbH, Kaufingerstraße 24, 80331 München, Germany

www.ingramcontent.com/pod-product-compliance
Lightning Source LLC
Chambersburg PA
CBHW062035270326

41928CB00036BB/2310

* 9 7 8 1 1 3 8 6 1 9 1 7 3 *